The
NATURE
of PORTLAND

A Fun, Friendly Guide to Portland-Area Plants & Animals

Photo, Tracy Ave

LeeAnn Kriegh

Tempo Press
Bend, Oregon

ISBN 978-0-9975215-1-1

Author: LeeAnn Kriegh, LeeAnn@natureofbooks.com
Designer: Sarah Craig, sarahcookdesign.com

Cover photo credits: background, spine, trillium, and heron by Tracy Aue; beaver by Steve Hersey

In loving memory of M.A. Willson
photographer, traveler, friend

TABLE OF CONTENTS

ACKNOWLEDGMENTS

It takes years to produce a book like this, years full of other commitments and unexpected challenges. Sarah Craig steered into the slide and stuck with me to create a book that's even more beautiful than our first. She's an extraordinary graphic designer and even better friend.

At the back of the book are brief biographies for each photographer. Let me add upfront that I know many of you will not read this book, opting instead to simply admire these people's photos. To you, dear non-reader, I say: I don't blame you. The photos are spectacular, and I'm profoundly grateful to those who shared their work.

The experts below taught me, with great patience, about Portland's plants and animals, so I could share my understanding with you. I'm indebted to them for reviewing sections and chapters more times than we'd care to recall. The best parts of this book are due to their insights and explanations; the errors are all mine.

Plants

- Rick Shory, plant guru (rickshory.wordpress.com)
- Mandy Tu, Plant Taxonomist & Herbarium Curator, Hoyt Arboretum
- Mitch Bixby, Botanic Specialist, City of Portland Environmental Services (invasives)
- Barb Morris, writer and naturalist (barbmorris.com) (wildflowers)

Birds

- Chuck Gates, creator of Oregon Birding Site Guide, ecaudubon.org
- Shawneen Finnegan, birder and artist (shawneenfinnegan.com)
- Joe Liebezeit, Staff Scientist & Avian Conservation Manager, Portland Audubon
- Jay H. Withgott, science and environmental writer
- P.K. Lichen, author of *Kidnapping the Wild One*
- Irene Liu, researcher/producer, Cornell Lab of Ornithology

Wildlife

- Sue Anderson, naturalist (butterflies)
- Rich Hatfield, Senior Conservation Biologist, Xerces Society (bees)
- Alan St. John, herpetologist and author of *Reptiles of the Northwest* and *Oregon's Dry Side: Exploring East of the Cascade Crest* (amphibians and reptiles)
- Leslie Bliss-Ketcham, Samara Group (samarapdx.com) (mammals)
- Caitlin LaBar, lepidopterist and author (northwestbutterflies.com) (butterflies)
- Daniel Hilburn, entomologist, ODA, retired (damselflies and dragonflies)
- Eric Forsman, OSU, Dept. of Fisheries & Wildlife, retired (mammals)
- Leslie Carraway, OSU, Dept. of Fisheries & Wildlife (mammals)

Many other professionals were incredibly generous with their time, including Dan van den Broek, Angie Kimpo, Dominic Maze, Jim Moore, Robert Michael Pyle, Deb Quinlan, and Stefan Schlick.

Thanks, too, to Brenda Kinoshita, Mary Fehrs, and other friends who've listened to me drone on about dragonfly eyes and duck sex for the past six years. Your support means the world. And to Lorna Hickerson, thank you for making this book, and my life, so much better.

Photo: Tracy Aue

Photo: Dave Rein

Photo: Kermit Williams

Photo: Marlin Harms

Photo: Tracy Aue

INTRODUCTION

Portland presents a Rorschach test of sorts: Do you see an urban metropolis of concrete and cars? Or do you see a city teeming with plants and animals of all sorts in backyards, parks, and natural areas?

It is both, of course.

The place we now call Portland was once home to dozens of villages and thousands of Indigenous people, some who stayed year-round and others who came and went with the seasons. They knew what the so-called "settlers" would only belatedly discover: that this damp, temperate interior valley is a remarkably fertile place, able to support a vast array of life.

By the time city founders Asa Lovejoy and William Overton arrived in 1843, the land was not entirely wild—Multnomah, Clackamas, and other Native bands and tribes had managed it successfully for centuries—but it was lavishly green, with six-feet-thick Douglas-firs and western redcedars standing tall and spreading their arms wide in what we now call downtown Portland.

In those days, bears and cougars roamed the forests, wolves howled in the West Hills, and trails were carved by the hooves of thousands of deer and elk. Today, many

Photo: Tracy Aue

of those old wildlife trails are paved roads, and you probably won't hear a wolf or see a cougar or bear (jokes aside). But even now, over 175 years later, Portland remains a little bit wild.

The streets are alive with squirrels scurrying up poles, crows cawing overhead, and some 218,000 street trees shading 650,000 Portlanders. Head a few miles out to Forest Park to hear woodpeckers and wrens and to see a dozen shades of green. A bit farther from the city, you can revel in the buzz and trill of thousands of birds on Sauvie Island and view the April eruption of pink and blue wildflowers at Camassia Natural Area.

The notion that cities are where people live is not wrong, but it is incomplete— Portland proves that. This is an urban area where nature still rises up and through our civilized veneer. If your Rorschach test suggests otherwise, fear not: The pages ahead will lift the veil and help you appreciate the richness that remains and the wildness that is, still, all around us.

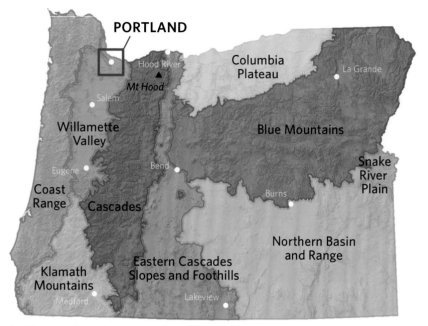

PORTLAND

Columbia
Plateau

La Grande

Hood River

Mt Hood

Salem

Willamette
Valley

Blue Mountains

Eugene

Bend

Snake
River
Plain

Burns

Coast
Range

Cascades

Northern Basin
and Range

Klamath
Mountains

Eastern Cascades
Slopes and Foothills

Medford

Lakeview

Level III ecoregions of Oregon (epa.gov). Map: Deb Quinlan, Deschutes GeoGraphics

WHERE ARE WE?

Most of this book is about which plants and animals are native to Portland, where you can go to see them, and how best to enjoy them. The map above hints at the larger story of why certain species, including our own, find the Rose City to be such a welcoming place to live.

As you might gather by looking out your window, Portland is an especially lush, verdant place. The city's richness stems from its location, nestled between the Coast Range to the west and the Cascade Mountains to the east. Here, at the northern tip of the Willamette Valley, lies one of the greenest, most fertile lands on the continent, bordered to the north by the country's fourth-largest river and split down the middle by the river that gives the valley its name.

Portland's prime location, and its associated mild climate, goes a long way toward explaining why, as Portland author Ursula K. Le Guin wrote, "All our streets began in the forest, once upon a time." More broadly, it's why our fair city features not only the temperate forests for which we are best known but also wetland areas, oak savannas, and an array of other habitats.

Those different environments support the abundance of plants and animals described in this book, the turtles and maples and eagles that have long made their homes here, living in forests, along rivers, under our feet, and in our backyards.

Now, isn't it time we got to know this life-sustaining place, and these wild neighbors of ours, a little bit better?

HOW TO USE THIS BOOK

Some people, mostly my friends, will display this book in their bathrooms. Others will read it from cover to cover. And still others will toss it in their backpack so they'll have it handy when exploring local parks and trails. However you choose to use it, take note of these features to get the most out of every page.

Best times to look for birds and wildflowers

Common and scientific names of over 360 species

PINK TO RED OR RED-PURPLE

Western Starflower (*Lysimachia latifolia*)

Blooms: Late spring to early summer
Late spring is a magical time to explore trails in the Portland area. Among the many pleasures are seeing fern fronds unfurling and colorful blossoms emerging on wildflowers like this one.

Western starflower's delicate pinkish blooms stand out against the backdrop of the plant's big, broad, deep-green leaves (*latifolia* roughly translates to "broad-leaved"). Lots of flowers have a starry shape, but species like this one earn the starflower moniker by virtue of their wafer-thin flower stalks, upon which the blooms seem to float in the air like stars.

The flower stalk's too thin to see here.
Photo: M.A. Willson

ID tips: Perennial, 2–12 in. tall. Look for a whorl of 4–7 broadly oval leaves (up to 3.5 in. long) with pointed tips. Up to a few star-shaped pink flowers (up to .75 in. wide) bloom on thin flower stalks, each with 5–7 pointed petals.

Locations: Locally common in shady, moist woods, including at Oxbow Regional Park, Hoyt Arboretum, Camassia Natural Area, and Powell Butte Nature Park.

Trails and parks within 30 minutes of downtown where you can see every species

Plain-language descriptions to help you identify each species

Fun and informative natural history, ecology, and stories

At the back of the book, you'll find "treasure hunts" for 10 locations in the Portland area where you can find the species described in the main chapters. Because reading about plants and animals is fun. But getting outside to experience and connect with nature is what *The Nature of Portland* is all about.

Photo: M.A. Willson

Photo: Tracy Aue

Photo: Tracy Aue

TREES & SHRUBS

There's a certain irony to Portland being such a tree-loving, tree-protecting place. This is Stumptown, after all, named for the remains of thousands of trees cut down by early settlers who whitewashed the stumps so they could see their way home at night.

It's tempting to think lingering guilt from that legacy drives current Portlanders to identify and count every tree on every street (218,000 in all), and to honor hundreds of our biggest, oldest, and most significant trees as Heritage Trees.

In truth, even in the mid-1800s many Portlanders recognized the value of trees, protecting the Park Blocks and Washington Park, for instance, even as the hillsides

Photo: M.A. Willson

Photo: Tracy Aue

Photo: Ed Jensen

Photo: Tracy Aue

Photo: Tracy Aue

Photo: Tracy Aue

just beyond were being logged. By 1880, the city had made it illegal to destroy or even injure shade and ornamental trees—with offenses punishable by fines or jail terms.

Maybe we've always known that native trees are central to what makes this place home. What would Portland be, after all, if you took away all the towering Douglas-firs and mighty western redcedars, all the sprawling maples and flowering dogwoods? Not to put too fine a point on it, but the trees of Portland also reduce noise, process stormwater runoff, and cool and purify the air we breathe.

And, no, I'm not forgetting about our humbler shrubs. This is not only Stumptown, after all, but also the Rose City. The spring blooms of red-flowering currant, the tasty blackberries of summer, the dazzling fall colors of vine maple—all our shrubs, as well as our trees, make this city healthier, more colorful, and more welcoming to all the animals, human and otherwise, who live here.

EVERGREEN TREES

Douglas-firs with vine maples. Photo: Buddy Mays

Douglas-fir *(Pseudotsuga menziesii)*

With all due respect to California (redwood), Idaho (western white pine), and Washington (western hemlock), Oregon's state tree, the Douglas-fir, offers far and away the best combination of statewide historical, cultural, and ecological significance.

It's estimated that eight of every 10 conifers west of the Cascades are Douglas-firs—look around any park in Portland, and odds are you'll see their distinctive swooping branches. The trees can live a thousand years, and given even a few hundred years, they become giants, second only to coast redwoods in height.

Many Native tribes relied on Douglas-firs for fuel, tools, and medicine, and later the trees David Douglas described as "one of the most striking and truly graceful objects in nature" were used to construct the railroad ties and telephone poles that helped make western expansion possible. Today, they're considered the most valuable timber tree in the world and are one of the country's favorite Christmas trees.

Although best known for the many ways they serve people, Douglas-firs are, as Henry David Thoreau noted of trees in general, "good for other things than boards and shingles." Both as living trees and as snags, Douglas-firs provide prime breeding and nesting habitat for all sorts of birds. Black bears strip the bark to get at the tasty cambium beneath, deer eat new shoots, small animals store seeds to feed themselves through winter, and a host of native plants grow in their understory. Simply put, our state tree benefits every living creature that lives on, under, or near it.

OLDEST DOUGLAS-FIRS

To see some of the oldest and largest Douglas-firs in the Portland area, head to Oxbow Regional Park, where you can walk among trees that started growing 800 years ago, around the time the Magna Carta was being drafted.

Look for droopy branchlets. Photo: Tracy Aue   *They're the world's second-tallest tree species. Photo: Buddy Mays*

ID tips: One of the world's tallest trees. Long limbs sweep upward with droopy branchlets. Cones have 3-pointed bracts that stick out between the scales, like a pitchfork or the hind end of a mouse. Soft but pointed needles (about 1 in. long) surround twigs like a bottlebrush. Old bark is thick and deeply furrowed. Buds are reddish-brown and pointed.

Locations: It's like finding hay in a haystack. Douglas-fir is the most common conifer (cone-bearing tree) in Portland and across the Pacific Northwest. Look for the trees in neighborhoods and at just about every natural area. Hoyt Arboretum alone has over 600 trees, and Oxbow Regional Park in Gresham has the region's tallest at 289 feet.

See the mice hind ends and tails? Photo: LeeAnn Kriegh

BIGGEST DOUGLAS-FIRS

The tallest tree in Portland is a 243-foot Douglas-fir on the bank of Balch Creek along the Lower Macleay Trail in Forest Park. At nearly half the height of the "Big Pink" U.S. Bancorp building in downtown Portland, that Heritage Tree is diminutive compared to the tallest Douglas-fir in the world, a 327-foot giant west of Roseburg. And that one's pint-sized compared to the 465-foot Douglas-fir that was cut down in Washington in 1897.

Grand Fir *(Abies grandis)*

Grand fir is Oregon's most common true fir, and the only one that grows at lower elevations west of the Cascades. In wet, shady areas, these attractive evergreens can reach heights of well over 200 feet.

It's a true fir, so cones perch upright on branches.
Photo: Ed Jensen

Grand firs are thin-barked and disease-prone, but if you're in the market for a Christmas tree, they're tough to beat. When young, the trees are symmetrical pyramids with horizontal branches and flat sprays of needles that seem specially designed to hold ornaments. That flat arrangement is a common adaptation for species that grow in the shade, so they can make the most of the limited sunlight available under taller trees like Douglas-firs.

Break off and crush a needle or two of grand fir to savor the unmistakable tangerine aroma. You can also use your fingernail to puncture a resin blister on younger trees, which will release another pleasant scent.

ID tips: Shiny green needles (up to 2 in. long) tend to splay in 2 flat rows, like Alfalfa's hair on "The Little Rascals." Needle undersides have 2 white stomatal lines; tips are soft, blunt, and slightly notched on lower branches. Buds (often in 3's) are rounded at the tips, not pointy like on Douglas-firs. Look for upright cones in the treetops.

Locations: Usually in moist conditions, mixed with Douglas-fir. Look for them at just about any wild area, including Tryon Creek State Natural Area and Laurelhurst Park.

Needles are shiny, blunt, and soft.
Photo: Ed Jensen

FACTS ABOUT TRUE FIRS

The hyphen is a tip-off that Douglas-firs aren't true firs, which are all in the *Abies* genus. You can tell grand fir is the real deal by these traits:

- The cones perch upright on the topmost branches, like small birds.
- Needles are "friendly like firs," meaning the ends are blunt, not sharp.
- Gently pull the needle of a true fir off its twig and it'll leave a smooth scar.

Pacific Madrone *(Arbutus menziesii)*

Who can resist the colorful, voluptuous arms of these beauties? The bark on madrone trunks and branches peels away in papery red strips to reveal a startlingly smooth green-gold interior—and that's only one of this tree's many attractions.

Spring brings sweetly scented white flower clusters (madrone was a finalist for Oregon state flower), and in late fall, the trees are adorned with red-orange fruits popular with thrushes, doves, and other birds.

In stark contrast to straight-up evergreens like Douglas-firs, madrones lean, twist, and otherwise contort themselves to reach for the sun (or, as Edward Jensen writes in *Trees to Know in Oregon*, to seek "a better view of the world").

If they were easy to transplant and didn't shed so many leaves and berries, I have a hunch there'd be many more of these peeling wonders in Portland-area backyards.

ID tips: Portland's only native broadleaf evergreen tree is famous for its peeling bark. Leaves (3–6 in. long) are shiny, oval, and leathery. Clusters of fragrant, urn-shaped white flowers persist into early summer (look for clear windows near the base of each flower). Orange-red fruits have a bumpy surface.

Locations: Not common but found here and there in sunny forest openings and edges, including at Tryon Creek State Natural Area, Camassia Natural Area, Hoyt Arboretum, and Cooper Mountain Nature Park.

One of the true beauties of the tree world.
Photo: Ed Jensen

Outer bark strips away to reveal a clammy green-gold underlayer. Photo: Ed Jensen

WHY EXFOLIATE?

Madrones and paper birches are two of many tree species that actively shed, or exfoliate, their bark. Odd, isn't it, when other trees like Douglas-firs instead build up thick, protective bark? While thicker bark helps trees survive fire, the prevailing theory is that peeling bark is an adaptation that originated millions of years ago to help some species shed parasites, fungi, and epiphytes such as mosses and lichens.

Reddish fruits have bumpy skins.
Photo: Ed Jensen

Purplish scales peel away to reveal rose-colored inner bark. Photo: Ed Jensen

Female trees produce red arils that contain poisonous seeds. Photo: Ed Jensen

Pacific Yew *(Taxus brevifolia)*

To understand Pacific yew, you first need to know that it's very different from the better known and closely related English yew *(T. baccata)*.

The longer-lived English yew is a popular ornamental known as the "tree of death" for its toxicity—there's a reason the witches in Macbeth added "slips of Yew" to their lethal brew. Pacific yew's seeds, needles, and twigs are likewise poisonous, but the tree is famous not for its toxicity but rather for its healing powers.

In 1962, a botanist took a sample of Pacific yew bark from Washington's Gifford Pinchot National Forest as part of a study exploring the potential medicinal benefits of various plants. Lo and behold, scientists discovered that the bark contained a compound (paclitaxel) that could be used to fight cancer.

Decades later, the resulting drug, Taxol, was approved to treat ovarian, breast, and other cancers. Given how common cancer is—and how uncommon and slow-growing these trees are—it's fortunate that by the mid-1990s a synthetic form of Taxol was developed, so producing the lifesaving drug no longer requires killing Pacific yews.

ID tips: Our smallest conifer has a disheveled, shrubby appearance and a contorted trunk and limbs. Bark is thin with purplish outer scales. Broad, flat needles (up to 1 in. long) are soft and of uniform length, with pointy tips. Needle undersides don't have obvious white stomatal lines. Instead of woody cones, look for reddish arils (fleshy red pulp around a poisonous seed) on female trees.

Locations: Here and there in moist understories, frequently shaded by Douglas-firs. Look for yews at Tryon Creek State Natural Area, Forest Park, and Cooper Mountain Nature Park.

TAKE A TREE WALK

With the help of thousands of volunteers, Portland Park & Recreation's Urban Forestry division has created remarkably detailed maps of the city's trees. Take a look online to get to know the trees growing along Portland's streets and at your favorite parks. portlandoregon.gov/parks/article/433143#map.

Ponderosa Pine *(Pinus ponderosa)*

Ponderosa pines are one of the most common and attractive tree species east of the Cascade Mountains. Take a hike near the town of Sisters to walk among towering old-growth ponderosas and smell their sweet vanilla or butterscotch aroma.

In Portland we don't have nearly so many of these beautiful trees, but you can find pockets of the Willamette Valley variety, including the huge Pearson Pine on NE 29th and Fremont that was planted in 1885.

Ponderosa seeds are preferred cuisine for chickadees, evening grosbeaks, finches, nuthatches, sparrows, and towhees, as well as beavers, porcupines, chipmunks, squirrels ... the list goes on.

Even when ponderosas die, they're valuable as sturdy snags (standing dead trees) that northern flickers and other birds drill holes into, excavating homes for themselves and later for squirrels, smaller birds, and other short-term renters.

ID tips: This is the only native Northwest conifer with needles in bundles of 3. Bark ages from gray to orange. Needles are very long (up to 9 in.) and cones are large (3–5 in. long), with prickly scales.

Locations: Here and there in sunny, dry habitats, including at Tryon Creek State Natural Area, Tualatin Hills Nature Park, Powell Butte Nature Park, and Cooper Mountain Nature Park.

A typical cathedral of old-growth ponderosas.
Photo: M.A. Willson

Is there anything more beautiful than a pondo?
Photo: Kim Elton

"If you're seeing, not just looking, then when you observe that tree growing in the forest, or the water bubbling up from the ground, or the sanderling on the shore, you are getting connected. That is what makes the difference. You begin to see yourself *in* a context rather than think you *are* the context."

— Neal Maine in *A Generous Nature: Lives Transformed by Oregon*

Note the drooping tops and branch tips. Photo: Ed Jensen

Western Hemlock
(Tsuga heterophylla)

Famed naturalist E.O. Wilson once wrote, "When you've seen one ant, one bird, one tree, you have not seen them all."

That sentiment certainly holds true for Portland's native tree species, each of which has evolved unique methods for survival. For instance, western hemlocks grow more slowly and to lesser heights than Douglas-firs, but they're twice as leafy so they can take advantage of the limited sunlight that's available under the giants.

Western hemlocks also have shorter lifespans than Douglas-firs, but they make the most of their limited years, growing together in dense stands that produce more wood per acre than most other forest types.

Even when hemlocks succumb early to wind, insects, or fungal infections, their lives are not exactly over because many fallen trees become nurse logs for the next generation.

When you come across logs and stumps in an old forest, see if you can't find one—or a row of—hemlock saplings growing right out of the decaying wood. Hemlocks produce hundreds of small cones every year, and each houses up to 40 seeds that sometimes end up nestled in the rich soil of a nurse log.

Nurse logs hold tree seeds up above the forest floor, where they would otherwise have to compete with ferns and other plants. The roots of hemlock saplings grow around and through the decaying logs, eventually leaving twisty arms of aboveground roots with openings where their nurse log used to be.

PORTLAND'S BEST-SMELLING TREES AND SHRUBS

Many trees and shrubs offer a reward to those who stop to smell the flowers ... or leaves or bark. These are among those worth a whiff:

- Black cottonwood leaves and buds
- Elderberry flowers
- Grand fir sap and needles
- Ponderosa pine bark
- Mock-orange flowers
- Rose flowers
- Osoberry leaves

Big trees, tiny cones. Photo: Ed Jensen

ID tips: Look up! Hemlock crowns are narrow, and the leader (topmost stem) typically has a distinctive droop. Branch tips droop too, like fingers pointing down. Cones are very small (up to 1 in. long). Soft, flat, blunt needles are all under 1 in. long (shortest of any native conifer) and distinctive in that they vary in length and spread in different directions, creating a disheveled appearance.

Locations: Western hemlocks are most common in older forests just outside the city, under the canopy of Douglas-firs and other trees (air pollution limits their success in cities). Look for them here and there in Portland neighborhoods and at Sauvie Island, Hoyt Arboretum, and Tryon Creek State Park.

Needles are under an inch long and of varying lengths. Photo: Ed Jensen

TREES VS. STARS

Are there more trees on Earth or stars in the Milky Way? According to a 2015 study in *Nature*, there are far more trees—about 3 trillion in all, or 422 trees for every person on Earth. (Stars number "only" in the hundreds of billions.) The news isn't all good: The same study found that about 15 billion trees are cut down each year.

Trunks become fluted over time.
Photo: Tracy Aue

Western Redcedar *(Thuja plicata)*

Western redcedar is also known as arborvitae—literally "tree of life"—which might be all you need to know about this majestic evergreen.

Western redcedar grows primarily in a wide band that begins in northern California, runs up the west side of Oregon and Washington, and continues into British Columbia, where it's the official tree. As you might intuit, these giants like things cool and moist—120 inches of rain a year isn't too much.

Throughout the Northwest, western redcedar was used by Native tribes from cradle to grave. The wood is fragrant, rot-resistant, easy to carve, and lightweight, and the bark is thin but tough and soft enough for weaving. Thus, babies could wear diapers made of shredded bark and sleep on mattresses made of the same. The bark was also made into skirts, hats, and other clothing, and woven into rope, mats, and baskets.

Indigenous people living near modern-day Portland used redcedar planks to erect longhouses large enough to house a hundred people, and to build massive seafaring canoes that reached over 60 feet long and eight feet wide.

Want more? According to anthropologist and ethnobotanist Daniel Moerman, this tree has a longer list of medicinal uses by Native peoples than any other plant in North America.

Unfortunately, we don't have many remaining groves of redcedars. Compared to Indigenous people who tried to avoid killing the trees by peeling off thin planks, Euro-American settlers were far less discriminating.

If you've seen the cathedral-like stands of old-growth western redcedar that remain in places like Vancouver Island, you know the legacy we've lost to extensive logging of these trees of life, which can grow to more than 200 feet and live for well over a thousand years.

Tiny cones appear all over the fern-like sprays.
Photo: Ed Jensen

You can run your hand along the bark without getting splinters. Photo: Ed Jensen

ID tips: Tall, wide tree with a fluted base. Reddish-brown bark runs in vertical strips, like a cat clawed it. Leaves are yellow-green and scale-like, arranged in flattened, fern-like sprays. Look for white, butterfly-shaped stomatal patterns on the underside of the leaves. Woody cones are cinnamon-colored and tiny (up to .75 in. long).

Locations: Small groves can be found in shady and moist habitats, including at Tualatin Hills Nature Park, Powell Butte Nature Park, Cathedral Park, and Tryon Creek State Natural Area.

Look for butterfly-shaped stomatal lines.
Photo: Ed Jensen

"This is the land of the tree of ample hips and full baskets, the one known in the Salish languages as Maker of Rich Women, as Mother Cedar. No matter what the people needed, the cedar was ready to give, from cradleboard to coffin, holding the people."
— Robin Wall Kimmerer, *Braiding Sweetgrass*

A hillside in fall, dotted with the yellow of bigleaf maples. Photo: Ed Jensen

Bigleaf Maple *(Acer macrophyllum)*

Walk along just about any forested trail in the Portland area and you'll see leafy trees clothed in rich green mosses, with licorice ferns poking out from the trunks at odd angles. The trees are bigleaf maples, the largest maple species in the world and the second most common native hardwood in the Pacific Northwest (behind alder).

Spring blooms hang in clusters.
Photo: M.A. Willson

To confirm it's a bigleaf maple, look for the giant leaves that give the tree its name. In spring and summer, the foot-wide green leaves offer shade; in fall, they turn a golden yellow that contrasts beautifully with surrounding evergreens; and in winter, the leaves' browning remnants cushion area trails.

As Donald Peattie notes in his lyrical guide to western trees, bigleaf maple leaves "do not form an oppressive shade—windless and somber—but they act, rather, like lattices, letting the light through but not the heat of the day."

The flowers and fruits of bigleaf maples are less appreciated but no less appealing. In spring, see if you can spot dangling clusters of greenish-yellow flowers when they emerge just before and with the first leaves. In summer, keep an eye out for connected pairs of samara fruits that are called helicopters or whirlibirds for the way they twirl as they fall to the ground.

Leaves are divided into five lobes. Photo: Tracy Aue

ID tips: Bark is furrowed gray-brown at maturity, often covered in moss. Clusters of small greenish-yellow flowers are soon followed by huge leaves (8–12 in. across). Leaves look like outstretched hands with 5 fingers (lobes), each pointed at the tip. Pairs of hairy winged seeds, or samaras (1.5–2 in. long), emerge in midsummer. Leaves turn yellow in fall.

Locations: Very common in areas with full to partial sun, usually under conifers. Look for them along most trails at sites including Forest Park, Hoyt Arboretum, Kelley Point Park, and Tryon Creek State Park.

WHY MAPLES LIKE MOSSES

Most bigleaf maples are draped in mosses, ferns, and other plant life. One study found the average weight of all those epiphytes on a bigleaf maple is about 78 pounds! Mosses and other green stuff benefit the trees by collecting nitrogen and other valuable nutrients from the air and sponging up water and holding onto it through dry summer months. Small roots grow from maple branches to absorb the collected nutrients and water.

Cottonwoods provide some of our best fall colors.
Photo: Tracy Aue

A large cottonwood on Sauvie Island.
Photo: Tracy Aue

Leaf undersides are much lighter in color.
Photo: Ed Jensen

Black Cottonwood *(Populus trichocarpa)*

Who says it doesn't snow much in Portland? Head to local lakes, rivers, and streams in late spring and you could find yourself caught in a veritable whiteout of cottony fluff falling from black cottonwoods. The tree's seeds are built to fly, with silky white hairs attached to carry them far and wide.

Cottonwoods' small seeds don't have much in the way of stored carbohydrates, so they have to land in moist sites where they can germinate right away. The trees are not shade tolerant, so open, disturbed areas are best. In those sweet spots, cottonwoods grow faster than any other native tree, racing to beat the competition to the sunlight. Like red alders, they do a lot of good along the way, stabilizing riverbanks with their thickly stitched roots and providing food and shelter for wildlife.

Cottonwoods are the tallest native broadleaf trees in the West, and their sprawling crowns make ideal habitat for large birds like eagles and ospreys. In Portland, cottonwoods are also home to great blue heron rookeries that stand out in winter at sites such as Sauvie Island and Heron Lakes Golf Course.

ID tips: Branch tips and the tree's triangular leaves (3–6 in. long) have pointy ends, are sticky, and smell sweet when new. Leaves flash pale undersides. Mature trees have deeply furrowed gray bark; young bark is gray or white. Droopy male and female catkins appear on separate trees in early spring.

Locations: Along Portland waterways, including at Kelley Point Park, Ross Island, and Sauvie Island. Willamette Park has one cottonwood with a diameter of more than 6.5 feet.

DID YOU KNOW?

Not to point the finger, but if cottonwoods make you sneeze, you can blame male trees. In spring, they release pollen that's near the top of the allergen scale. The later "snow" attached to the seeds of female trees doesn't cause allergic reactions, but the fluffy stuff is frequently blamed because it's so noticeable and happens to coincide with the release of unseen grass pollen.

Cascara *(Rhamnus purshiana)*

You've seen cascara—I know you have. It's just that you might not have noticed it, or if you did, it may have registered only as an unremarkable understory tree with leathery leaves, gray bark, and no other distinctive characteristics to help you distinguish it from the rest of the big green world.

Let's try to make cascara memorable, beginning with the fact that the cured bark can be used as a laxative. That led some clever folks to call the tree "chitticum" because the, uh, "chit" will come after eating it. The bark has been peeled for that and other medicinal purposes for more than a century; in 1924 the total harvest in Portland was estimated at 6,000 tons.

If you really haven't seen cascara in the wild, it's probably because of the harvest of the bark, which continues to this day. You can help make up for that by planting cascara in your yard, where its small flowers will entice pollinators, and its berries will feed cedar waxwings and other birds.

Cascara is a small, easily overlooked tree.
Photo: Ed Jensen

ID tips: Short tree (up to about 40 ft. tall) or shrub with gray bark splotched with patches of white lichen. Elliptic to spoon-shaped leaves are 2–6 in. long. Leaves alternate along the stem, can be leathery, and have parallel veins that stick out like ribs, especially on leaf undersides. Greenish flowers cluster in leaf axils (the angle just above where each leaf attaches to the stem). Fruits ripen from green to red to black.

Locations: Relatively common but never in large numbers. Look in moist, deeply shaded locations, including at Forest Park, Tryon Creek State Natural Area, Powell Butte Nature Park, and Hoyt Arboretum.

Another name is cascara sagrada (Spanish for "sacred bark"). Photo: Ed Jensen

HERITAGE TREES

Nothing shows off Portland's love of trees better than the Heritage Tree program. Since 1993, City Council has recognized more than 300 trees for their outstanding size, age, or historical or horticultural significance—you've probably seen the plaques on eye-catching trees around town. I've pointed out a few Heritage Trees in these pages. Search online for detailed guides, walking tours, and more.

Fruits ripen from green to red to black.
Photo: Ed Jensen

Cherries on the waterfront. Photo: Tracy Aue

Petals from a 'Kwanzan' tree on NE Schuyler Street. Photo: Rick Shory

Winter-blooming cherry. Photo: Tracy Aue

Cherries (*Prunus* spp.)

Bitter cherry (*P. emarginata*) is Portland's only native cherry tree, a humble, multi-stemmed tree that produces white flowers in spring and red fruits that, as the name implies, you'll want to leave for birds and squirrels.

The city is much better known for its ornamental cherries, especially the hundred 'Akebono' (*P. x yedoensis*) cherry trees that line Tom McCall Waterfront Park to honor the memory of Japanese Americans interned during World War II.

You can also see about 25,000 ornamental cherry and plum trees lining streets in Portland neighborhoods. One example of how they got there: In 1961, facing prejudiced zoning and city disinvestment, Opal Strong and other African-American leaders in the Albina District organized a neighborhood committee and obtained federal funds to revitalize their communities, in part by planting 'Kwanzan' or 'Kanzan' (*P. serrulata*) cherry trees along Albina's streets.

ID tips: Bitter cherry is a multi-stemmed tree with reddish-brown to gray bark marked by horizontal lenticels (raised pores that allow gas exchange). Yellowish-green leaves are finely toothed along the sides and rounded or slightly notched at the tip.

Locations: Ornamentals are all over the city, and bitter cherry is scattered across moist, sparsely wooded areas, including at Tualatin River National Wildlife Refuge and Willow Creek Nature Park.

CHERRY HISTORY

Bing cherries, the most popular commercial variety, got their name from Ah Bing, a Chinese foreman who worked in Seth Lewelling's cherry orchards in Milwaukie. According to the Oregon Historical Society, Mr. Bing worked the orchards for 35 years and may have helped Lewelling develop the famous variety (or the name might honor Mr. Bing's years of service).

In 1889, his work contract fulfilled, Mr. Bing traveled to China. He never returned, possibly because the Chinese Exclusion Act of 1882 sanctioned the deportation of legal residents and made it difficult for Chinese-Americans to re-enter the U.S.

Black Hawthorn (*Crataegus douglasii*)

To identify hawthorns, remember the two elements of their name: "haw" is an old term for the apple-like fruits that dangle in small clusters and "thorn" refers to the thorns that poke out from the branches—both are distinctive features of hawthorn trees. As suggested by Emily Dickinson ("Covert in April / Candid in May"), you can also time the arrival of the blooms.

Black, or Douglas, hawthorn is the only native species that's prevalent in Portland, but we also have several non-natives, the most widespread of which is the weedy common hawthorn (*C. monogyna*).

Black hawthorns sometimes grow as multi-stemmed shrubs, so they're a popular nesting option for birds. The fruits are also a favored food source through winter. Because the fruits ferment over time and become alcoholic, you might see drunken birds staggering through the air—a funny sight but one that's dangerous for the birds.

ID tips: Hawthorns are the only trees with both conspicuous woody thorns (up to .75 in. long on black hawthorn) and leaves tipped with irregular teeth or lobes. Their bark is shaggy, often shredded. Clusters of edible but seedy fruits mature to black.

Locations: Occasionally seen in moist sites in open areas, including at Sauvie Island and Tryon Creek State Natural Area.

May flowers of black hawthorn.
Photo: Ed Jensen

Note the teeth across the ends of the leaves.
Photo: Ed Jensen

Ouch! The stiff thorns of black hawthorn.
Photo: Mark Leppin

FUN FACT

Hawthorn trees have many other common names such as hag thorn and thorn apple. Because they typically bloom in May, the trees are also known as "May flowers"—the source of the name for the Mayflower ship that brought the Puritans to Plymouth in 1620.

Each compound leaf has 5-9 leaflets.
Photo: Ed Jensen

Oregon Ash *(Fraxinus latifolia)*

Oregon ash is a common tree that doesn't get a lot of love or attention, but it does yeoman's work along rivers, streams, and wetland edges, where it provides shade, erosion control, and food and nesting sites for birds and other wildlife.

This is the only native ash tree in the Pacific Northwest, but you'll also come across various ornamental ashes that are beloved for their fall colors.

The looming threat to all ash species is the spread of the emerald ash borer, an invasive beetle from Asia first identified in Michigan in 2002. The beetle has been found in dozens of states, and if and when it reaches Portland, it could decimate our local ash populations. Threats like that are one reason it's critical to plant a diversity of tree species across Portland.

ID tips: Oregon ash is our only native tree with oppositely arranged, pinnately compound leaves (box elder shares the trait but isn't locally native; elderberries also share the trait but are shrubs). Each compound leaf has 5-9 pointed leaflets. Bark is grayish-brown with diamond-shaped fissures. Winged fruits (samaras) that look like canoes hang in dense clusters.

Locations: Common in wetlands, floodplains, and other areas with moist soils, including at Smith and Bybee Wetlands, Cathedral Park, Jackson Bottom Wetlands Preserve, and Fernhill Wetlands.

Trees can be 80 feet tall.
Photo: Ed Jensen

Samaras hang singly, not paired like maples.
Photo: Ed Jensen

> **"Trees do most of the things you do, just more slowly. They compete for their livelihoods and take care of their families, sometimes making huge sacrifices for their children. They breathe, eat and have sex. They give gifts, communicate, learn, remember and record the important events of their lives."**
>
> — Barbara Kingsolver
> in *The New York Times*

It's the official flower emblem of British Columbia. Photo: Tracy Aue

Pacific Dogwood *(Cornus nuttallii)*

You won't find any forests or large stands of Pacific dogwoods. These beautiful flowering trees are an occasional sight worth savoring, especially in spring, when their showy white blooms stand out in contrast to the fresh greenery that surrounds them. In fall, dogwoods announce themselves once again when their leaves turn a vibrant purple, orange, or red, and their blooms sometimes reappear.

Pacific dogwoods are popular with wildlife and in landscapes, but they (as well as some non-native dogwoods, London planetrees, American sycamores, and other species) are prone to attack by a fungal disease called anthracnose that causes leaves to brown and drop in summer.

Leaf veins curve toward the tip. Photo: Ed Jensen

Because of anthracnose, as well as climate change and other threats (see Oregon ash at left), the city is planting—and encouraging you to plant—a variety of tree species.

ID tips: Leaves are oppositely arranged and tapered at both ends, with veins that curve toward the leaf tip (different from cascara). The white-pink bracts on the blooms are big (up to 2.5 in. long and wide) and have pointed tips; they surround a cluster of greenish-white flowers. In fall, leaves turn red and clusters of bird-friendly red fruits appear.

Locations: Fairly common in the shade of other trees and at forest edges and roadsides. Hotspots include Forest Park, Tryon Creek State Natural Area, Powell Butte Nature Park, and Washington Park.

CANINE CONNECTION?

Portlanders love both dogs and dogwoods, but I'm sorry to say there's no real connection between the two words. The tough wood of dogwood was made into skewers that were called "dags," which led to the word "dagwood" and then "dogwood."

An oak tree in North Plains. Photo: Tracy Aue

Oregon White Oak *(Quercus garryana)*

I feel like I'm writing about a family member. When I lived on Sauvie Island, I grew to love the oaks that dot the island's pastures and line its popular trails. After lightning struck one lonely old tree in the back field, tearing an enormous gash in its side, my neighbors and I walked out in a somber procession to witness the damage—to see it and feel it, like visiting an aging loved one after a heart attack.

Oaks have always had that kind of impact on people. Thousands of years ago, the Greeks hailed the "oak god" Zeus, and today oaks are the national tree or symbol of more than a dozen countries, including our own.

History

When David Douglas arrived in the Willamette Valley in the 1820s, the broad crowns of Oregon white oak sprawled across lowlands and hillsides. As late as the 1850s, surveyors recorded about 150,000 acres of oak habitat in the core of the Portland area. Now, nearly all that habitat is either gone or fragmented.

The trees grew so profusely because fire—both lightning-caused and set by the area's original inhabitants—created the open habitat they need. After Euro-American settlers moved in, most oak habitat was converted to agricultural fields, and elsewhere fire suppression allowed conifers to crowd out sun-loving oaks.

Native peoples cultivated oaks because the trees produced tons of acorns that could be eaten and traded, and post-fire savannas provided rich habitat for harvestable plants such as common camas, as well as open space for hunting deer and elk.

What was true then remains true today: Oak habitat is among the richest and most varied in Portland, supporting more than 300 native species, including at-risk animals such as acorn woodpeckers and red-legged frogs. The trees are larval hosts for at least five butterflies, the acorns and high-protein foliage feed a long list of wildlife species, and the hollow trunks and limbs make ideal nesting sites.

Get to Know Oaks

Marooned oaks like the one my neighbors and I mourned are sprinkled across Portland, but preserving and creating swaths of oak habitat is more ecologically important than loving individual trees. To understand why, find an old oak near you and take a moment to get to know the life it supports:

- Listen for birds, squirrels, and insects.
- Look around the tree's base at all the native plants that live in its shade.
- Pick up an acorn and think about how that little nut has fed people and wildlife for millennia.
- In late summer, listen for native wasps trying to break out of galls, or round, ball-like growths. Native wasps lay eggs on oak leaves and twigs, the tree grows a protective covering around the eggs, and non-stinging gall wasps mature inside.

ID tips: In open areas, their crowns can be as wide as the trees are tall (up to about 65 ft.). Bark is gray with shallow fissures. Alternate leaves have 7–9 mostly rounded lobes. Acorns are thumb-size with a rounded tip and distinctively thin cap.

Locations: Small stands tend to be on south-facing slopes in open, sunny areas. Some oaks on Sauvie Island are over 300 years old. Other sites include Oaks Bottom Wildlife Refuge, Camassia Natural Area, and Cooper Mountain Nature Park.

Our native oak has 7–9 rounded lobes.
Photo: Tracy Aue

Oregon oak acorns have thin caps.
Photo: Ed Jensen

Some galls get mighty large.
Photo: Ed Jensen

BIG OAKS FEED SMALL CATERPILLARS

Oaks are one of the best native trees for insects. Douglas Tallamy, a professor of entomology and wildlife ecology, counted 410 caterpillars at head height on a native oak (in his case, an eastern white oak), versus one caterpillar on an ornamental pear tree. The next day he surveyed two more trees, with similar results: 233 caterpillars on the white oak versus only one caterpillar on a non-native pear tree.

Woodpeckers love the soft trunks.
Photo: Ed Jensen

Note the thin, flat petiole. Photo: Ed Jensen

Quaking Aspen *(Populus tremuloides)*

There aren't many quaking aspen stands remaining in Portland or elsewhere in the Willamette Valley, but it's still a tree worth knowing.

When you come across an aspen grove, you might notice that many of the trees are the same sex and roughly the same size—that's because they're clones. There's a parent root system a few inches underground, from which new trees (ramets) sprout.

One quaking aspen clone in Utah is said to have 47,000 trees attached to the same root—making it arguably the single largest organism in the world.

Aspen groves are wonderfully species-rich places. Sit for a while and you'll hear the buzz and chirp and flutter of activity all around you. Aspen leaves are popular with insects, providing good hunting for birds and bats. Elk drop their calves in aspen stands, dozens of bird species nest in the trees, beavers and other rodents eat the tree parts and surrounding vegetation, and all of the above activity entices predators ranging from hawks to coyotes.

To deepen your appreciation of aspen groves, listen as the leaves rustle in the wind, or "repeat the wind's gossip," as novelist Richard Powers describes it. The soothing sound resembles that of a waterfall.

ID tips: Slender trees grow in groves and have chalky white bark marked with black scars. Roughly triangular leaves dangle like earrings on flattened petioles and have pale-green undersides that flash in breezes. Leaves turn yellow, gold, or red in autumn.

Locations: Here and there along streams and in forest openings, including at Tualatin River National Wildlife Refuge and Camassia Natural Area.

DID YOU KNOW?

Look closely and you might notice a greenish tinge to the bark of quaking aspen trees. That's chlorophyll that allows the trunks to continue photosynthesizing even after leaves drop in autumn.

Red Alder *(Alnus rubra)*

Foresters long viewed red alder as a weed of a tree that competed for light and nutrients with more desirable conifers. But in fact red alder is a healer that hides in plain sight, moving into sites that have been burned, logged, or flooded to rapidly restore life, before dying off to make room for other species to thrive.

Millions of alders line just about every pond, river, and stream across the Northwest—far more than oaks or maples or any other broadleaf tree. As writer William Dietrich notes, "If you're not sure which tree is an alder, put on a blindfold and walk into the woods. The first big-leaf tree you bump into will probably be one."

Alders don't turn pretty colors in fall or produce tasty berries, but don't underestimate or overlook them: Ecologically speaking, these are among our most beneficial trees. Alder roots have clusters of coral-like bacteria nodules on them. The tree feeds sugars to the bacteria, and in turn the bacteria converts atmospheric nitrogen captured in the soil into a water-soluble form that's nutritious for the tree.

In just five years, alders can grow as tall as a three-story building. Photo: Ed Jensen

That symbiotic relationship with bacteria is why alders can grow in muddy banks and other sites where other species can't. But alders don't simply enrich their own lives; their roots and fallen leaves leak nitrogen into the surrounding soil, feeding other plants, and some leaves land in the water where they nourish phytoplankton. As foresters eventually discovered, if you plant Douglas-firs with alders, the Doug-firs grow bigger and healthier than they do alone.

Leaves fold lightly in the middle, like tacos. Photo: Ed Jensen

Speaking of supporting life, red alders also provide forage for deer and elk, nesting spots for birds, and construction material for beavers. And, as if all that weren't enough, their root systems help hold banks together and prevent erosion.

ID tips: Small to midsize trees, usually with white crustose lichen growing on the trunk, creating a mottled gray-white look. Leaves (2–6 in. long) are a darker green above and lighter below, with

Left: The long male catkins produce pollen. Right: Female catkins look like tiny woody cones. Photos: Ed Jensen

margins rolled under slightly (helpful for ID). Leaves are doubly sawtoothed, with blunt serrations along the margins. Male catkins (4–6 in. long) are much longer than female catkins, which look like inch-tall pinecones; both emerge in fall and persist through winter.

Locations: Most common along forested waterways toward the coast and Mt. Hood, but look for them in Forest Park and places like Tideman Johnson City Park.

Fruits are oblong. Photo: Ed Jensen

Western Crabapple (*Malus fusca*)

Cultivated apple trees were developed from humble, shrubby crabapple trees like this one largely to produce alcoholic cider. Bite into a western crabapple fruit, and you'll understand why the cultivation was necessary—they're small, hard, and sometimes tart (the Quileute name for the tree translates as "hurts the tongue").

Honeycrisps are far more popular for snacking, but for your backyard you can't go wrong with western crabapples. From late April to June, they produce the fragrant and attractive white blossoms typical of cultivated apple trees, and in summer, their small "apples"—oblong and less than an inch long—feed finches, cedar waxwings, and other birds.

Look for crabapples growing wild in swampy woodlands. They're one of relatively few tree species comfortable with having their feet wet year-round—a feature those fancy honeycrisp trees can't match.

ID tips: Very similar to black hawthorn. Leaves have toothed and sometimes lobed margins. Stems have blunt spurs (short shoots), not sharp thorns. White to (rarely) pink flowers appear in small clusters. Fruits are yellow to red and oblong, not round like hawthorn fruits.

Locations: Occasionally seen in moist, sunny areas, including at Reed College, Forest Park, and Tryon Creek State Natural Area.

Spurs are not sharp like on hawthorns. Photo: Ed Jensen

Leaf margins are toothed or lobed. Photo: Ed Jensen

BIG FRUIT FOR BIG ANIMALS

Next time you spread avocado on your toast (or pay $12 for someone to do it for you), consider that you're eating the flesh of a large—very large—fruit. Which raises the question: Why do some trees expend so much energy producing humongous avocados (and guavas, papayas, etc.) instead of producing lots of small fruits like crabapples?

Researchers believe the answer is that large fruits (those not developed more recently by plant breeders) are holdovers, or "ghosts of evolution," that evolved to appeal to megafauna, including mammoths and truck-sized ground sloths that roamed the Earth until about 13,000 years ago.

Willows (*Salix* spp.)

Just about any wild place where water meets land, you'll find thicket after thicket of willows with their distinctive yellowish (or sometimes reddish) stems. Exactly which willow species you'll see is a whole lot harder to say because Oregon has several dozen that hybridize and are notoriously difficult to tell apart.

Four of the bigger and more common willow species in the Portland area are Columbia River (*S. exigua*), Pacific (*S. lasiandra* var. *lasiandra*), Scouler (*S. scouleriana*), and Sitka (*S. sitchensis* var. *sitchensis*).

All willows are hugely important to the environment. They help stabilize streambanks, and they shade the water, keeping it cool for fish and smaller animals. Songbirds nest in willow thickets, their early blooms provide one of the first spring food sources for native insects, and lots of larger animals like beavers rely on the trees for food.

Not for nothing, willows are also beautiful trees that give us some much-needed color through our long winter months.

ID tips: Leaves are simple, alternate, and usually long and thin (like canoes). Male and female flowers appear early in spring on separate trees. Female catkins develop seeds with white tufts of cottony down that float long distances in the wind or water. Like cottonwoods, willows can also reproduce via broken branches and stem fragments.

Locations: Willows grow along pretty much every river and stream in the Portland area.

A willow along the Willamette River.
Photo: Tracy Aue

Hairs carry seeds, leaving the empty capsules at right.
Photo: © Al Schneider, swcoloradowildflowers.com

 WILLOW MEDICINE

Ancient peoples discovered that chewing willow leaves and bark helped reduce aches and fever. The reason is that willow contains salicin, which the body turns into salicylic acid. In the 1890s, German chemist Felix Hoffman developed an altered version of salicin called acetylsalicylic acid. His employer was a little company called Bayer, and they named the new drug aspirin.

SHRUBS

Red bracts support twin sets of berries.
Photo: Tracy Aue

Black Twinberry *(Lonicera involucrata)*

Blooms: Spring to summer

It might surprise you to learn that this is the most common and widely distributed honeysuckle in the West. Unlike most of its brethren, black twinberry is a shrub, not a vine, and it's not invasive. In fact, it's native, hardy, colorful, and a great choice for gardens.

Hummingbirds and butterflies are attracted to the tubular yellow flowers of black twinberry, and many humans are attracted to the pretty pairs of black berries that stand out in contrast with the reddish bracts that support them.

Twinberry's glossy berries are variously described as inedible or too bitter to bother with (coastal tribes called them "crow berry" and "monster's food"). Better to leave them for birds and other wildlife.

ID tips: 2–10 ft. tall. Leaves (1–5 in. long) are dark green, oval to elliptic, pointy-tipped, and opposite one another along the stem. In spring and early summer, look for pairs of yellow tubular or trumpet-shaped flowers, supported by 2 leaf-like bracts that turn from green to purplish-maroon and later support pairs of black berries.

Locations: Fairly common on moist ground at the edge of woods and along streams, including at Powell Butte Nature Park and Tualatin Hills Nature Park.

FOREST SCAVENGER LIST

This scavenger list for the young and young at heart is adapted from *Sharing Nature with Children* by Joseph Cornell. Don't pick or remove parts from living plants, especially at Portland parks, but look for the items on the ground at local natural areas.

- ☐ A feather
- ☐ A seed
- ☐ Exactly 12 of something
- ☐ A pine cone
- ☐ Something round
- ☐ Five pieces of human-made litter
- ☐ Something perfectly straight
- ☐ Something beautiful
- ☐ Something white
- ☐ Something that makes a noise
- ☐ Something soft
- ☐ Something that reminds you of yourself

California Hazelnut *(Corylus cornuta)*

Blooms: Very early spring

I believe it is every native Oregonian's right to roll our eyes at the astronomical sums charged for fancy "hazelnuts."

When I was young, we talked on phones that were tethered to the wall, we rolled down car windows using our arms, and we picked the nuts formerly known as filberts off the ground for pennies a pound at area orchards.

The filberts we ate fell from imported filbert trees probably introduced to Oregon by French settlers. It was English settlers who called this similar native shrub a hazelnut. In 1981, the Oregon Filbert Commission wisely decided to apply that more appealing term to the nuts they were producing on their filbert trees. Since

Cornuta means "horned," referring to the pointy husks. Photo: Mark Leppin

then, hazelnut prices have risen, they've been named Oregon's official nut, and the Willamette Valley has become by far the leading U.S. supplier of hazelnuts.

While the hazelnut industry relies on cultivated, blight-resistant trees, the California hazelnut is a wonderfully beneficial native shrub that grows easily in backyards and natural areas across Portland. It's the first shrub to bloom in the city, its dangling male catkins opening as early as January to release pollen that travels to tiny red female flowers—and to the noses of allergy sufferers.

In fall, California hazelnut leaves turn a golden yellow and paired nuts develop on the branches. Go ahead and try to outrace squirrels, birds, and other wildlife to the nuts (they're free).

ID tips: Shrub or small tree, up to 13 ft. tall. Yellow-brown male catkins (2–4 in. long) dangle from branches in late winter to early spring, along with inconspicuous female flowers (only the red reproductive parts protrude from gray-brown buds). Softly hairy leaves, oblong to oval, emerge next and have doubly sawtoothed margins. In fall, the fuzzy leaves turn bright yellow and paired nuts develop, enclosed in husks that stick out past the nuts to form a beak.

Locations: Common in moist forest openings and edges, including at Powell Butte Nature Park, Hoyt Arboretum, and Tryon Creek State Natural Area.

Other names include beaked hazelnut and western hazel. Photo: Mark Leppin

Male catkins release pollen in spring. Photo: LeeAnn Kriegh

Red stigmas stick out of early-spring flowers. Photo: Rick Shory

It's also called steeplebush or rose spirea. Photo: WinterCreek Nursery

Douglas Spiraea (*Spiraea douglasii*)

Blooms: All summer

There are lots of spiraeas, both wild and cultivated, but with its tall pink to red blooms, Douglas spiraea, or hardhack, is by far the best-known native species. By early summer, spiraea's fuzzy blooms look like cotton candy on a stick, attracting a bevy of butterflies, hummingbirds, and other pollinators. The colorful summer blooms eventually turn dark brown and persist that way through winter.

Douglas spiraea grows naturally only in flat, low, wet spots, where it spreads to form dense stands. As a fast-growing, deep-rooted shrub, it supports streambanks and provides a convenient hiding spot for birds, amphibians, and other small critters.

ID tips: 3–7 ft. tall. Oblong to elliptic leaves are toothed only across the tips and spiral in an alternate fashion along the stems. Best known for long (4–6 in.), erect, pink to red flower clusters in July and August.

Locations: Stands are common in open, moist, and disturbed areas, including Tryon Creek State Natural Area and Oaks Bottom Wildlife Refuge.

Long stamens create that fuzzy look.
Photo: Tracy Aue

A gorgeous cluster of red elderberries. Photo: M.A. Willson

Elderberries *(Sambucus* spp.*)*

Blooms: Spring to early summer

It's not easy to tell a small tree from a tall shrub. David Allen Sibley of birding fame provided one of the simpler distinctions when he said, "If you can walk under it, it's a tree; if you have to walk around it, it's a shrub." By that definition, most elderberries qualify as shrubs—but not all, since you can certainly walk under some grand old specimens.

Leaves are long and opposite each other on the stems. Photo: LeeAnn Kriegh

In the wild, the long compound leaves of elderberries make them relatively easy to identify even when they're not covered in cream-colored flowers or colorful berries. The west side of the Cascades is best known for red elderberries *(S. racemosa),* which have cone-shaped flower clusters, but you also might spot blue elderberries *(S. cerulea)* that have flatter sprays of flowers.

Elderberries are renowned for their medicinal uses, and they're terrific plants for wildlife. The flowers lure hummingbirds and other pollinators, and birds, squirrels, mice, raccoons, and other species eat the fruit—something you should generally avoid (although blue elderberries are delicious when cooked).

ID tips: Large shrub to small tree, up to 26 ft. tall. Ash-like leaves are long and opposite in arrangement, with each leaf pinnately divided into long leaflets. Yellow-white flowers bloom in flat sprays on blue elderberry and in a tall cone shape on red elderberry, followed by clumps of berry-like fruits.

Locations: Red elderberry is common in forests and waterside at sites including Mt. Tabor, Reed College canyon, and Powell Butte Nature Park. Blue elderberry isn't common in Portland, but you can find it near Oaks Amusement Park and at Fernhill Wetlands and Hoyt Arboretum.

All native huckleberries are edible and great for gardens. Photo: Tracy Aue

Huckleberries *(Vaccinium spp.)*

Blooms: Spring

It's one of the classic Oregon backcountry experiences to stumble upon a patch of huckleberries and stop to savor a handful of the little jewels. Ah, the joy of "eating wildness," as author Asta Bowen described it. The best-tasting huckleberry species are thinleaf or black huckleberry *(V. membranaceum)* and oval-leaf huckleberry *(V. ovalifolium).*

Note the shelf-like branches of red huckleberry. Photo: Ed Jensen

Now for the bad news: Those delights don't grow in Portland, where we have to settle for the tart and sparse berries of red huckleberry *(V. parvifolium)*, a common species that grows out of rotting logs and stumps in area forests. Evergreen huckleberry *(V. ovatum)*, which bears small blue-black berries, is also popular in backyard plantings.

Needless to say, post-Columbus immigrants did not discover huckleberries. For thousands of years, Native peoples spent late summer and fall up in the mountains picking, preserving, and eating the berries. They also used controlled wildfires to create and maintain berry patches since many huckleberries prefer open, sunny areas and can re-sprout from their roots after fire.

ID tips: 1–12 ft. tall. Red huckleberry branches often parallel the ground like shelves. The delicate leaves are oval to elliptic and alternate along the stems. Single, urn-shaped green to pink flowers hang down; berries are red. Evergreen huckleberry has leathery, lance-shaped leaves, finely toothed and paler underneath (popular in floral arrangements). Pink, urn-shaped flowers hang in dense clusters of up to a dozen; berries are small and bluish-black.

Locations: Common in forest openings and wet meadows, including at Powell Butte Nature Park, Tryon Creek State Natural Area, and Forest Park.

Look for leathery leaves and urn-shaped blooms. Photo: Ed Jensen

Kinnikinnick (*Arctostaphylos uva-ursi*)

Blooms: Late spring

Let us count the year-round virtues of kinnikinnick: It grows easily in backyards without being terribly aggressive, it's drought-resistant and cold-tolerant, it forms mats that help prevent erosion, its urn-shaped blooms appeal to hummingbirds and bees, it has evergreen leaves that change color in fall, and its red berries feed local wildlife into winter.

For those reasons and more, it's easy to see why kinnikinnick is among Portland's most popular native groundcovers.

Birds are the primary beneficiaries of the berries, but bears love them too, leading to the other common name of bearberry. Native peoples and early pioneers sometimes dried and smoked the leathery leaves, typically mixed with tobacco and other leaves and bark. That's where we get the word "kinnikinnick," an intertribal word for the smoking mixture.

ID tips: Prostrate shrub, up to 20 in. tall. Low-growing mats have shiny, leathery leaves (up to 1 in. long) that tend to be obovate, meaning they're egg-shaped and widest near the tip. Clusters of urn-shaped flowers are white to pink and appear in late spring, followed by red, mealy fruits.

Uva means "grape" and ursus means "bear"; the berries are "bear's grapes." Photos: Ed Jensen

Locations: Uncommon in open to partially shaded areas, including at Camassia Natural Area and Oxbow Regional Park.

Crush and rub a leaf and it will foam into a lather.
Photo: M.A. Willson

Mock-Orange (Philadelphus lewisii)

Blooms: Late spring to midsummer

Mock-orange's bright and delicately fragrant flowers were popular as wedding decorations in the early 1900s, and their blooms remain one of the great beauties of spring. In May and June, make a point of finding a mock-orange shrub so you can sniff the snow-white flowers—some have the sweet aroma of orange blossoms.

Mock-orange is not especially prolific in the wild, but you can spot it here and there in area parks and forests. Better yet, plant it in your own backyard. It's an adaptable shrub that grows well in full sun to partial shade, in soils ranging from dry to moist. Just make sure to buy this native species, not the European import, *P. coronarius*.

ID tips: Up to about 10 ft. tall. Oval leaves are oppositely arranged on the stem, each prominently 3-veined. Leaves turn a soft yellow in fall. Fragrant flowers can be up to 1 in. in diameter; each has 4 showy white petals and a center with lots of golden-yellow stamens.

Locations: Common in moist woods and conifer forests, including at Tryon Creek State Natural Area, Oaks Bottom Wildlife Refuge, and atop Mt. Tabor.

Waves of oceanspray in summer.
Photo: Ed Jensen

Oceanspray (Holodiscus discolor)

Blooms: Late spring to early summer

If you're not sure why a Portland-area shrub would be called oceanspray, just wait until June, when cascading sprays of white flowers dangle from the ends of this common shrub's arching branches, often with buzzing bees aboard.

Native tribes used oceanspray wood to make fish hooks, knitting needles, and arrow shafts, after hardening it with fire, and Euro-American settlers found the wood hard enough to use as pegs that took the place of nails. These days, you might want to plant oceanspray on steep, crumbly banks where its sturdy roots will hold soil in place (salal is another good choice). Oceanspray is also a host plant for several native butterfly species, including Lorquin's Admirals.

ID tips: 1-20 ft. tall. Alternate leaves (up to 3 in. long) are oval with shallow lobes along the margins and paler undersides. Summer brings dense clusters (up to 1 ft. long) of tiny white to cream-colored flowers that later turn darker cream and then brown. Dry brown fruits hang in clusters through winter.

Locations: Common in moist woods and rocky areas, including at Hoyt Arboretum, Mt. Tabor, and Tryon Creek State Natural Area.

Orange Honeysuckle *(Lonicera ciliosa)*

Blooms: Late spring and early summer
Honeysuckles tend to be a little creepy, or sometimes a lot creepy, clambering up and over walls and trees and anything else that gets in their way. This particular climber is one of a handful of wildlife-friendly honeysuckle vines native to the Pacific Northwest.

As with most honeysuckles—another native you might come across is pink honeysuckle *(L. hispidula)*—orange honeysuckle has tube-shaped flowers designed to accommodate the long bills of hummingbirds.

While some other honeysuckles use a sweet scent to entice pollinators, this one depends on its colorful blooms to beckon not only hummingbirds but also butterflies and other insects.

ID tips: Trailing or twining vine, 6–10 ft. tall (depending on what it has climbed up). Opposite pairs of leaves (1–4 in. long) have paler undersides; the upper 1–2 pairs of leaves are fused like a platter just below the flowers. Flowers (about 1 in. long) splay outward at the tips, displaying the reproductive parts. Orange-red berries are generally considered inedible.

Locations: Occasionally seen on the outskirts of forested areas and oak woodlands, including at Forest Park, Tryon Creek State Natural Area, and Hoyt Arboretum.

Upper leaves are fused like a platter.
Photo: M.A. Willson

Note the holly-like leaves.
Photo: M.A. Willson

It's also called mahonia.
Photo: Tracy Aue

Oregon Grape *(Berberis* spp.)

Blooms: Early spring

Should Oregon's state flower be a fragile showstopper—a cultivated peony like Indiana's or a peach flower like Delaware's? Nah, no thanks. Ours is this common and useful shrub that provides essential wildlife habitat, is a handsome and hardy addition to gardens, and can be made into a bold yellow dye, a tasty jelly and wine, and medicine to treat everything from itchy eyes to syphilis.

On this side of the Cascades, you're most likely to come across Cascade Oregon grape *(B. nervosa)* in forested areas. You also might spot the much taller, and appropriately named, tall Oregon grape *(B. aquifolium),* the species that was named our state flower in 1899. East of the Cascades, you'll see a lower-growing species called creeping Oregon grape *(B. repens).*

All Oregon grapes bloom early in spring, which makes them especially valuable to native pollinators. When bees and others visit the flowers, the anthers literally spring to action and, like a king wielding a scepter, deposit pollen on the insects' heads. (Touch the stamens inside the flowers to see how it works.)

ID tips: Holly-like, with dark-green, jagged-edged, pointy-tipped evergreen leaflets. Yellow flowers grow in clusters; dark berries emerge summer to fall. Cascade Oregon grape maxes out at about 3 ft. tall and has 7–23 flat, narrow leaflets, each with 3 veins. Tall Oregon grape can reach at least 6.5 ft. tall and generally has 5–9 leaflets, each wavy and deeply glossy, with 1 midvein.

Locations: Very common in a variety of habitats, including forest understories and other moist areas. Look for Oregon grapes just about everywhere you go, including at Mt. Tabor and Forest Park.

THE STORY BEHIND OUR STATE FLOWER

In 1890, the Oregon Horticultural Society formed a committee to nominate a state flower. For more than two years, the committee fought over (er, debated) Washington lily, trillium, blanket flower, madrone, and Oregon grape. Finally, in 1892 the committee forwarded its nomination of Oregon grape to the Oregon Legislature ... which sat on it for seven more years. Only after the Oregon Federation of Women's Clubs rallied the support of women statewide did the legislature finally adopt the attractive and useful Oregon grape as state flower.

Osoberry *(Oemleria cerasiformis)*

Blooms: Early spring

Osoberry, formerly called Indian plum, has a brief burst of fame early each spring, when it's one of the very first plants to bloom in Portland. Bumblebees and other hungry pollinators depend on the sprightly clusters of greenish-white flowers, which also give a lift to our heavy winter hearts.

Once the blooms are gone, osoberry disappears. Or, okay, it doesn't actually disappear, but it recedes into the forest greenery where it largely goes unnoticed until early spring rolls around again.

Make a point of identifying this shrub, and you'll be rewarded: The leaves have a pleasant cucumber smell when crushed. And those delicate flowers? Female plants tend to have fewer flower clusters and a nice scent (some say it too resembles cucumber), while male plants have more inflorescences and give off an odeur de dirty socks, or possibly cat urine.

The leaves look like Tinker Bell's wings.
Photo: Tracy Aue

ID tips: Large shrub to small tree, 5–20 ft. tall. Lance-shaped leaves (2–5 in. long) alternate along the stem and have paler undersides. Bell-shaped, greenish-white flowers hang in clusters, opening in late winter or early spring. On female plants, clusters of 1–5 plum-like fruits mature from yellow or orange to red or dark purple.

Locations: Common along rivers and streams and other moist areas, including at Forest Park, Hoyt Arboretum, Tryon Creek State Natural Area, and Sauvie Island.

You'll have to race birds and rodents to the precious berries. Photo: Ed Jensen

WHY ARE BUMBLEBEES SO HUNGRY IN SPRING?

Where do bumblebees go in winter? Well, all the males and non-queen females die before winter. That leaves the survival of bumblebee species up to young, pregnant queens who, all alone, try to stay alive in abandoned rodent holes, under our garden sheds, and wherever else they can find shelter. Many queens die over Portland's long winter months, but the survivors emerge in early spring, desperately hungry for nectar (sugar) and pollen (protein). To support bumblebees and all our other native bee species, plant early-blooming plants like osoberry and Oregon grape in your yard.

Snowball-shaped flower clusters get ready to burst. Photo: M.A. Willson

Pacific Ninebark *(Physocarpus capitatus)*

Blooms: Late spring or early summer

Most ninebark species—including a number of ornamental cultivars and this native shrub—are colorful all year long, earning their reputation in the landscaping industry as "four-season charmers."

In spring, lobed leaves emerge on Pacific ninebark, along with white puffballs of flower clusters that contain red-tipped stamens. In summer, the flowers give way to reddish-brown fruits surrounding yellow seeds. In fall, the leaves turn a pretty rosy-brown. And in winter, the bare branches show you where ninebark got its name, as the branches shred a few layers (not really nine) to reveal bronze-colored bark.

ID tips: 5–8 ft. tall. Leaves alternate along the stem and have 3–5 lobes with sawtoothed margins. White flowers bloom in domed clusters. Shredding bark is orangish-brown to bronze.

Locations: Fairly common along streambanks and in open woods, including at Tryon Creek State Natural Area, Tualatin Hills Nature Park, and Hoyt Arboretum.

Note the colorful pollen. Photo: LeeAnn Kriegh

The scientific name means "rose tree with big leaves." Photo: Tracy Aue

Pacific Rhododendron *(Rhododendron macrophyllum)*

Blooms: Spring through summer

One of the many highlights of late spring and summer in Portland is walking past spectacular displays of rhododendrons in yards and parks across the city. Those rhododendrons are cultivated ornamentals, but if you head out on a trail near the coast or in the Cascades, you can enjoy plenty of examples of this wild native.

Pacific rhododendron became Washington's state flower after a competition in 1893. Every state needed to choose a flower to represent it at the World's Fair in Chicago, and Washington's competition came down to the Pacific rhododendron and a clover. Universal suffrage wouldn't come for nearly three more decades, but on this subject only women were allowed to vote, and they wisely chose the rhody.

That's the real story of how this plant became Washington's state flower, although in his book on Northwest natural history, Daniel Mathews offers a tongue-in-cheek alternative, suggesting that Washington chose the Pacific rhododendon "to make up for having fewer of them than Oregon."

ID tips: Evergreen up to 13 ft. tall, resembling a small tree in shade and a dense bush in the open. Large (3–6 in.) leaves are leathery, smooth (no hairs), and usually elliptical. Showy clusters have 10–20 flowers each.

Locations: Not found naturally in the Portland area, but it's at Marquam Nature Park and is common along the Oregon Coast and in the Cascades. Washington Park, and many streets in Portland are good places to see ornamental rhododendrons.

Say it with me: "Leaves of three? Let it be!" Photo: Tracy Aue

Leaves turn red in late summer.
Photo: Evelyn Sherr

Poison Oak (*Toxicodendron diversilobum*)

Blooms: Late spring to early summer

As the botanist John Howell observed, there's a lot to love about poison oak (stay with me here): "In spring, the ivory flowers bloom on the sunny hill or in sheltered glade, in summer its fine green leaves contrast refreshingly with dried and tawny grassland, in autumn its colors flame more brilliantly than in any other native ..."

Ah, but there is the one "great fault," as Howell also noted: Poison oak is poisonous, albeit only to people (wildlife love it). Touch those dreaded leaves of three—or handle dogs or clothing that have touched the plants—and after one to three days, or sometimes longer, you'll regret it. A single drop of the plant's urushiol oil causes deeply irritating itching and stinging that lasts up to several weeks.

If your skin touches any part of poison oak—even dead poison oak—wash right away with soap. You should also wash anything else that may have touched the plant, including your clothes, dogs, hiking poles, and loved ones. Never put poison oak in a burn pile because its smoke can severely irritate your nose, throat, and lungs, as wildland firefighters know all too well.

ID tips: 3–10 ft. tall; sometimes a tree-climbing vine. Stems are reddish-brown or gray. Leaves are divided into 3 (sometimes 5) round to oblong leaflets (up to 5 in. long by 3 in. wide). Leaf margins can be smooth, wavy, or lobed, similar to native oak leaves. Leaf tops tend to be shiny and smooth. Flowers are small, white-green, and inconspicuous. White fruits appear in bunches in late summer. In fall, leaves turn beautiful hues of red and coral.

Locations: Common in woodlands and on rocky slopes. Watch out for it along many trails, including at Camassia Nature Park, Tryon Creek State Natural Area, and Cooper Mountain Nature Park.

Gooseberries have prickles; currants like this one don't. Photo: M.A. Willson

Red-flowering Currant *(Ribes sanguineum)*

Blooms: Early spring

Plant lovers get a little protective—dare I say even grouchy—when the plants they care most about are harmed by the less-worshipful public.

Such was the case for my favorite cranky botanist, Martin Gorman, who wrote in the early 1900s of red-flowering currant: "Of all our native wild flowers this beautiful shrub suffers most at the hands of the low, ignorant and vicious individuals with which all our cities are infested."

Ribes fruits are edible, but these are tasteless to sour. Photo: Mark Leppin

Gorman's concern was with the "Sunday rabble" who would dig up and transplant this beauty into their gardens. These days, I like to think we know better and will instead head to local nurseries to buy red-flowering currant, which rewards us with its burnt-umber bark and bright foliage—and its absolutely stunning early-spring clusters of blooms that attract scores of hummingbirds and other pollinators.

Along with its status as one of Portland's most beautiful native species, another reason to plant red-flowering currant in your yard is that its flowers have a delightfully sweet aroma that rivals that of mock-orange, oceanspray, wild roses, and other popular native shrubs.

ID tips: Up to 13 ft. tall. Leaves alternate along the stem, each with 3–5 lobes. Beautiful white to red flowers hang in clusters of 10–20 flowers. Blue-black berries are edible but not tasty.

Locations: Common in forests, along streams, and in restored areas, including at Reed College canyon, Sauvie Island, Hoyt Arboretum, and Forest Park.

How can you identify a dogwood? By its bark.
Photo: Ron Halvorson

A cluster of dogwood fruits. Photo: Kim Elton

Red-osier Dogwood
(Cornus sericea)

Blooms: Late spring to summer

In winter, take a look at the shrubs lining area waterways. What colors do you see? Odds are there will be lots of thin, yellowish stems—those are likely willows. There will also be some thickets of red stems that typically belong to red-osier dogwood.

Also called western, creek, or redstem dogwood, red-osier dogwood is common in backyards and wetland areas across much of North America. It's one of the prettiest native shrubs in Portland, with its flashy stems and large clusters of white flowers that start to bloom in May. The fruits that arrive in summer are eaten by robins, cedar waxwings, and other birds.

When you look at the rounded clusters of red-osier dogwood flowers, you might think it strange that it's related to other dogwoods, including Pacific dogwood trees and bunchberry wildflowers. But look closely at one small white flower in a cluster, and you'll see that it's a miniature version of our other dogwood blooms, with four small white petals (not bracts, in this case) surrounding a golden middle.

Look for: Up to 13 ft. tall. New stems are dark red to purplish, graying with age like the rest of us. Leaves are arranged opposite one another on stems. Leaves are typically 2–4 in. long and oval to elliptic with pointed tips. Both flowers and fruits are white to creamy in color and appear in tight, rounded clusters.

Found: Common along area waterways, including at the Columbia Slough, Kelley Point Park, Tryon Creek State Natural Area, and Oaks Bottom Wildlife Refuge.

Roses (*Rosa* spp.)

Blooms: Late spring to summer

The Rose City is a rose-obsessed place, home both to the Rose Quarter, where the Blazers play, and the International Rose Test Garden in Washington Park, where over 650 varieties of roses grow.

Wild roses are found all across Portland, but there are only three native species: baldhip (*R. gymnocarpa*), Nootka (*R. nutkana*), and swamp (*R. pisocarpa*). All three form dense thickets that shelter birds and other wildlife.

A few general tips to tell the species apart: Baldhip rose is a smaller shrub with up to three flowers in a loose cluster. The brown sepals fall off the hips when they mature (hence the name).

Nootka rose is named for the Nootka Sound of Vancouver Island. It has stout thorns where its leaves emerge and singular, large flowers that bloom in May.

Swamp rose, which grows in swampy areas, has clusters of flowers and blooms up to a month later than Nootka.

Not to confuse you further, but you also might see exotic roses such as multiflora rose (*R. multiflora*) and a non-native species called dog rose (*R. canina*) that has hooked prickles and football-shaped hips.

ID tips: Baldhip is the smallest native rose, a scraggly, weak-stemmed shrub that grows up to 5 ft. tall, often in deep shade, and has soft, straight prickles and rounded leaflets with double-toothed edges. Nootka rose can grow up to 10 ft. tall and has big, single flowers (2–3 in. across) and large hips (up to 1 in. long). Swamp rose has sharply pointed leaflets, clusters of up to 20 flowers, and smaller hips than Nootka.

Locations: Common in lots of moist areas, forest slopes, and roadsides, including along the Springwater Corridor Trail, at wetland areas, and at Forest Park.

Large, mostly single flowers suggest this is a Nootka rose. Photo: Tracy Aue

Baldhip rose, one of our three natives. Photo: Evelyn Sherr

It's also known as Oregon wintergreen. Photo: Evelyn Sherr

*Urn-shaped flowers are a hallmark of the heath family.
Photo: Mark Leppin*

Salal *(Gaultheria shallon)*

Blooms: Spring through summer

Salal has it all: beauty, tastiness, historic interest, and ecological value. It's probably the most common shrub west of the Cascades, a typically hardy and resilient Oregonian that shades our forest floors with its leathery leaves.

Back in 1806, Lewis and Clark noted salal's value to wildlife, including the elk they saw eating its leaves, and to Native people who dried the purple berries into cakes and loaves said to weigh up to 15 pounds. You can still stain your tongue blue on the berries David Douglas called "by far the best in the country"—although, as naturalist Daniel Mathews notes, that was before Douglas encountered huckleberries.

Perhaps because it spreads by rhizome and grows to unpredictable heights, salal is not terribly popular among gardeners, nor is it much remarked upon by hikers. Florists know about salal, however—they make millions off its foliage, which is frequently used as a backdrop for bouquets.

ID tips: Up to 6.5 ft. tall. Forms dense thickets. Stems feel sticky and twigs zig-zag slightly between nodes. Oval leaves are leathery and alternate along the stems. Urn-shaped white to pale-pink flowers dangle from stem tips. Blue to blackish berries are juicy in early to midsummer, turning mealy over time.

Locations: Very common in forests, roadsides, and riverbanks. Look for it in any forest, including at Forest Park, Hoyt Arboretum, and Tualatin Hills Nature Park.

YUM! PORTLAND'S TASTIEST NATIVE FRUITS

I think these are some of the best-tasting fruits in Portland, but by all means conduct your own research. Just follow a few simple rules: Make sure you know what you're eating, don't pick fruits at City of Portland Parks, and leave plenty for wildlife and the next hiker on the trail.

- o Huckleberries
- o Salal
- o Salmonberry
- o Thimbleberry
- o Trailing blackberry
- o Wild and woodland strawberries

Salmonberry *(Rubus spectabilis)*

Blooms: Early to midspring

I was surprised to read that some people don't like the flavor of salmonberries. Insipid? Mealy? I beg your pardon! To be fair, flavors vary from one patch of clones to the next, but my childhood nostalgia insists that all salmonberries have a faintly sweet taste that will make you want to play outside for a few more hours.

You'll find thickets of salmonberries growing in moist—very moist—areas, where the boldly colored flowers attract bees and hummingbirds as early as March. Salmonberry fruits are among the first of the season, which is a boon to area birds, squirrels, and other wildlife that also eat the leaves and stems.

Spectabilis means "spectacular."
Photo: Evelyn Sherr

Stories abound about where salmonberry's name originated. Among other possibilities, it may refer to the color of the fruits, individual drupelets' resemblance to salmon eggs, or the fact that salmonberries ripen at roughly the same time as spring Chinook salmon runs begin.

ID tips: 6.5–13 ft. tall, forming thickets. Yellowish to red-brownish stems peel with age and have prickles. Most leaves are divided into 3 sharply toothed leaflets; the terminal leaflet is larger than the 2 lower leaflets, which each have a small lobe like the thumb of a mitten. Flowers have 5 pink to magenta petals. Fruit color varies (yellow, orange, red, or rarely black).

Locations: Common in moist woods and along streams, including along Johnson Creek, at Powell Butte Nature Park, and in Forest Park on the Lower Macleay Trail and others.

They're among the first fruits of summer.
Photo: Tracy Aue

"It is a grand fact that you cannot make the fairer fruits or parts of fruits [a] matter of commerce; that is, you cannot buy the highest use and enjoyment of them. You cannot buy that pleasure which it yields to him who truly plucks it. You cannot buy a good appetite even. In short, you may buy a servant or slave, but you cannot buy a friend."

— Henry David Thoreau, *Wild Fruits*

They're pretty, but don't eat them. Photo: M.A. Willson

Snowberry *(Symphoricarpos albus)*

Blooms: Spring to summer

Take a walk in the woods on either side of the Cascades, and you'll have a hard time not coming across common snowberry. You might not notice the bare-branched shrubs in the coldest months, but they'll catch your eye in late spring and summer, when leaves emerge and the shrubs are covered in small pink and white flowers.

Even better is the big autumn show, when white fruits appear all over the many stems. Most of the fruits, commonly called popcorn, hang on through winter, in part because they're a last-ditch option for wildlife. They're also a last-ditch option for us because they taste more like soap than popcorn, and may be toxic in large quantities.

ID tips: 2–6 ft. tall. Opposite leaves are usually small and oval, but they can vary quite a bit; some leaves can be lobed like poison oak. Bell-shaped pink to white flowers are .25 in. across. White fruits grow in small clusters.

Found: Very common in forests and forest openings, including at Hoyt Arboretum, Sauvie Island, and Tualatin Hills Nature Park.

WHY SOME BERRIES TASTE SO BAD

Great-tasting wild berries—we're looking at you, huckleberries—are juicy and filled with sugar. Those berries attract birds and other wildlife that help spread the seeds. Like red-osier dogwood and many other plants, snowberry takes a different approach, producing dry, astringent, bacteria-resistant berries that get passed over—at first. In fall and winter, when juicier berries are long gone, snowberries and their sour ilk become the only game in town.

Thimbleberry *(Rubus parviflorus)*

Blooms: Spring and early summer
Thimbleberry is a stingy shrub that produces a few scant handfuls of delicious fruits; such cruelty! Some people will tell you thimbleberries have a bland taste, and they'll likely say the same of salmonberries. Tastes vary, but let's be clear that these people are wrong.

Thimbleberry's benefits go beyond its tasty berries (technically a bunch of drupelets around a hollow core). It's also a wonderfully useful native shrub that provides cover for wildlife, controls erosion on slopes, and draws pollinators to its wide-open white flowers.

Leaves are big and very soft. Photo: M.A. Willson

Because fruits ripen a few at a time and are too soft to pack and ship, you'll have to enjoy thimbleberries where you find them, whether that's along the road, in forested areas, or in your backyard.

ID tips: 2–9 ft. tall, often forming dense thickets. Stems are brown, shredding, and prickle-free (unlike salmonberry stems). Soft leaves are large and fuzzy, with 3–5 finely toothed lobes, pointed at the tips. Up to 15 white flowers bloom in clusters. Fruits are dark red when ripe.

A tasty, thimble-sized fruit. Photo: Ed Jensen

Locations: Common in open woods and roadsides, including at Forest Park, Powell Butte Nature Park, Hagg Lake, and Cooper Mountain Nature Park.

You'll see lots of thickets like this one. Photo: Ed Jensen

One of our prettiest and most common shrubs. Photo: M.A. Willson

Vine Maple *(Acer circinatum)*

Blooms: Spring

If fall is your favorite season of the year, odds are vine maple is one of your favorite shrubs. Its brilliant yellow, orange, and scarlet colors are one of the surest signs that autumn has arrived.

Leaves turn gorgeous colors in fall.
Photo: M.A. Willson

Vine maples aren't really vines, and with enough sunshine they can even grow into decent-sized trees—look for an enormous old one along the Hawthorn Trail at Hoyt Arboretum. Deeper in the forest understory, vine maples twist and contort and sprawl along the forest floor in a slow-motion quest for sunlight. Individual branches can grow right into the forest floor, forming new roots and more chances to creep along in search of the sun.

In addition to providing eye candy for hikers, vine maple provides nourishment for wildlife. Deer and elk forage on its leaves and bark, which are especially valuable food sources in winter, and other animals dine on its seeds, buds, and flowers. In spring, white and wine-red flowers that are tucked under the leaves offer nectar to bees and butterflies. All these benefits—as well as its glorious fall colors—are why vine maple is one of Portland's most popular native shrubs for landscaping.

ID tips: Shrub or small tree, up to 20 ft. tall. Bark is typically greenish to red. Leaves are opposite one another on the stems, usually with 7–9 lobes that are sharply toothed and pointed at the tips. Flowers have showy white petals and red sepals. Samaras turn reddish and then brown at maturity.

Locations: Common in a variety of habitats, especially along waterways. Look for vine maples in Forest Park, Oaks Bottom Wildlife Refuge, Tryon Creek State Natural Area, and lots of other parks across Portland.

Western Serviceberry
(*Amelanchier alnifolia*)

Blooms: Spring to early summer

In June and July, look in wild places for the cheerful splashes of white that are a hallmark of western serviceberry.

As befits a popular and widespread shrub, this one goes by many other common names, including juneberry (for its bloom time in some areas), Saskatoon (the Canadian city was named after it), shadbush, and my favorite: pigeon berry.

Serviceberry is a terrific choice for backyards, where in addition to its showy white flowers in spring and early summer, it produces tasty fruits in late summer and colorful foliage in fall.

Serviceberry fruits are edible, but I've been told ours are not as delicious as those found east of the Cascades and in Montana and Canada. A late-summer road trip might be in order to perform detailed field research.

ID tips: Shrub or small tree, 3–40 ft. tall. *Alnifolia* refers to the alder-like leaves that alternate along the stem and are elliptic to round, with prominent "teeth" only across the top third or half of the leaf (like Bart Simpson's hair). Star-shaped flowers have 5 narrow petals. Purple-black fruits can be eaten fresh or dried.

Locations: Occasionally seen in the forest understory, on hillsides, and in oak woodlands at places such as Powell Butte Nature Park and Cooper Mountain Nature Park.

They're classified as shrubs but can reach 40 feet tall.
Photo: Tracy Aue

The flowers smell like apple blossoms.
Photo: M.A. Willson

WHERE DID SERVICEBERRY GET ITS NAME?

Legend has it that serviceberry's common name comes from the eastern U.S. and Canada, where its early-spring flowers indicated that the ground had thawed and it was time to dig graves and have funeral services for loved ones who had died over the winter. A related story is that serviceberry was one of the only blooms available for those early-spring funerals. More likely, "service" refers to the many services provided by the shrub or is a transformation of the word "sorbus" that originally referred to a similar plant.

Creamy clusters of clematis blooms. Photo: Ron Halvorson

The fluffy tails help seeds disperse.
Photo: Ron Halvorson

Western Clematis
(Clematis ligusticifolia)

Blooms: Summer

Western clematis is, as a friendly botanist told me, "that viny thing" that climbs up and over fences, shrubs, and trees. You'll see it, as well as lots of cultivated clematis varieties, hanging on trellises and dangling over doorways across Portland.

In the wild, tangled mats of western clematis, or virgin's bower, stabilize streambanks and provide nesting spots for birds. In summer, its flowers feed bees, butterflies, and other native pollinators.

Look closely to tell female and male flowers apart: Male flowers have lots of stamens tipped with cream-colored to greenish pollen, while female flowers have lots of pistils and sterile stamens with no pollen.

ID tips: Climbing, sprawling vine with opposite leaves, pinnately compound and usually divided into 5–7 leaflets. Dense clusters of creamy to white flowers bloom all summer in dense clusters. In fall, look for fluffy-tailed fruits.

Locations: The invasive *C. vitalba* is much more common in the Portland area, but once in a while you'll see native western clematis along rivers, creeks, and roadsides, including at Oaks Bottom Wildlife Refuge and Camassia Natural Area.

FRIEND OR FOE?

Western clematis is a helpful native vine that doesn't tend to grow out of control. It's sometimes called old man's beard, which is confusing because that's also the common name for an exotic, invasive clematis, *C. vitalba* (pg. 120). A key difference is that western clematis usually has strongly toothed leaflets, whereas *C. vitalba* has mostly entire (untoothed) to gently lobed leaflets.

Photo: Tracy Aue

Photo: M.A. Willson

Photo: Tracy Aue

Photo: Tracy Aue

Photo: Tracy Aue

Photo: Edmund Hertz

Photo: Tracy Aue

Photo: Tracy Aue

Photo: Tracy Aue

WILDFLOWERS

Portland is a very, very green city, thanks in large part to the 150 or so days of rain we get each year. It's even green in winter, when thousands of evergreens remain, well, evergreen, and moss continues its steady takeover of the city.

We should celebrate all that verdant splendor, but it's only human to tire even of good things that are available in such abundance. Which brings us to spring and the electric current of hope that jolts us when at long last we see flowers blooming in colors other than green.

Photo: Tracy Aue

Photo: Tracy Aue

Photo: Tracy Aue

Photo: Evelyn Sherr

Photo: M.A. Willson

Trilliums are traditionally thought of as the first wildflower of spring in Portland, their emergence so deeply anticipated that they get their own festival. More whites follow, from small strawberries to drooping fairybells and foaming foamflowers. It's not only whites: blue camas lilies, yellow violets, orange poppies, and other stunners paint Portland-area forests, grasslands, and backyards from spring through fall.

Urban areas are home to lots of non-native blooms too, and this chapter highlights a few of them. But mostly the focus is on our most common native wildflowers—the ones that still grace wild areas in and near town and, in many cases, that we can plant in our own yards to support wildlife and make Portland a more colorful place.

WHITE OR WHITISH
3 OR 6 PETALS

The leaves are technically ovate (oval, wider at the base).
Photo: Gerald D. Carr

Edible fruits are yellow to red.
Photo: Tracy Aue

Clasping-leaved Twisted-stalk (*Streptopus amplexifolius*)

Blooms: Late spring to early summer

Clasping-leaved twisted-stalk is indeed a twisted plant that has earned its place in the *Streptopus* ("twisted foot") genus. The stems have nodes that cause a bit of zig and zag, and most unusually, the flared flowers dangle from delicate, sharply kinked stalks. Take a close look at how the base of each leaf basically surrounds, or clasps, the stem, and you'll understand where this plant got the rest of its convoluted name.

ID tips: Perennial, 1–3.5 ft. tall. Sharply tipped leaves (2–6 in. long) are oblong to oval, have sharp tips, and alternate along the stem. Bell-shaped flowers are tucked under the leaves on twisty stalks, with petal tips flared and curving upward. Half-inch berries are yellow to red.

Locations: Fairly common in moist, rich soils in forests and streamsides, including at Tryon Creek State Natural Area and Forest Park.

LEARN THE LINGO

Millions of plant and animal species have yet to be identified, but those we know of have a two-part scientific name, the genus and species, as in *Homo sapiens*. These clues can help you understand what the names mean, so they'll make more sense and be more memorable.

***douglasii, menziesii*, etc.:** Many terms ending in "i" or "ii" refer to historic figures such as David Douglas and Archibald Menzies.

-flora: "flowers" (*grandiflora* means "large flower"; *uniflora* means "one flower")

-folia, -folius: "foliage"

grandi-, max-, macro-: "big"

occidentalis: "western"

-phylla, -phyllum: "leaves" (*hydrophyllum* means "water leaf"; *heterophylla* means "different types of leaves")

uni-, bi-, tri-, hex-, etc.: The number of particular plant parts

Fairybells (*Prosartes* spp.)

Blooms: Early to late spring

We have a couple fairybells in Portland: Smith's fairybells (*P. smithii*) and more common Hooker's fairybells (*P. hookeri*). Both are perennials with drip tips—long, pointed, deeply veined leaves that channel rainwater off the leaf surface.

Smith's and Hooker's fairybells are named after giants in the field of botany. Sir James E. Smith founded the Linnean Society of London, published numerous books, and made future nature writers weep in envy by contributing 3,348 articles to one publication—in just 11 years.

Not to be outdone, all Sir Joseph Dalton Hooker did in his 94 years was sail the world identifying hundreds of plants, direct the Royal Botanical Gardens at Kew, and aid his pen pal, Charles Darwin, in refining and spreading the word about the latter's little theory on natural selection.

My favorite story about Hooker's diligence: On cold and snowy Desolation Island in the Indian Ocean, where Captain Cook had found fewer than 20 plant species, Hooker identified more than 150, including frozen lichens he gathered by sitting on them till they thawed.

Hooker's fairybells are a great groundcover for shade gardens.
Photo: M.A. Willson

Smith's fairybells hide their stamens inside the blooms.
Photo: Tracy Aue

ID tips: Both are perennials, 1–3 ft. tall. Leaves are oval with pointed tips, alternating along the stem. Hooker's blooms are shorter and hang like bells with stamens dangling down (Smith's hang nearly straight and conceal the stamens within). Hooker's stems and leaves are hairy, not smooth like Smith's. Hooker's flowers are in clusters of 1–3; Smith's clusters have up to 7 flowers.

Locations: Hooker's fairybells are common in moist wooded areas, including Oxbow Regional Park, Graham Oaks Nature Park, and Forest Park. Smith's are in similar areas but are less common. Head toward the coast to see both at Saddle Mountain.

DID YOU KNOW?

Why do so many flowerheads nod, or point toward the ground? One reason might be to avoid rain. Dangling flowers are also tough for crawling insects to reach. Bees, on the other hand, have the requisite gymnastic skills and benefit plants because they're terrific pollen carriers.

They're pretty plants that quickly cover the ground.
Photo: M.A. Willson

False Lily of the Valley
(*Maianthemum dilatatum*)

Blooms: Late spring

False lily of the valley is a beautiful backyard groundcover, so long as you don't mind that it really will cover your backyard.

Also known as snakeberry for its spotted fruits, false lily of the valley is in the same genus as false Solomon's seal and shares that plant's habit of spreading rapidly by rhizome. The two also share the unfortunate "false" moniker, in this case referring to the plant's resemblance to lily of the valley (*Convallaria majalis*), a native of Europe and Asia that's popular in bridal bouquets.

The fruits of false lily of the valley were eaten by various Native tribes, although nature writer Daniel Mathews notes that they did so "unenthusiastically." You can try a few, or leave the bitter berries for birds, rodents, and other creatures that presumably have more enthusiasm for them.

ID tips: Perennial, 4–15 in. tall. Deeply lined, heart-shaped leaves alternate on stems and can reach 8 in. long. Fragrant flowers are clustered around a thin stalk, like a hot dog on a stick. Pea-sized berries age from green to speckled to red. Oddly, the plant parts are in 4's instead of the usual 3's or 6's of the lily family.

Locations: Common in moist forests, including at Forest Park, Hoyt Arboretum, and Powell Butte Nature Park.

Blooms often flare up and back.
Photo: Tracy Aue

Eastern species are called trout lilies because of their mottled leaves. Photo: Tracy Aue

Oregon Fawn Lily (*Erythronium oregonum*)

Blooms: Spring

Everyone loves a lily, from the trilliums that announce spring in Portland to the blazing-orange glory of tiger lilies. From April through early June, one of the city's prettiest lilies is this one, with its lantern-like blossoms dangling gracefully from long stems.

Oregon fawn lily's long and mottled leaves are distinctive, giving rise to the common name. With a little imagination, you can see their resemblance to the spotting on a fawn.

ID tips: Perennial, 6–16 in. tall. A pair of smooth to wavy-edged leaves (4–9 in. long and about half as wide) emerge from the bulb. Leaves are mottled white, brown, and green (avalanche lily lacks the mottling). Each stem has 1–3 flowers (1–2 in. wide).

Locations: Fairly common in meadows and woodlands, including at Forest Park, Kelly Butte Natural Area, Cooper Mountain Nature Park, and Canemah Bluff Nature Park in Oregon City.

False Solomon's Seal
(Maianthemum racemosum)

Blooms: Spring to early summer

False Solomon's seal is saddled with an unfortunate name, forever labeled a pretender to the "real" Solomon's seal (*Polygonatum* spp.) that's in a different genus, isn't native to the Northwest, and has different-looking blooms that hang under its leaves. As writer F. Schuyler Mathews grumbled, "We might as well call a Frenchman a false Englishman."

Large leaves alternate along the stem.
Photo: Tracy Aue

What's true about false Solomon's seal is that it's a big, beautiful, showy understory plant with clustered flowers that have a lusciously sweet scent. Its "false" name purportedly stems from its lack of medicinal qualities compared to species in the *Polygonatum* genus.

ID tips: Perennial, 1–3 ft. tall, with arching stems. Oblong to oval leaves with pointy tips alternate along the stem and are about 3-7 in. long. Clusters of 20 or more fragrant white flowers appear at stem ends. Edible but insipid berries ripen from green to red.

Locations: Common in moist and other soil types in forested areas such as Powell Butte Nature Park, Kelly Butte Natural Area, Jenkins Estate, and Forest Park.

The genus roughly translates as "May blossom." Photo: Kermit Williams

Starry False Solomon's Seal
(Maianthemum stellatum)

Blooms: Late spring to midsummer

To tell starry false Solomon's seal from false Solomon's seal (above), look at the blooms. They are, in fact, starry, with each six-petaled flower spread wide on its own stalk. The leaves are also smaller and narrower than those of false Solomon's seal and have pronounced parallel veins.

ID tips: Perennial, 1–2.5 ft. tall, with arching stems. Alternate leaves are 2–5 in. long, lance-shaped to elliptic, with pointed tips. Up to about 15 dainty, star-like white flowers appear at stem ends, just above the leaves. Berries ripen to dark blue or reddish-black.

Locations: Common in moist soils in area forests, including at Forest Park, Tualatin Hills Nature Park, and Hoyt Arboretum.

Blooms are open and star-like.
Photo: Tracy Aue

Flared petals reveal the reproductive parts.
Photo: Tracy Aue

You can see why it's also called duck's foot.
Photo: LeeAnn Kriegh

Look for mottled leaves. Photo: Kermit Williams

Small white flowers bloom in summer.
Photo: Kermit Williams

Inside-Out Flower *(Vancouveria hexandra)*

Blooms: Late spring to early summer

Inside-out flowers are named for the way their white blooms seem to be pulling themselves backward so far they're going to turn the flower inside out. As with shooting stars *(Dodecatheon* spp.), the blooms droop and swept-back petals reveal the flower's petticoats, or more precisely the reproductive parts. Inside-out flower is a can't-miss plant for gardens: low maintenance and virtually pest free, with pretty leaves shaped like duck feet.

ID tips: Perennial, 8–18 in. tall, often in dense patches. Compound, 3-lobed leaves grow from the base with a lot of heart-shaped leaflets. White sepals and petals bend backward and flare out along long, slender stalks.

Locations: Prefers shady, semi-moist conditions (a Portland specialty). Sites include Hoyt Arboretum, Camassia Natural Area, and Forest Park.

Rattlesnake Plantain *(Goodyera oblongifolia)*

Blooms: Summer

If you've got a thing for orchids, as many people do, but you also want to fill your yard with native plants, rattlesnake plantain is a terrific choice. Yes, it's an orchid, and yes, it's native to the Portland area (other native options include fairy slipper orchids and white bog orchids).

The "rattlesnake" part of the name refers to its mottled leaves. The snakeskin-like pattern led settlers to mistakenly believe the plant could be used to treat rattlesnake bites. In summer, look under older Douglas-firs and western hemlocks for tall flowering spikes with small white flowers.

ID tips: Perennial, 7–16 in. tall. At the base, evergreen rosettes have leathery, lance-shaped to elliptic leaves mottled with white veins. In midsummer, a short, leafless flowering spike emerges bearing white flowers.

Locations: Sparse in the understory of older forests. Look for patches in the West Hills and at Mt. Talbert Nature Park.

> "I am very poorly today & very stupid & hate everybody & everything. One lives only to make blunders. I am going to write a little Book for Murray on orchids & today I hate them worse than everything so farewell & in a sweet frame of mind, I am
> **Ever yours"**
> — Charles Darwin, in a letter to Charles Lyell

To briefly enjoy the vanilla scent, dry a leaflet on your car dash. Photo: M.A. Willson

Vanilla Leaf (*Achlys triphylla*)

Blooms: Spring to midsummer

You can readily identify vanilla leaf by its three fan-shaped leaflets and the white flower spike that stands erect in summer. Go ahead and give the large leaflets a sniff—but expect to be disappointed. Their vanilla scent emerges only when they're dried, leading this plant to be "plucked unsparingly by idle boys" who sold bundles on Portland street corners.

That quote is from Martin Gorman, a botanist who wrote in the early 1900s that people would hang the bundles in their homes and shops to savor the vanilla fragrance as the leaflets dried. Gorman, a droll guy, added, "Were it generally known that any long continued inhalation of this odor is injurious, the practice of hanging up the leaves in bedrooms would undoubtedly be stopped."

Flower spikes can be over a foot tall.
Photo: M.A. Willson

ID tips: Perennial with flower spikes up to 16 in. tall. The 3 wide, flat leaflets (each part of a compound leaf) have wavy outer edges; the smallest middle leaf resembles a goose foot. Flowers have white stamens that make them look fuzzy (*Achlys* means "mist" and probably refers to the flowers).

Locations: Very abundant in shady forests and near streams, including at Forest Park, Hoyt Arboretum, and Powell Butte Nature Park.

FUN FACT

Orchids are named after the shape of their roots, which resemble testicles (*orchis* in Greek). This is also why the Middle English name for an orchid is bollockwort.

Trilliums are a traditional sign of spring in Portland. Photo: Kermit Williams

Western Trillium *(Trillium ovatum)*

Blooms: Early spring

Portland may be the Rose City, but in March it's western trilliums that draw folks out of their homes to trod down muddy forest trails hoping to see that spark of white that means spring—spring at last!—is on its way.

They're also called wake-robins because they bloom just as robins start singing. Photo: Tracy Aue

Portlanders cherish trilliums for many reasons beyond the timing and beauty of their blooms. The leaves and flowers are large and easy to recognize, making them a favorite among children, and the plants are common but not so ubiquitous as to be overlooked or taken for granted.

To deepen your admiration of trilliums, first consider their longevity: Most of the blooms sprout from underground stems (rhizomes) that can be as old as us—70 years or more.

It's sacrilege to pick a trillium not only because doing so deprives other people of the flower's beauty but because the aging rhizome needs its above-ground parts to provide food through photosynthesis. The rhizome stores the nourishment so it's ready to put out early blooms the following spring.

Most trilliums spread by those underground rhizomes, which is why you'll see so many plants growing in patches alongside trails. Trilliums also spread to new areas via seeds that are carried by ants or deposited by deer, but it can take six to eight years for a seed to turn into a blooming plant.

Blooms fade to purple. Photo: Kermit Williams

Another way to appreciate trilliums is to look closely at their sepals, petals, stamens, styles, and leaves. You'll find they're all in multiples of three, a trait typical of lilies. See the three green sepals that support the three petals? And the six pollen-tipped stamens within the flower?

When you hear that trilliums are in bloom, don't delay—you'll need to act fast to see them. Their blooms come early and don't last long, fading from white to purple after only two or three weeks. That's what Shakespeare was referring to when he wrote in "A Midsummer's Night Dream" that Cupid's arrow "fell upon a little western flower, / Before milk-white, now purple with love's wound."

Plant parts are in multiples of three. Photo: M.A. Willson

Whether due to a love dart or not, when the flowers turn purplish, they effectively signal to bees and other pollinators that they should move along and get their protein-laden pollen from the next white trillium along the trail.

ID tips: Perennial, 4–18 in. tall. All parts are in 3's. Large horizontal leaves can reach 8 in. long, and are typically oval and wider at the base (ovate), with no petioles. Showy petals (1–2.5 in.) age from white to purple.

Locations: Common in lots of moist, shady woods. Forest Park and Tryon Creek State Natural Area are hotspots, but they're also at Hoyt Arboretum and many other nature parks and trails.

FRIENDS OF TRYON CREEK

TRILLIUM FESTIVAL

Don't miss the Trillium Festival each April at Tryon Creek State Natural Area, where you can see lots of trilliums, buy native plants, learn about local natural history, and load up on great nature art and books from the nature store. You can also become a member of the Friends of Tryon Creek, the group that's been presenting the festival since 1980.

Look for long leaves and clusters of white flowers. Photo: Paul Slichter

Leaves are shaped like arrowheads.
Photo: Gerald D. Carr

Wapato *(Sagittaria latifolia)*

Blooms: Summer

No offense to Laurent Sauvé, the French dairyman for whom Sauvie Island is named, but I prefer the name (if not the spelling) suggested by Lewis and Clark: Wappatoe Island.

Wapato is a wild potato—not at all related to the common potatoes we eat today—and was a major food source and trade item for the Multnomah tribe of the Chinook Indians who lived on the island. Women would paddle canoes out on lakes and ponds, hop into cold water that sometimes rose to their armpits, and sift through the mud with their feet to locate and loosen the buried tubers. Then they hauled the chestnut-sized treasures home to roast and eat fresh or to store for trading and winter eating.

In addition to its historical value, wapato offers an interesting lesson in how some plants survive while living mostly underwater. From the bottom of lakes and ponds, wapato's rhizome sends a shoot up to the surface of the mud, where it forms a knob from which leaves, roots, and a long flowering stalk grow. The flowering stalk is the only part that rises above the water's surface, where it soaks up energy from the sun. Meanwhile, the rhizome and fleshy tubers are kept safe under the mud—except when dug out by muskrats or people's toes.

ID tips: Perennial, 1–3 ft. tall. Large leaves (up to 1 ft. long) and tall flowering stems rise above the water. Leaves are deeply veined and shaped like an arrowhead (sagittate). White flowers bloom on the leafless flowering stems.

Locations: Occasionally seen lining water edges at Sauvie Island, Jackson Bottom Wetlands Preserve, Oaks Bottom Wildlife Refuge, Smith and Bybee Lakes, and Fernhill Wetlands.

> "Wappatoe Island is ... high and extremely fertile ... with ponds which produce great quantities of the ... bulb of which the natives call wappatoe."
> — Meriwether Lewis

4 PETALS

Bunchberry *(Cornus unalaschkensis)*

Blooms: Late spring to early summer
You know what would look great in your backyard, under the red-osier dogwood shrub that's growing under your Pacific dogwood tree? This beautiful dogwood groundcover, of course.

Look closely at the millimeter-long flowers in the middle of each bunchberry bloom. Each tiny flower sticks up an antenna that acts like a tripwire. When a pollinator brushes against the antenna, the flower bud bursts opens in less than half a millisecond, launching pollen off its spring-loaded stamens to coat the pollinator. No big deal—it's just the fastest plant movement ever recorded.

It's native to Portland but more common at higher elevations. Photo: M.A. Willson

ID tips: Perennial groundcover, 4–8 in. tall. Look for 4–6 pointy-tipped leaves surrounding stems in a whorl. Atop each whorl sits a single bloom with 4 whitish bracts surrounding tiny flowers. Red-orange fruits have little flavor.

Locations: Uncommon in moist, shady forests in Portland, including at Tualatin River National Wildlife Refuge. See if you can find the one patch by a picnic shelter at Hoyt Arboretum.

Four white bracts support tiny flowers. Photo: M.A. Willson

5 WAYS TO HELP NATIVE PLANTS

1. Stay on trails to avoid trampling trailside plants.

2. Don't pick wildflowers, which robs them of their ability to reproduce.

3. Scrape mud and dirt from your boots before each hike, so you don't introduce invasive species to new areas.

4. Learn to identify native plants through books, workshops, and groups like the Portland chapter of the Native Plant Society of Oregon.

5. Share what you notice along the trail with friends and family. Stay curious and make learning fun.

*Aparine is from the Greek "to seize."
Photo: Paul Slichter*

Bedstraw *(Galium* spp.*)*

Blooms: All summer

Several species of bedstraw grow in Portland, and their other common names (sticky willy, grip grass, and cleavers) hint at what to expect when you touch them. Their clingy plant parts help them hitch rides on passing animals—including you—to spread to new locations.

Fragrant bedstraw *(G. triflorum),* which has a vanilla-like aroma when dried, used to be stuffed in mattresses to improve their smell. If you tire of the offerings at Portland's 2,500 coffee shops, the seeds of another species, *G. aparine,* can be roasted and ground to create what's said to be a tasty coffee substitute.

ID tips: Climbing to erect or sprawling annuals or perennials. Feel for bristliness on the leaves and stems. Thin leaves grow in whorls, and flowers are tiny and white.

Locations: Very common in meadows, wetlands, and streambanks, including at Oaks Bottom Wildlife Refuge, Tryon Creek State Natural Area, Sauvie Island, and Forest Park.

Flowers are a little small to be called enchanting. Photo: Paul Slichter

Enchanter's Nightshade *(Circaea alpina)*

Blooms: Late spring to early summer

Sometimes common names are a little (or a lot) misleading. Enchanter's nightshade isn't related to species in the toxic nightshade family, and while the small white flowers are pretty enough, they're not especially enchanting.

The thing is, scientific names can be misleading too. *Circaea* derives from the Greek sorceress Circe, who turned Odysseus's men into swine—a little grandiose for this groundcover. Despite its *alpina* species name, enchanter's nightshade is found on forest floors, not in alpine habitats. And small and low-key as it is, it's in the same family as much showier fireweeds and fuchsias.

ID tips: Perennial, 5–14 in. tall. Leaves (1–2.5 in. long) are oval and opposite one another on the stem. Leaf margins can be smooth to slightly toothed. Erect flower stems bear clusters of 8–12 tiny white flowers.

Locations: Locally common in moist forests, including at Hoyt Arboretum and Forest Park.

5 PETALS

Look for the single black dot on each berry. Photo: Tracy Aue

Baneberry *(Actaea rubra)*

Blooms: Spring to early summer

Baneberry will indeed be the bane of your existence, if you try to eat its poisonous red or occasionally white berries (or the leaves or roots). There's a strong hint in the common name: "Baneberry" comes from the Anglo-Saxon word *bana,* meaning "murderous."

One berry will taste really bad, two are said to be enough to kill a child, and a handful could easily make an adult violently ill. Such toxicity is unusual in the Portland area, where most native berries are edible in at least small quantities, even if they're not always very appetizing.

ID tips: Perennial, 1-3 ft. tall. Up to 4 large (up to 2 ft. long), compound leaves emerge from lower stem. Leaflets have pointed tips and irregularly toothed edges. Flower clusters resemble a white ball or bottlebrush head. July brings a dense cluster of glossy red (occasionally white) berries.

Locations: Moist soils in area forests, including at Tryon Creek State Natural Area and Forest Park.

White blooms appear in dense clusters.
Photo: Tracy Aue

INEDIBLE BERRIES

Always check a field guide—or two—before you eat any wild fruit. Baneberry berries can be deadly, and the others on this list range from bitter and unpleasant to downright poisonous.

- Baneberry
- Black twinberry
- Cascara
- Poison oak
- Pacific yew—this tree's fruits contain a dangerously poisonous seed
- Snowberry

White clover petals can be tinted pink. Photo: Gerald D. Carr

Clovers like this red clover are popular with bees. Photo: Evelyn Sherr

Clovers (*Trifolium* spp.)

Blooms: Midspring to late summer

Did you hear the one about the Portlander who grew a field of clover and a lawn broke out? If you have a swath of sod, you no doubt have patches of clover, especially white clover (*T. repens*). Depending on your aesthetic preferences, that isn't necessarily a bad thing.

Clovers are legumes that fix nitrogen, so they're often used as a cover crop to restore soil health. They also provide protein-rich forage for many small critters (insects, voles, robins) and big ones (deer and bears).

White and red clover (*T. pratense*) are both true clovers in the genus *Trifolium*, which hints at the fact that they have three leaflets, not a lucky four. The odds of finding a four-leaf clover are about one in 10,000, making it a worthy summer mission for bored kids.

Another way to enjoy clovers, since there's not exactly a shortage: Pick a few flowers and suck or chew on their bases to taste the sweet nectar.

ID tips: Non-native perennials. White clover is 2–4 in. tall, with runners that form mats. Red clover is up to 2 ft. tall, with leaflets .5–1.5 in. long. Leaflets of both often have a white "V" on top.

Locations: Both white and red clover are extremely common. White clover is found in just about every Portland lawn.

DID YOU KNOW?

Plants need nitrogen, but they can't absorb it directly from the air. To turn it into a usable substance, species like clover have bacteria-filled nodules on their roots that absorb and convert nitrogen found in air pockets in the soil. This "nitrogen fixing" capability fertilizes nearby soil and is what makes clover a great cover crop.

Photo: Tracy Aue

Foamflower *(Tiarella trifoliata)*

Blooms: Summer

Foamflower's common name refers to its tiny white flowers, which bloom in loose clusters on tall stalks, creating a frothy or foamy appearance. It's one of Portland's many native saxifrages, and its delicate blooms make it arguably the prettiest of them all.

ID tips: Perennial, 6-24 in. tall. Large basal leaves (1-8 in. across) can be simple, with 3-5 lobes, or compound (with 3 leaflets). Leaves are coarsely toothed along the margins, and there are sometimes smaller leaves on the flowering stalks.

Locations: Common in moist soils in area forests and along streams, including at Forest Park, Hoyt Arboretum, Camassia Natural Area, and Tryon Creek State Natural Area.

Leaves at the base can be eight inches across.
Photo: Walter Siegmund

Cow Parsnip *(Heracleum maximum)*

Blooms: Late spring to early summer

The carrot or parsley family is big and diverse, featuring everything from invasive giant hogweed to deadly water and poison hemlocks. Think of cow parsnip, the largest native species, as the friendly family member that does a lot of good for wildlife.

Cow parsnip's sprawling compound umbels teem with life, including bees, wasps, gnats, flies, beetles, butterflies, and other pollinators that view its blooms as a veritable buffet of nectar and pollen.

Large, wide leaflets differentiate it from water or poison hemlock. Photo: M.A. Willson

ID tips: Perennial, 3-10 ft. tall. Grooved stems have long hairs and a strong odor. Huge leaves (6-16 in. long, 8-20 in. wide) are divided into 3 coarsely lobed and toothed leaflets. Compound umbels can be a foot wide.

Locations: Occasionally seen on roadsides, ditches, and forest edges, including along the Springwater Corridor Trail and at Tryon Creek State Natural Area.

The flowers have a fetid aroma best enjoyed by flies.
Photo: Tracy Aue

Grandiflora ("large flowers") is misleading; they were the largest in a previous genus. Photo: Evelyn Sherr

Fringecup *(Tellima grandiflora)*

Blooms: Spring to early summer

Multiple websites claim that eating fringecups will improve the night vision of woodland elves. I'm not sure how that research was conducted, but even if you don't know any elves (or their eyesight is just fine), you can plant fringecup as a backyard groundcover that doesn't require much attention and produces a pretty spike of fragrant and edible flowers each spring.

Fringecup, foamflower, and piggyback plant are all in the saxifrage ("stone-breaker") family that got its name either from the fact that the plants grow in rocky areas or from the superstition that they can be used to treat kidney stones.

You can recognize most plants in the saxifrage family by their basal (ground-hugging) rosette of leaves and their tendency to produce tall, leafless flowering stalks.

ID tips: Perennial 1–3 ft. tall. Leaves at base are broad (1–4 in. long and wide) and coarsely toothed with shallow lobes. Lots of fragrant flowers bloom on long flower stalks (up to 3 ft. tall). Similar to piggyback plant, but these blooms are a different color and fringecups don't have plantlets on their leaves.

Locations: Abundant in many moist forests, streambanks, and meadows, including at Powell Butte Nature Park, Jenkins Estate, Hoyt Arboretum, Camassia Natural Area, and Forest Park.

Its common name refers to the fringe of colorful petals. Photo: Evelyn Sherr

Goat's Beard (*Aruncus dioicus*)

Blooms: Early summer

Tired of all those small, subtle wildflowers that dot the landscape? Then you'll love goat's beard: It's big—up to six feet tall and about that wide—and bold, with numerous lanky plumes of creamy-white flowers that feed native pollinators.

Flower plumes resemble garden plants in the Astilbe genus. Photo: Georges Jansoone

Use a hand lens to determine whether you're looking at a male or female flower. Male blooms are fluffier-looking because they're loaded, with stamens, while comparatively svelte female flowers have only three to five pistils.

ID tips: Perennial, 2–6 ft. tall. Stems have large compound leaves (up to 2 ft. long). Oval leaflets are up to 6 in. long with pointed tips and sharply toothed margins. Look for long plumes of creamy-white flowers.

Locations: Found in moist soils in area forests, including at Oxbow Regional Park, Graham Oaks Nature Park, and Forest Park.

Spent blooms in late summer. Photo: Tracy Aue

Pacific Waterleaf (*Hydrophyllum tenuipes*)

Blooms: Spring to summer

When walking along forested trails in Portland, have you noticed that many understory plants have large leaves that splay horizontally? There's a reason: Like us, they're trying to soak up as much of the forest's limited sunlight as possible. Unlike us, they're able to use photosynthesis to convert that sunlight into energy.

Leaves are big and deeply lobed. Photo: Evelyn Sherr

As its name suggests, Pacific waterleaf is a water lover: *Hydrophyllum* is from the Latin *hydro* ("water") and *phyllos* ("leaf"). Because it spreads by underground rhizomes, you'll be hard-pressed to find just one Pacific waterleaf— usually there's a whole colony.

ID tips: Perennial, 1–2.5 ft. tall. Leaves (3–8 in. wide) are split into 3–5 deeply lobed leaflets with jagged teeth. Long stamens make flowers look fuzzy and form scorpion tail-like clusters called helicoid cymes. Flowers can be white, yellow, or purplish.

Locations: Extremely common in moist, shady forests and streamsides. Large patches grow at Powell Butte Nature Park, Hoyt Arboretum, and Forest Park.

Take a close look at the colorful pollen on the long stamens. Photo: Evelyn Sherr

68

Look inside flowers for a surprise: orange pollen! Photo: Kermit Williams

Indian Pipe *(Monotropa uniflora)*

Blooms: Midsummer

Indian pipe is also known as ghost-plant or corpse-plant, but fear not: It's not a ghost or goblin, and it doesn't feed off the dead. It's a flowering plant in the same heath family as blueberries and rhododendrons, but it goes about its business in a much different way than those more common plants.

You'll see Indian pipe growing in places where the sun don't shine—which is possible because it doesn't have chlorophyll and doesn't photosynthesize. It's an epiparasite that saps sugar from mycorrhizal fungi that are connected to nearby tree roots. That might sound problematic, but the fungal network also supplies nutrients to the trees.

ID tips: Perennial, 4–10 in. tall. Clusters of white stalks turn black at maturity. One nodding flower sits atop each stem. At maturity, the pipe uncurls so the plant and its fruit point toward the sky. Phantom orchid *(Cephalanthera austiniae)*, the only somewhat similar plant you might see, doesn't have nodding flowers.

Locations: Rare in shady woods, including at Tualatin Hills Nature Park, Forest Park, Kelly Butte Natural Area, and Tryon Creek State Natural Area.

FUN FACT

When a neighbor gave Emily Dickinson a watercolor painting of Indian pipes, the poet responded: "That without suspecting it you should send me the preferred flower of life, seems almost supernatural, and the sweet glee that I felt at meeting it, I could confide to none."

C. perfoliata *leaves form a saucer.* Photo: Tracy Aue   C. sibirica *is also known as candyflower.* Photo: Joan Amero

Miner's Lettuce (*Claytonia* spp.)

Blooms: Spring

Miner's lettuce is one of the best-known edible plants, famously eaten by early miners and prospectors who wanted to stave off scurvy and lose weight (kidding about the latter). Its modern claim to fame is as an overpriced salad green—"America's gift to salad!"—served up at four-star restaurants.

In Portland-area forests, you'll see lots of both *C. sibirica* (aka candyflower) and *C. perfoliata*, and sometimes hybrids of the two. Their leaves tend to be tastier earlier in spring. As to which tastes better, some say *C. perfoliata* is the clear winner, but see for yourself; just pick leaves sparingly, and never pull up entire plants.

ID tips: *C. perfoliata* is generally 2–16 in. tall, with leaves fused to form a saucer-like disk beneath white to pale-pink blooms. *C. sibirica* is 2–24 in. tall, with oblong to triangular leaves opposite on the stalk and small clusters of flowers with pink candy stripes on the petals.

Locations: Abundant in area forests. Look for both species in the understory at Powell Butte Nature Park, Forest Park, Hoyt Arboretum, and Camassia Natural Area.

Small-flowered Alumroot (*Heuchera micrantha*)

Blooms: Late spring to early summer

North America is home to dozens of *Heuchera* species, commonly called coral bells or alumroot. At local nurseries, you'll see a wide array of *Heuchera* hybrids and cultivars, with colorful names like Purple Palace, Peach Flambé, and Green Spice.

This humbler native, the aptly named small-flowered alumroot, grows along rocky crevices where its extensive root systems help prevent erosion. Alum is an astringent that's been used to treat everything from sore throats to syphilis-related inflammation.

ID tips: Perennial, 6–24 in. tall. Forms mounds with hairy leaves on long petioles. Leaves are broadly oval to oblong, 1–3 in. long, with 5–7 lobes and toothed margins.

Locations: Relatively common in moist sites along streams and on rocky slopes and cliffs, including at Camassia Natural Area and Canemah Bluff Nature Park.

Micrantha ("small-flowered") *refers to the tiny flowers.* Photo: M.A. Willson

Petals often have candy stripes. Photo: M.A. Willson

"Sorrel" means "sour" and hints at the tart taste. Photo: M.A. Willson

Oregon Oxalis (*Oxalis oregana*)

Blooms: Spring and summer

Plants can't run away from their problems. When times get tough, they either find a creative way to adapt or they die trying. This groundcover, also called redwood sorrel, has, like a true Portlander, found a way to adapt to both too much sun and too much rain.

When happily shaded in a forest understory, Oregon oxalis splays its leaves out to soak up as much sunshine as possible. When the sun gets too strong, the plant folds up in minutes to avoid the direct hit—you can watch it happen! When conditions improve, oxalis leaves unfold over about a half-hour. The leaves also fold up when rain falls and at night. All these opening and closing movements in response to conditions have the fabulous name of nyctinasty.

ID tips: Creeping perennial, 2–8 in. tall. Shamrock-like leaves clump together. Leaves are divided into 3 heart-shaped leaflets with maroon undersides. Showy, solitary white to pink flowers bloom upright, often with pinkish striations on the petals.

Locations: Common on shady, cool, undisturbed forest floors. Forest Park is a good place to look.

Note the "blood" in the middle of the bloom. Photo: Tracy Aue

Queen Anne's Lace (*Daucus carota*)

Blooms: Summer to early fall

My mom loved Queen Anne's lace for its beauty and commonness. As weeds go, it's a lovely one, named after the 18th century British monarch who, legend has it, pricked her finger with a needle while making lace, resulting in a drop or two of her blood appearing in the center of each inflorescence (the "blood" is really a purple flower).

It might be pretty, but Queen Anne's lace is considered a nuisance plant in Portland and a noxious weed in Washington, in part because it can interfere with crop production. Its bad reputation among some is furthered by its general resemblance to the deadly poison hemlock.

ID tips: Non-native biennial, 1–4 ft. tall. Leaves (up to 6 in. long) are pinnately divided like fern leaves. First year, there's a basal rosette of leaves. Second year, upright stems have alternating leaves with flat to slightly rounded flower clusters (umbels).

Locations: Very common in roadsides, fields, pastures, and meadows, including at Fernhill Wetlands, Cooper Mountain Nature Park, and Tryon Creek State Natural Area.

Trailing Blackberry (*Rubus ursinus*)

Blooms: Late spring to early summer

Our two native blackberry species, trailing blackberry (aka Pacific blackberry or dewberry) and the less common western blackcap (*R. leucodermis*), offer a summer treat along Portland-area trails.

You've probably seen trailing blackberry spread—and spread and spread—into tangled masses. Berries galore, right? Not always. If those masses are all male, you'll be disappointed to discover no berries at all.

In July or August, if you spot a mass of sun-drenched female trailing blackberry, count your blessings. The berries are aromatic and delicious—far superior to the never-say-die, highly invasive Himalayan (*R. armeniacus*) and cutleaf (*R. laciniatus*) blackberries that blanket so much of the city.

ID tips: Vines are up to 18 ft. long and 1.5 ft. tall. Stems are slender with mostly straight prickles (Himalayan has thick, grooved stems and stouter prickles). Leaves are usually divided into 3 leaflets (non-native blackberries have 5). White to pink flowers are 1–2 in. across.

Locations: Very common in wooded areas, vacant lots, and roadsides, including at Forest Park, Camassia Natural Area, and Hoyt Arboretum.

Leaves are usually in groups of three. Photo: Tracy Aue

Flowers are usually white. Photo: Evelyn Sherr

"The apple orchards will be in fruit; the air thick with the smell of warm mint and blackberry—ah, I hear my native land a-beckoning to me."
— Ken Kesey, *Sometimes a Great Notion*

They grow lower to the ground than woodland strawberries. Photo: Ron Halvorson

Wild Strawberry *(Fragaria virginiana)*

Blooms: Late spring

In the 1600s, Roger Key quoted a doctor as saying of strawberries, "God could have made, but God never did make, a better berry." More recently, English author Charlotte Mendelson wrote that strawberries are "the point of summer." I know of few Portlanders who would disagree.

Most of the larger cultivars you can buy at stores or U-pick in June were derived from wild strawberry and coast strawberry. Our native strawberries are arguably even more delicious than cultivated varieties and will grow happily in your backyard.

ID tips: Perennial, 2–6 in. tall, with long runners. Lower-growing than woodland strawberry, with 3 blue-green leaflets that have less prominent veins. Flowers grow among the leaves, not inches above like woodland strawberry blooms.

Locations: Common in forest openings and along streambanks, including at Forest Park, Cooper Mountain Nature Park, and Tryon Creek State Natural Area.

These strawberry plants can be a foot tall. Photo: Evelyn Sherr

Woodland Strawberry *(Fragaria vesca)*

Blooms: Late spring

Both wild and woodland strawberries are wild, and both grow in woodlands. Their differences are subtle—the bluish hue of wild strawberry leaflets, the greater height of woodland strawberry blooms.

For a berry-eating adventure, try finding and comparing the taste of these two species. Then head west to sample coast strawberries (*F. chiloensis*), arguably the most delicious of Oregon's native strawberry species.

ID tips: Perennial, 4–12 in. tall. Unlike wild strawberry, leaflets often have an extended terminal tooth (like they're sticking out their middle finger). The fruits, which botanically-speaking aren't true berries, emerge by midsummer.

Locations: Common in forested areas with moist, well-drained soil (fruits aren't common because they require ample sunshine). Look for them at Forest Park, Cooper Mountain Nature Park, and Tryon Creek State Natural Area.

> "Wild, or Alpine, strawberries are a far better bet than tame ones. They grow (cf. Nature) anywhere—in a pot, along a wall—and they are gloriously fragrant, sweetly sharp, the essence of wooded childhood holidays. Add four tiny ones to your overpriced city-bought granola; they will taste like magic."
> — Charlotte Mendelson in *The New Yorker*

COMPOSITE

The species name millefolium *refers to leaves beings divided into a thousand parts. Photo: Ron Halvorson*

Many insects drink nectar and rest on the flowers. Photo: M.A. Willson

Common Yarrow (*Achillea millefolium*)

Blooms: Late spring and summer

The botany joke (!) goes that if you forget the genus of this common plant, "ah-kill-E-ah" (roughly, "I'll kill ya"). It's a name worth knowing because clumps of these pollinator-friendly white flowers are readily spotted across Portland, along with cultivars with yellow, hot pink, and other supernatural colors (and names like Strawberry Seduction).

Over the years, yarrow has been smoked, snorted, eaten, brewed as a beer, and sipped as a tea. Native peoples and soldiers in the Civil War applied it to open wounds, and others have used it to address less bloody concerns, including baldness and evil spirits.

ID tips: Perennial, up to 3 ft. tall. Soft, hairy, highly dissected (fern-like) leaves are gray-green. Many tiny white flowers are grouped together in mostly flat-topped clusters.

Locations: Very common in open places all across Portland, including roadsides, vacant lots, and trailsides at Forest Park and Tryon Creek State Natural Area.

> **"To the lover, especially of birds, insects, and plants, the smallest area around the well-chosen home will furnish material to satisfy all thirst of knowledge through the longest life."**
> — Mary Treat, *Home Studies in Nature*

They're attractive weeds with a pleasant aroma.
Photo: Evelyn Sherr

An Ochre Ringlet dropping by for a sip of nectar.
Photo: Lori Humphreys

Oxeye Daisy (*Leucanthemum vulgare*)

Blooms: All summer

This is the original "She loves me, she loves me not" flower, its powers of deduction now largely replaced by online quizzes. Oxeye daisies are so omnipresent they're barely noticed, but stop and sniff one this summer—they have a pleasant aroma similar to chrysanthemums.

Oxeye daisies are generally considered invasive, noxious, or simply weedy, so if you don't have a romantic affection for them, dig them up before they go to seed.

ID tips: Non-native perennial, 1-2 ft. tall. Leaves at base can be pinnately lobed to toothed (up to 5 in. long); leaves are smaller on stems. One flowerhead (about 1-3 in. across) typically blooms per stem.

Locations: Common in sunny clearings, roadsides, and meadows, including at Tryon Creek State Natural Area and Forest Park.

Smell the sweet scent of the flowers.
Photo: Gerald D. Carr

Petasites, from the Greek for "broad-brimmed hat," refers to its broad leaves. Photo: Tracy Aue

Palmate Coltsfoot (*Petasites frigidus*)

Blooms: Early to midspring

Put yourself in the place of a plant in winter: It's cold and wet, with hardly any sunlight to convert into energy. Come February or March, you'd be able to attract loads of hungry pollinators (who have also suffered through winter), if only you could send up early blooms. But how can you do that, after so many months of dormancy, and with so little sunlight peeking through the clouds?

Like trilliums, palmate coltsfoot pulls off the early-blooming trick by storing nutrients in its stout underground rhizome. As soon as spring arrives, it's among the first plants to produce flowers—even before putting energy into producing the big leaves that recharge the rhizome through summer.

ID tips: Perennial, 4-25 in. tall. Flowering stalk shoots up in early spring, topped by rounded flower clusters. Big leaves (up to 16 in. wide), coarsely lobed and toothed, then emerge from the base with long leafstalks and fuzzy undersides.

Locations: Occasionally seen along streamsides, roadsides, and wet forest areas. Look for patches at Hoyt Arboretum, the Reed College canyon, and Tryon Creek State Natural Area.

Pathfinder (*Adenocaulon bicolor*)

Blooms: All summer

Pathfinder is known as the tracker's friend because when large animals tramp through a patch, they overturn the arrowpoint-shaped leaves, exposing silvery undersides. It's said that you can use this trick to retrace your steps if you get lost in the woods, although a compass might be more dependable.

Like other low-lying, big-leaved plants that grow in deep shade, pathfinder's greatest benefit is in creating a cool, protected area under its leaves where organic matter can be decomposed to enrich the soil and help other plants thrive.

Bicolor refers to the leaves: green on top, whitish on the bottom. Photo: Evelyn Sherr

ID tips: Perennial, 3–40 in. tall. Inconspicuous flower bouquets bloom atop spindly stems. Triangular leaves are large (1–10 in. long), grow mostly at the base, and are dark green on top and white-fuzzy underneath.

Locations: Common in moist, shady forests, including at Forest Park, Hoyt Arboretum, and Powell Butte Nature Park Nature Park.

Pearly Everlasting (*Anaphalis margaritacea*)

Blooms: Mid to late summer

Pearly everlasting is a survivor. Hardy and easy to grow, it perseveres even in gravelly soils and can be so successful it's deemed weedy. Its trichomes, or hairs, help reduce water loss, prevent overheating, and stave off spittlebugs that struggle to penetrate the dense hairs.

Pearly everlasting's blooms resemble sunnyside-up eggs, with white bracts surrounding yellow disk flowers. Its pretty name comes from the pearly white color of the bracts and the fact that in dried

The flowers have a musky odor. Photo: Susan Berger

flower arrangements the bracts last long after the yellow disk flowers have wilted.

ID tips: Perennial, 8–47 in. tall. Leaves are linear, narrow, and alternate with woolly undersides. Blooms have tiny yellow disk flowers in the middle, surrounded by several overlapping series of white bracts.

Locations: Common in dry, open, grassy areas, especially roadsides (more common at higher elevations, including near Mt. Hood). Look for it at Cooper Mountain Nature Park and Tualatin Hills Nature Park.

WHAT'S A DISK FLOWER?

At a glance, pearly everlasting looks like it bears clusters of 25 or so flowers. But look at just one of those "flowers" that's yellow in the middle and white on the outside. That right there is a bouquet of flowers! The yellow part is a cluster of tiny, tubular disk flowers. Put a single yellow disk flower under a microscope and you'll see it has all the sexual parts of a complete flower.

Macrophyllum *refers to its large leaves.*
Photo: Evelyn Sherr

The golden flowers resemble buttercup blooms.
Photo: Evelyn Sherr

Largeleaf Avens *(Geum macrophyllum)*

Blooms: Spring and summer

This buttery bloom belongs in the buttercup family, right? Nope—it grows alongside buttercups, but it's in the rose family. Right, so it's a cinquefoil? No again.

Despite its yellow, five-petaled flowers, largeleaf avens is not a cinquefoil. The key distinction is minor but interesting to see with a hand lens: Largeleaf avens' style, the tube-shaped part of the female sexual organ, has a curlicue twist near the tip, like a pig's tail.

While looking closely at one of the flowers, imagine there's a black spot in the middle. Because indeed there is one, only we can't spot it because our eyes can't see ultraviolet wavelengths. Many pollinators can, and the black dot acts as a nectar guide to draw them in for a sip.

ID tips: Perennial, 8 in.–3.5 ft. tall. Leaves (up to 18 in. long) are pinnately compound; terminal leaflet is several times larger than others. Flowering stems are hairy, and stem leaves are smaller than those at the base. At stem tips, look for 3–10 flowers.

Locations: Common in moist soil of woods and open areas, including at Powell Butte Nature Park, Hoyt Arboretum, and Oaks Bottom Wildlife Refuge.

Common Mullein (*Verbascum thapsus*)

Blooms: All summer

As weeds go, mullein isn't all that bad. Yes, common mullein and moth mullein (*V. blattaria*) take over a lot of territory, but mostly mullein thrives in areas that are inhospitable to other plants. If it's causing you problems, pull it up before it releases its thousands of seeds.

Nothing else looks quite like mullein, with its towering stalks of yellow flowers. Note how the large leaves clasp the stem—that's so they can direct rainwater down to the roots. The velvety leaves can be made into a tea, and hikers sometimes use them as toilet paper (be careful; some report adverse skin reactions). The stalks have also been dried and used as "witches' torches," after dipping the tops in wax.

ID tips: Non-native biennial, up to 6–8 ft. tall. Year one, soft leaves (up to 20 in. long) form a basal rosette. Year two, look for straight, hairy stalks, topped by dense spikes (racemes) of yellow flowers that typically bloom a few at a time.

Locations: Common in disturbed areas (roadsides, vacant lots, overgrown yards, the I-5 corridor) and natural areas such as Cooper Mountain Nature Park and Tryon Creek State Natural Area.

They're not really as tall as downtown buildings.
Photo: © City of Portland

Stonecrops (*Sedum* spp.)

Blooms: Midsummer

Sedums, or stonecrops, are readily identified by their location (rocky, gravelly sites), succulent leaves (fleshy, water-filled), and flowers (usually bright yellow, with pointed petals).

Four *Sedum* species grow in the Portland area, but all are rare in the wild. Head east of town to see them in abundance along rocky trails (Iron Mountain is one hotspot). You can also see and plant them closer to home in sunny, well-drained yards and rock gardens.

ID tips: Perennials, about 2–9 in. tall. Mat-forming succulents have fleshy leaves that form rosettes. Pretty yellow flowers bloom in summer.

Locations: Rare on rocky outcrops and gravelly areas. Look for them at Camassia Nature Park and in urban rock gardens.

"Succulent" comes from the Latin for "juice" or "sap." Photo: Rick Schory

Summer brings golden blooms. Photo: Tracy Aue

The leaves are easily confused with those of marijuana plants. Photo: M.A. Willson

Slender Cinquefoil *(Potentilla gracilis)*

Blooms: Late spring to early summer

Pardon the anthropomorphizing, but slender (or graceful) cinquefoil is a downright cheerful wildflower. How can you not smile at those wide-open golden blooms and heart-shaped petals? The cheer continues through late summer and fall, when the plants produce attractive seedheads and colorful foliage.

Slender cinquefoil is rare in Portland, which is too bad because it's a good source of nectar and pollen for insects and a host plant for native butterflies. Beware that there's a similar-looking plant called sulphur cinquefoil *(P. recta)* that's invasive. It's not easy to tell the difference, but one clue is that our long-stemmed native rarely forms the dense patches indicative of *P. recta.*

ID tips: Perennial, 8 in.–3.5 ft. tall, covered in silky hairs. Leaves are divided palmately (like the fingers of a hand) into 5–7 sharply toothed leaflets. Leaflet undersides are hairy. Look for loose clusters of saucer-shaped flowers (not cup-shaped like buttercups).

Locations: Rare in meadows, roadsides, and open forests. Look for it at Cooper Mountain Nature Park, Vale Park, and area nurseries.

Ranunculus *is Latin for "little frog" (both frogs and buttercups live near water). Photo: M.A. Willson*

Western Buttercup *(Ranunculus occidentalis)*

Blooms: Spring

As you might surmise, buttercups are named for the butter-rich color of their blooms. What's less known is that nectar-rich buttercups are poisonous. Their stem juices can blister your skin, so don't let children put buttercup parts in their mouths; let bees and other pollinators do the touching.

Most buttercups you'll see in Portland are non-native. Creeping buttercup *(R. repens)* slinks along the ground and spreads like mad. Even less pleasant is lesser celandine *(R. ficaria)*, a mat-forming invasive species. Be careful what you buy at nurseries and big-box retailers: The more upright buttercups are the natives to look for.

ID tips: Perennial, 4–30 in. tall, with single stem. Leaves are deeply 3-lobed and toothed, arising from the base and alternating on erect stalks.

Locations: Here and there in moist soils. Look for it at Cooper Mountain Nature Park and Sauvie Island.

Creeping buttercup leaves crowd out native plants. Photo: LeeAnn Kriegh

Go ahead and smell violets, but most have ketones that'll dull your sensory receptors. Photo: Evelyn Sherr

Stream Violet *(Viola glabella)*

Blooms: Spring to summer

Who doesn't love violets? They're a classic symbol of virtue, faithfulness, and humility, and the state flower of four states (roses lay claim to only three).

Further upstaging roses, violets are the traditional Valentine's Day flower because it's said that St. Valentine crushed some blooms that grew outside his prison cell to make ink. Then he used the ink to write notes on the leaves—notes delivered to the correct recipients by remarkably cooperative doves.

Maroon veins guide pollinators.
Photo: Evelyn Sherr

Stream violets are common in moist forested areas, which happens to describe most wild areas near Portland. You also might see two other natives: evergreen violets *(V. sempervirens)* are low-growing with yellow flowers, and early-blue violets *(V. adunca)* have purplish blooms. Other pink, purple, or white violets are usually New Jersey's state plant, the common blue violet *(V. sororia)*.

ID tips: Perennial, up to 1 ft. tall, with roughly heart-shaped leaves at the base that are toothed along the margins and come to a sharp tip. Half-inch flowers are deep yellow. Look for the eyelash-like maroon veins on the lower 3 petals.

Locations: Common in wet forests, including at Forest Park, Mt. Tabor, and Hoyt Arboretum.

DIY FLOWERS

Single people can take heart in the reproductive strategy of violets. Each spring they open up their beautiful flowers for fertilization by traditional means. But they also have a backup plan called cleistogamy ("closed marriage"), through which they produce non-opening, self-pollinating flowers that create their own seeds—no partner required.

They're found along waterways. Photo: Tracy Aue

Yellow Monkeyflower (*Erythranthe guttata*)

Blooms: All summer

If you look at this summer wildflower and see the face of a monkey, more power to you. I don't see that, nor have I experienced what the Flower Essence Society describes as monkeyflower's ability to help us overcome "the specific worries and fears that can vex us in everyday life, from the child's fear of the dark, to adolescent shyness, to the timidity of an elderly shut-in."

But that's not to say the buttery monkeyflower blooms you'll encounter along area waterways aren't worth a closer look. In fact, you should take a very close look and touch their reproductive parts. I know, I know, but it's not as creepy as it sounds. The pistil ends in a sticky, touch-sensitive stigma designed to trap pollen. Take a blade of grass and touch the lobes at the tip of the stigma—they'll snap closed, like a Venus flytrap.

ID tips: Annual or perennial, 3 in.–3 ft. tall. Oval to round leaves are toothed with a pointed tip. Flowering stalks tend to have more than 5 flowers (up to 1.5 in. across) near the top. The lower 3 petal lobes are larger than the upper 2 lobes and have red dots in the throat.

Locations: Occasionally seen in wet areas, including at Sauvie Island, Cooper Mountain Nature Park, and Hoyt Arboretum.

The upper petal has two lobes; the lower has three. Photo: Joan Amero

> "True, a beargrass plant can't read, or write, or think abstract thoughts. Well, I can't turn sunlight into food or re-sprout after wildfire. Let's not quibble over who is the more miraculous."
> — Pepper Trail in *High Country News*

COMPOSITE

Canada Goldenrod *(Solidago elongata)*

Blooms: Late summer to fall

It fills my heart to see lemon-yellow goldenrods blooming in late summer and into fall, when most other native wildflowers have folded up their tents, as it were. Hundreds of butterfly, moth, bee, and bird species rely on goldenrods for late-season food and shelter.

Goldenrod has other uses too. It contains a lot of latex, which in the 1920s captured the interest of Henry Ford, who sought a domestically produced rubber substitute. His friend Thomas Edison experimented on 17,000 plants before cultivating a strain of goldenrod with raised levels of latex. After Edison died, the former slave and renowned scientist George Washington Carver continued his work, but Carver soon passed away and petroleum-based rubber substitutes became the favored solution.

ID tips: Perennial, 1–5 ft. tall. Long, narrow leaves with pointed tips alternate up hairy stems that are topped with tall, fluffy clusters of golden flowers. It's tough to tell goldenrod species apart; use a detailed field guide for help.

Locations: Common in moist meadows and sunny disturbed areas, including clearings and roadsides. Look for them at Tryon Creek State Park, Powell Butte Nature Park, and Mt. Tabor.

Leaves are long and narrow. Photo: Tracy Aue

Do wildlife a favor and plant goldenrod in your yard.
Photo: Tracy Aue

DID YOU KNOW?

Many people blame goldenrod for their late-season allergies. It looks guilty because it blooms at the right time—but goldenrod has heavy pollen transferred by insects. The real culprit is windblown pollen from ragweed and other plants.

82

*Petals tend to be lighter in color toward the tips.
Photo: M.A. Willson*

*Eriophyllum ("woolly leaf") and lanatum ("woolly")
refer to its hairiness. Photo: M.A. Willson*

*The tips of the petal-like structures are toothed.
Photo: Tracy Aue*

Oregon Sunshine *(Eriophyllum lanatum)*

Blooms: Spring and summer

I like to think of Oregon sunshine as our unofficial state flower. It's a sun lover that has, like many of us, adapted to tolerate a little less sun and a little more shade. It's also hardy like Oregonians, which is why you'll see it blooming in dry, sandy, rocky, thin-soil conditions both east and west of the Cascades.

Also in true Oregonian fashion, the several varieties of Oregon sunshine wear a lot of wool. Scores of white hairs cover the stems, leaves, and leaf-like bracts, leading to its other common name of woolly sunflower. Its hairiness is the easiest way to distinguish it from the many similar DYCs, or damned yellow composites.

ID tips: Perennial subshrub, 4–40 in. tall. Looks grayish because of dense white hairs. Typically grows in clumps with several upright flowering stalks. Leaves (.5–3 in. long) are linear to oval. Yellow flowerheads are 1–2 in. across.

Locations: Here and there in dry meadows and rocky outcrops. Look for it blooming in May and June at Cooper Mountain Nature Park, Camassia Natural Area, and Canemah Bluff Nature Park in Oregon City.

Wall Lettuce *(Mycelis muralis)*

Blooms: All summer

Wall lettuce is named for its tendency to grow on and near walls in Europe, but in Portland you're much more likely to see it dotting the forest floor and spreading into your backyard. Native to northern Europe, wall lettuce is a weed worth knowing, if only because you'll see so much of it in gardens, on roadsides, and along hiking trails. It's related to garden lettuce, and the leaves are edible—but more bitter than you might like.

ID tips: Non-native annual to perennial, 2–3 ft. tall. Pinnately divided leaves (1.5–7 in. long) clasp branched stems. It starts as a basal rosette of leaves, then develops flowering stalks. Pale-yellow flowers look like they have 5 petals, but they're composite, with many flowers in each flowerhead.

Locations: Common in forests, meadows, and disturbed areas, including at Powell Butte Nature Park, Hoyt Arboretum, and Forest Park.

NO OBVIOUS PETALS

Skunk Cabbage (*Lysichiton americanus*)

Blooms: Early spring

Set aside the off-putting name for now and just look at this dazzling yellow beauty! It's a huge wildflower, at least by Portland standards, that brightens swampy areas in early spring with a golden bloom that's as certain a harbinger of spring as our better-known trilliums. Yet for some reason there are no festivals to honor skunk cabbage.

Probably most people never get past the name, which refers to the flower's skunk-like odor and the young leaves' resemblance to cabbage leaves. The foul odor is less pronounced in this western species than in the eastern (*Symplocarpus foetidus*), and in any case, nobody's suggesting skunk cabbage be used for floral displays.

Here's the real kicker that I hope will win you over to the skunk cabbage appreciation society: It's one of the only plants in the world that generates its own heat! That's why you'll see skunk cabbage rising up through the spring snow on Mt. Hood. In a

They have the largest leaves of any plant native to Portland.
Photo: M.A. Willson

study in Ontario, Canada, the outside temperature was 37 degrees, but inside the eastern skunk cabbage bloom the temperature was a toasty 61 degrees.

Along with enabling skunk cabbage to burn through early-spring snow, the plant's thermogenic (heat-producing) capability helps it defend against frost and spread its fetid scent far and wide. As you might imagine, insects in the cold days of March and early April are attracted to the warm blooms—and perhaps confused into thinking they're smelling rotting corpses. Which, okay, might not be an attractive image to end on, but it would make for a heck of a festival.

Look for: Perennial, up to 3 ft. tall. Early spring, a large (up to 8 in. long) yellow bract (spathe) emerges, partially surrounding a greenish-yellow flowering stalk (spadix). On the upright stalk are lots of yellow-green bumps, which are the flowers. Later in spring, huge, glossy, elliptical leaves, each up to 5 ft. long, form a basal rosette that persists through fall and into winter.

Found: Here and there in marshes and other perennially saturated soils, including in the Johnson Creek watershed, Reed College canyon, and Tryon Creek State Natural Area. It's more common toward the coast and Mt. Hood.

> **"I have thought nature indifferent to humans, to one more human, but maybe the reverse is true. Maybe the world is already in love, giving me these gifts all the time, calling out all the time: take this. And this. And this. Don't turn away."**
>
> — Sharman Apt Russell, *Diary of a Citizen Scientist*

This cousin of opium poppies could cause you to flunk a urine test. Photo: Tracy Aue

California Poppy (*Eschscholzia californica*)

Blooms: Spring to fall

As its name suggests, California poppy is more common in California, where it's the state flower. But these hardy flowers are also native to Oregon; in fact, David Douglas collected their seeds in southern Oregon in 1826.

Until Euro-American settlers arrived, California poppies were probably restricted to gravel bars and grassy bluffs in the Portland area. Settlers expanded poppy habitat by clearing forests and creating more disturbed areas where the plant thrives. Now, both wild and introduced poppies bloom all over Portland, providing a long-lasting and pollen-rich resource to pollinators.

ID tips: Annual or perennial, .5–2 ft. tall. Plants are hairless and have deeply dissected leaves. One upright orange flower with 4 petals tops each long stalk.

Locations: Here and there on roadsides and rocky outcrops. Look for poppies planted in backyards and along highways, and farther afield at Dog Mountain.

True lilies like this one often have leaves arranged in whorls. Photo: M.A. Willson

Tiger Lily (*Lilium columbianum*)

Blooms: Early summer

Many plants, including water lilies and false lily of the valley, are called lilies but aren't in the lily family. The gorgeous tiger lily is the real deal: a lily that, like most, grows from a bulb and produces a tall, showy bloom.

You'll find lots of tiger, or Columbia, lilies in the Sandy River drainage and moist sites in the Columbia River Gorge. In Portland, count yourself fortunate if you spy even one splash of orange along a trail. When you do, be sure to get up close to appreciate the unusual spotted petals and orange anthers.

ID tips: Perennial, up to 8 ft. tall. Stems have multiple whorls of elliptic leaves with pointy tips (.5–4.5 in. long). Bell-shaped flowers (1–3 in. across) are bright orange with brown spots. Petals are flared back to show orange anthers.

Locations: Occasionally seen in drier forests, roadsides, and meadows. Look for them at Tualatin Hills Nature Park, Forest Park, and the eastern base of Powell Butte Nature Park.

PINK TO RED OR RED-PURPLE
3 OR 6 PETALS

Fairy Slipper Orchid *(Calypso bulbosa)*

Blooms: Late spring to early summer

It's also called calypso orchid.
Photo: Kermit Williams

The endlessly quotable and cranky botanist Martin Gorman wrote that the fairy slipper orchid has been "both plucked and dug up for potting so ruthlessly that its extermination is only a question of time"—and that was in 1904.

We do love our orchids, often to death, for their beauty and fragrance. Pollinators are likewise attracted to orchids, but the plants are notorious tricksters. Fairy slipper orchid's cruel trick is that it produces no nectar—zilch. Mature bees learn to avoid the flowers, so its success depends on fooling the next generation of inexperienced bees.

ID tips: Perennial, 3–7 in. tall. One long, wide leaf (1–2.5 in. wide) emerges from the base in autumn, overwinters, then withers in summer. A single flower emerges on an erect stalk. The common name refers to the lowermost "slipper" petal.

Locations: Rare in deep forests in the Portland area. Look for it at Mt. Talbert Nature Park, Oxbow Regional Park, and Jenkins Estate in Beaverton.

4 PETALS

Fireweed *(Chamerion angustifolium)*

Blooms: Summer

Fireweed can be weedy in gardens, but in the wild it soon gives way to others. Photo: Tracy Aue

After bombs fall on cities and fires burn through forests, fireweed is one of the first plants to rise up and restore life and beauty. It's most at home in deeply disturbed areas, including Portland trailsides, post-eruption slopes on Mt. St. Helens, and even post–World War II London, where its appearance in bomb craters earned it the nickname "bombweed."

Fireweed can be weedy in gardens, but it's one of my favorites because of all the good it does in the wild, where it helps to restore soil and prevent erosion before giving way to later-successional plants. Wildlife ranging from deer to muskrats eat fireweed shoots, lots of insects feed on it, and Native peoples have found many uses, from eating its shoots to crafting fishing nets from dried stem peelings.

ID tips: Perennial, up to 10 ft. tall. Stout stems have alternate leaves that are long (2–10 in.) and widest in the middle (lanceolate). Stems are topped by a dense column (raceme) of flowers.

Locations: Common in clearcut, recently burned, and otherwise disturbed areas. Look for it along roads and at Cooper Mountain Nature Park, Hoyt Arboretum, and Tryon Creek State Natural Area.

Look for purplish veins. Photo: Gerald D. Carr

Oaks Toothwort (*Cardamine nuttallii*)

Blooms: Early spring

Oaks toothwort is a pretty plant, also called spring beauty, that offers up one of our very first spring blooms. Its quirky, hard-to-pronounce name is a reminder of the doctrine of signatures: the idea that plants that resemble certain human body parts can be used to treat those parts.

The doctrine of signatures is where plants like toothwort, lungwort, and liverwort got their common names—but I hope it goes without saying that it's only a superstition. Please don't rely on rattlesnake plantain to treat snakebites or toothwort to treat toothaches.

ID tips: Perennial, 4–14 in. tall. Generally, leaves growing from the base have shallow lobes and those on the flowering stalk are divided into 2–5 leaflets (up to 1.5 in. long) with pointed tips. Petals are often lightly streaked with purple veins.

Locations: Common in moist soils in open forests, including at Hoyt Arboretum, Camassia Natural Area, Powell Butte Nature Park, and Sauvie Island.

Hummingbirds frequently pollinate bleeding hearts. Photo: Evelyn Sherr

Pacific Bleeding Heart (*Dicentra formosa*)

Blooms: Spring to summer

Pacific bleeding heart is pretty much the perfect plant for your backyard shade garden. It grows easily, needs little care, can bloom all summer, and attracts hummingbirds and other pollinators. Those drooping pink hearts are easy on the eyes too.

In late summer, watch for white seedpods to develop. Inside are black seeds, each with a white fat body, or elaiosome, attached. The fat bodies attract ants that lug their prizes back to their nests, where they dine on the oily fat bodies and discard the hard seeds.

The ants' waste disposal areas happen to be perfectly aerated, fertilized, and protected homes for the seeds to develop into next spring's bleeding hearts. Thousands of plants benefit from this hunt-and-gather process, which has the wonderful name of myrmecochory.

ID tips: Perennial, 8–16 in. tall. Fern-like, deeply dissected leaves sprout from the base and have a slightly waxy coating. Clusters of pink (sometimes white) flowers dangle from the long stems.

Locations: Common in moist soils in area forests. Enjoy them in April and May at Oxbow Regional Park, Graham Oaks Nature Park, and Gabbert Butte Natural Area.

5 PETALS

Stachys *means "ear of grain" and refers to the shape of the flower spike. Photo: Tracy Aue*

Cooley's Hedge-Nettle *(Stachys cooleyae)*

Blooms: Late summer

Have no fear! Cooley's hedge-nettle will not sting you, unlike the stinging nettles *(Urtica dioica)* that share the same moist soils.

Hedge-nettles are in the mint family, as suggested by their tubular flowers and minty aroma. If you're certain that the plant you're looking at isn't a stinging nettle, you can further assess its membership in the mint family by rolling a stem between your fingers. If the stem is square, it won't roll, and you can be pretty sure it's a type of mint.

Hummingbirds are drawn to tubular, reddish flowers like this one. Photo: Paul Slichter

ID tips: Perennial, up to 8 ft. tall. Square stems are covered with stiff hairs. Opposite leaves (2–7 in. long) are soft-hairy and oval, with rounded teeth along the margins. Tube-shaped flowers are clustered into whorls of 2–6 flowers per node.

Locations: Occasionally seen in moist forests, roadsides, and clearings, including at Tryon Creek State Natural Area and Forest Park.

AT LAST A PLANT NAMED AFTER A WOMAN!

Like the bridges of Portland, most wildflowers with human appellations are named after men. Not so Cooley's hedge-nettle. Botanist Grace Emily Cooley (1857-1916) collected the plant on Vancouver Island. She taught botany at Wellesley College and wrote a book on plants she collected while traveling in Alaska and British Columbia.

Henderson's is one of several shooting star species in Oregon. Photo: Gerald D. Carr

Henderson's Shooting Star
(*Dodecatheon hendersonii*)

Blooms: Early spring to early summer

One of P.G. Wodehouse's characters would have you believe that flowers are the souls of dead bunny-rabbits. That's difficult to test, but for now scientists are going with the idea that flowers evolved to attract pollinators.

The downward-facing dart of a shooting star is a classic example of a flower adopting a unique shape to attract a certain type of pollinator. Shooting stars lift their skirts to beckon bumblebees that buzz-pollinate the blooms, vibrating their flight muscles to dislodge protein-rich pollen held within dangling anthers.

ID tips: Perennial, 5–18 in. Reddish stems are bare, with a basal rosette of elliptic to oval leaves (1–6 in. long). Petals are bright magenta to lavender (sometimes white) and bent sharply back, with yellow and blackish bands around the white-edged base.

Locations: Rare in open woods and grassy areas. Try to spot shooting stars at Cooper Mountain Nature Park.

Do not ingest—or let your pet ingest—any part of foxglove. Photo: Tracy Aue

Digitalis *is from the Latin for "thimble." Photo: Tracy Aue*

Foxglove (*Digitalis purpurea*)

Blooms: Late spring

Foxglove is a big, beautiful weed from Europe that's poisonous to eat but medicinally famous as the original source for the heart drug digitalis. Digitalis is still used today to slow heart rates, giving the chambers more time to fill with blood.

If you make the mistake of pulling foxglove with your bare hands, you might feel what Oregon author and naturalist P.K. Lichen calls its "heart-thumping impact," as it works its way into your system. Wear gloves to avoid that sensation, and beware that every part of foxglove is toxic to dogs, cats, and horses.

ID tips: Non-native biennial, up to 6 ft. tall. First year, there's a basal rosette of leaves. Year two, an erect stem arises with dozens of pink, lavender, or white flowers. Hairy leaves are 4–12 in. long and oval, with toothed margins. Blooms are 1–3 in. long; look inside and you'll often see dark spots on the lower surface.

Locations: Locally common in open areas such as old clearcuts and roadsides with partial shade, including at Tryon Creek State Natural Area and Tualatin Hills Nature Park.

Meadow Checkermallow
(Sidalcea campestris)

Blooms: Late spring to early summer

There's a lot to love about meadow checkermallow, beginning with its looks: You could do worse than having dozens of pink blooms gracing your backyard on towering stems. If you've got a thing for underdogs, you'll also appreciate that this wildflower has been considered for state listing as a threatened or endangered species.

Still not sold? How about its role as host for at least five species of native butterflies? Or, if butterflies aren't your thing (what kind of person are you!), maybe you'll appreciate that meadow checkermallow is critical to the survival of a native bee species that specializes on three *Sidalcea* species in the Willamette Valley.

Smaller flowers are female (no anthers); larger ones are bisexual. Photo: Paul Slichter

ID tips: Perennial, 2-6 ft. tall, usually in clumps. Leaves are palmately veined and compound, like lupine leaves. Each leaflet is sharply pointed. Many pink or white flowers arise near the top of the flowering stem, with heart-shaped petals.

Locations: Uncommon in fields, grassy hillsides, and roadsides, including at Cooper Mountain Nature Park, Fernhill Wetlands, and Powell Butte Nature Park (near the top).

Purple Peavine *(Lathyrus nevadensis)*

Blooms: Late spring to early summer

You've probably eaten garden peas, snow peas, and sugar snap peas, which are all cultivated pea varieties. Purple peavine is related, but it's one of the wild pea species you'll find in clearings and drier areas across Portland.

To tell purple peavine from locoweeds and poisonous crazyweeds, look for string-like tendrils on the leaf tips. Vetches (*Vicia* spp.) also have tendrils, so distinguishing between a peavine and a vetch requires close examination. One way to tell them apart is to look at their pistils, or female reproductive parts (think of them as sex pistils). Vetch pistils are hairy all over; peavine pistils are hairy only on one side.

Look for clusters of a few flowers. Photo: Paul Slichter

ID tips: Perennial, 2-4 ft. tall. Pinnately compound leaves have 4-8 mostly opposite leaflets, ending with a branched and coiled tendril. Clusters of 2-4 flowers are generally pink to bluish. Leafy peavine (*L. polyphyllus*) has more leaflets and flowers.

Locations: Common in oak woodlands and occasionally seen in mixed forests, including at Tualatin National Wildlife Refuge and Lewis and Clark State Park.

The Haida call them "red rain-flowers"; pick one, and they say it will rain. Then again, if you don't pick one ... Photo: Susan Berger

A pretty and hardy perennial for rain gardens. Photo: M.A. Willson

Red Columbine (*Aquilegia formosa*)

Blooms: Summer

Have you ever smelled a red flower like this one? What you'll discover is that many red flowers smell like ... not much. That's believed to be because they've evolved to attract hummingbirds, which don't have a strong sense of smell but are drawn to the color red. Over the eons, red columbines have also increased the sugar content in their nectar to satisfy the ultra-high energy demands of hummingbirds.

Bees can't see the color red, but they do help pollinate at least some red, or western, columbine. That's why the plant is now seen growing up through British Columbia and into Alaska, where few hummingbirds fly.

ID tips: Perennial, up to 3 ft. tall. Leaves are lobed and may be divided into leaflets, similar to western meadow-rue. Flowers have 5 red sepals, 5 yellow petals fused into a rounded nectar spur (turning red), and a dangling cluster of yellowish stamens and styles.

Locations: Uncommon in moist, well-drained soils, including at Forest Park, Fernhill Wetlands, and Tryon Creek State Natural Area. They're also a popular option for native gardens.

A sea of rosy plectritis at Camassia Natural Area. Photo: Tracy Aue

Rosy Plectritis *(Plectritis congesta)*

Blooms: Spring

Do yourself a favor and head to a local meadow in late April or early May to see fields ablaze with the round pink clusters of rosy plectritis, often intermixed with the blue of common camas—it's a breathtaking sight.

Like other wildflowers that bloom early, rosy plectritis, or sea blush, is highly valued by hungry bumblebee queens emerging after long, cold, wet winters. Many other native bee and butterfly species likewise depend on early-spring blooms, making it especially important to mix them into our yards and gardens.

ID tips: Annual, 2–25 in. tall. Leaves at the base are spoon-shaped. Slender stems have opposite leaves with no petiole or leafstalk (they're sessile). Each flower in the dense, rounded clusters has 5 petals fused into a long tube, with a nectar spur protruding down toward the back.

Locations: Locally abundant in moist sites with some sun, including at Canemah Bluff Nature Park, Camassia Natural Area, and Cooper Mountain Nature Park.

POLLEN'S AMAZING JOURNEY

If a plant gets lucky, a microscopic pollen grain will land on its stigma, the sticky tip of the female sexual organ. But that's only the beginning of pollen's amazing journey. To become a seed, cells inside the pollen grain have to reach the ovule—but standing in the way is a long finger of nutrient-rich tissue called the style. So, the tiny pollen grain grows a straw-like extension called the pollen tube, which forges a path through the style. That tube transports the male sperm cells from the pollen grain to the ovule, where fertilization can, at last, take place.

The large blooms are a buffet for pollinators.
Photo: Kermit Williams

Plant this beauty to attract butterflies and other pollinators.
Photo: Gerald D. Carr

Showy Milkweed (*Asclepias speciosa*)

Blooms: Summer

Many different milkweed species are spread across the United States, but this is the only one native to the Portland area and thus is the one to shop for at local nurseries.

Milkweeds famously serve as host plants for the iconic Monarch butterfly, meaning they're the only plants Monarchs will lay their eggs on. Portland is not on the usual flight path for Monarchs, but they're sometimes seen here, and showy milkweed offers a bounty of nectar to all sorts of other insects too. Plus, its large flower clusters are a showstopper.

ID tips: Perennial, 1.5–4 ft. tall. Opposite leaves are thick, hairy, and large (3–7 in. long), often with a pointed tip. Big umbel-like clusters of rose-purple flowers top hairy stems.

Locations: Not found in the wild in Portland, but it's a fine choice for backyard plantings. If you're worried about milkweed spreading, plant it in containers.

Flower clusters can be a variety of colors.
Photo: Evelyn Sherr

Western Meadow-Rue (*Thalictrum occidentale*)

Blooms: Late spring to early summer

I might be revealing too much about my reading habits, but do you remember the character in *The Hunger Games* who cures Katniss's tracker jacker stings? The character is named Rue, likely after a medicinal plant of the same name.

"Rue" is also incorporated as part of the name of many unrelated plants—including this one—that have similarly bitter and medicinal leaves. Western meadow-rue is a pretty plant, but beware that you may "rue" planting it in your garden because it spreads quickly by rhizomes.

ID tips: Perennial, 1–3.5 ft. tall. Shiny and divided blue-green leaves have wedge- to fan-shaped leaflets. Loose flower clusters top purplish stems and are greenish-white to purplish-red.

Locations: Rare in forest openings and wet places, including at Forest Park. It's more common in the Columbia River Gorge and toward the coast at places like Saddle Mountain.

Western Starflower (*Lysimachia latifolia*)

Blooms: Late spring to early summer

Late spring is an especially magical time to explore trails in the Portland area, as birds are chirping, fern fronds are unfurling, and colorful blooms are emerging on wildflowers like this one.

Western starflower's delicate pinkish blooms stand out against the backdrop of the plant's big, broad, deep-green leaves (*latifolia* roughly translates to "broad-leaved"). Lots of flowers have a starry shape, but species like this one earn the starflower moniker by virtue of their wafer-thin flower stalks, upon which the blooms seem to float in the air like stars.

The flower stalk's too thin to see here.
Photo: M.A. Willson

ID tips: Perennial, 2–12 in. tall. Look for a whorl of 4–7 broadly oval leaves (up to 3.5 in. long) with pointed tips. Up to a few star-shaped pink flowers (up to .75 in. wide) bloom on thin flower stalks, each with 5–7 pointed petals.

Locations: Locally common in shady, moist woods, including at Oxbow Regional Park, Hoyt Arboretum, Camassia Natural Area, and Powell Butte Nature Park.

COMPOSITES

Canada Thistle (*Cirsium arvense*)

Blooms: Summer

I grew up thinking all thistles were bad and invasive—not true! Portland has several native thistles that are rich in nectar, provide rich habitat for native insects, and produce seeds that goldfinches and many other birds love.

If you have thistles, first use a field guide or call experts to determine if they're native. If so, count your blessings. If instead you have non-native Canada thistles you want to remove, pull up the stalks just before or after they bloom. Much of the underground stem will come up, robbing the rhizome of its strength (you'll need to repeat the process, sometimes for years). Digging only breaks up the rhizome and encourages spreading.

ID tips: Non-native perennial, 3–5 ft. tall (or taller). Basal rosettes of long leaves, each up to 8 in. long, have needle-like barbs. Stem leaves are smaller and deeply lobed, with long, poky spines. Blooms are pink to purple, like pom-poms.

Roots can spread over 20 feet and drill down 22 feet. Photo: © City of Portland

Locations: Common in open areas with poor soils, such as powerline corridors, roadsides, and industrial waste areas. Look for thistles at Tryon Creek State Natural Area and along the Multnomah Channel.

The forked white "teeth" in the center of the bloom are modified anther filaments. Photo: Kermit Williams

Cluster Lily (*Dichelostemma congestum*)

Blooms: Spring to midsummer

It takes a lot of energy for a plant to produce a bundle of large blooms instead of one or two small flowers. The advantage for species like cluster lily is that showy clusters can attract more pollinators that are likely to visit multiple flowers once they're in the neighborhood.

Cluster lilies—also called forktooth ookow, which rolls right off the tongue—used to be common around Portland, where they were an important food source for Native tribes. As we've replaced our prairies and oak woodlands with farms and dense stands of conifers, these flowers have become much less common.

ID tips: Perennial, 8–40 in. tall. The 3–4 leaves at the base are strap-like (lanceolate), each up to 4 in. long. Leaves may wither before the plant flowers. Leafless flowering stalks are topped by a ball-shaped cluster of 6–15 flowers.

Locations: Uncommon but found here and there in oak woodlands and thin-soil meadows. Cooper Mountain Nature Park is the best place to look.

Margaret Atwood describes the blooms as like "pastel water momentarily frozen in a splash." Photo: Tracy Aue

Oregon Iris (*Iris tenax*)

Blooms: Spring to early summer

Why plant non-native irises when you can plant this showy, hardy native instead? Oregon iris grows easily in well-drained soils and can survive in dappled shade to full sun. It's a perennial that'll come back each spring, spreading slowly to provide an eye-catching splash of violet in your backyard.

Do not mistake the beauty of irises for weakness. *Tenax* means "tough" or "tenacious," a trait Native peoples took full advantage of, braiding the leaves to make durable rope, bags, and nets. They also made snares that David Douglas described as tough enough to take down an animal as large as an elk.

ID tips: Perennial, up to 16 in. tall. Green, grass-like leaves (up to 14 in. long) emerge first in spring. By late spring, look for violet or occasionally blue, white, yellowish, or pinkish flowers with distinct veins.

Locations: Uncommon but found on hillsides and open wooded areas with well-drained soil. Enjoy them at Cooper Mountain Nature Park, Camassia Preserve, Kelly Butte Natural Area, and Tualatin River National Wildlife Refuge.

Common Camas *(Camassia quamash)*

Blooms: Spring

Common camas is one of the most culturally and historically significant plants in Oregon, a spring beauty that wars have been fought over and that was second only to salmon as a trade item for Native tribes in Oregon and Washington.

Among the Nez Perce, camas harvests could last months, with family groups digging in patches that they later burned to maintain the prairie-like habitat. Weeding was essential to remove death camas, which looks similar to common camas until its white flowers bloom. Women did most of the harvesting, using digging sticks to collect up to two tons of onion-like bulbs each year that they baked in stone-lined pits.

There's a constant buzz around camas.
Photo: Tracy Aue

Agricultural fields have overtaken much of its Willamette Valley habitat, but you can easily plant camas in your backyard. In April and May, you can also visit a few local natural areas to see stunning blue fields of camas, or what poet Lynn Ungar describes as "acres of sky."

ID tips: Perennial, 8–24 in. tall. Long, slender leaves (up to 2 ft. long) grow from the base, with a lighter-colored midrib. Upright stalks have blue to purple, occasionally white, flowers up to 1.5 in. wide. Yellow pollen contrasts beautifully with blue blooms. Great camas *(C. leichtlinii)* is much larger and less common.

Locations: Not widespread, but locally abundant in moist meadows at Cooper Mountain Nature Park, Camassia Natural Area in West Linn, Canemah Bluff Natural Area in Oregon City, and Mt. Talbert Nature Park in Clackamas.

The yellow anthers contain the pollen.
Photo: Kermit Williams

> **"The quamash is now in blume and from the colour of its bloom at a short distance it resembles lakes of fine clear water, so complete is this deseption that on first sight I could have sworn it was water."**
>
> — Meriwether Lewis

Camas is a must-have in native gardens.
Photo: M.A. Willson

5 PETALS

A field of lupines in bloom. Photo: Kermit Williams

*The distinctive leaves capture raindrops.
Photo: M.A. Willson*

Lupines (*Lupinus* spp.)

Blooms: Midspring to midsummer

J.K. Rowling's love of plants is sprinkled throughout her Harry Potter books. Herbology is a required subject at Hogwarts (taught by Professor Sprout), Harry's mother is named Lily, and Professor Lupin is ... a werewolf.

Why a werewolf? Probably because Rowling knew that "lupine" means "of wolves" or "wolf-like." It's believed that lupines got that name because they grow in poor soil, and it was wrongly assumed the plants were ravaging the soil like hungry wolves. The opposite is true: Lupines enrich poor soil through the wonders of nitrogen fixing—that's why they're able to grow in inhospitable places like the pumice plains of Mt. St. Helens.

Of the many different lupine species, riverbank (*L. rivularis*) and bigleaf (*L. polyphyllus*) are the two you're most likely to see in Portland. They're beautiful, beneficial wildflowers that provide food and drink to native bees and other insects, as well as to hummingbirds.

ID tips: Perennial, up to 5 ft. tall. Lupines have large, palmately compound leaves (like the spreading fingers of a hand). Flowers typically grow in whorls on tall, erect stems. Each flower has 5 petals: an upper (banner) petal that is centrally grooved, 2 side (wing) petals, and 2 keeled petals that protrude sharply forward.

Locations: Riverbank lupine is fairly common along riverbanks and in the city. Look for it and much taller bigleaf lupine at Powell Butte Nature Park, Howell Territorial Park, Sauvie Island, and Cooper Mountain Nature Park.

FUN FACT

The upper petals of lupines have white spots that guide pollinators to the nectar within. As the plant ages, look for the spots to turn magenta. That color change is believed to communicate to bees and other pollinators that the nectar is gone and they should move on to the next bloom.

American Vetch (*Vicia americana*)

Blooms: Midspring to midsummer

Whether you know it or not, you've no doubt walked past many, many vetches (there are about 140 species in the genus). They're so common that most people don't give them a second thought, which is a shame because they offer a host of benefits to both plants and animals.

Most common vetches in Portland are non-native—American vetch is the exception. It's a nitrogen fixer that fertilizes the soil around it, and it serves as a plentiful food source for birds, mice, deer, and other animals. Native people have used the plant as everything from an eyewash to a lucky charm.

ID tips: Sprawling perennial with stems up to 40 in. long. Leaves are pinnately divided, with 8-16 alternate leaflets (each up to 1.5 in. long). A pair of curly tendrils sticks out the end of each leaf. Clusters of 3-9 showy flowers grow along one side of flowering stalks.

Locations: Abundant in forests and meadows. You can see them at Tryon Creek State Natural Area and Ridgefield National Wildlife Refuge.

Vicia is derived from the Latin vincio ("to bind").
Photo: © Al Schneider, swcoloradowildflowers.com

Self-Heal (*Prunella vulgaris*)

Blooms: Late spring to late summer

If only self-heal, or heal-all, really could cure all that ails us. Alas, it's not a magical remedy for our every existential ache and physical pain, but the plant is edible and has been used to treat sore throats, fevers, high blood pressure, and more.

Self-heal is a fast-grower beloved by bees and butterflies, but beware that it can grow out of control in yards. Like oregano and thyme, it's a member of the mint family, even though it doesn't give off a minty odor.

ID tips: Perennial, 4-20 in. tall. Creeping to upright stems bear opposite leaves that are lance-shaped to oval (about 1-2.5 in. long), with smooth margins. Clusters of purple, pink, or white flowers appear in dense, stubby spikes at stem tips.

Locations: *Vulgaris* means "common," and this sun lover is just that, especially in disturbed soils. Look for it at Tryon Creek State Natural Area, Forest Park, Hoyt Arboretum, and Willamette Park.

July is peak bloom time. Photo: Tracy Aue

It's a beautiful and easy-to-grow winter annual.
Photo: Ron Halvorson

Note the maroon tinge under the leaves.
Photo: Ron Halvorson

Small-flowered Blue-eyed Mary
(*Collinsia parviflora*)

Blooms: Spring

Next Easter, after hunting down all the eggs hidden around your house, head out on another quest to find this beauty in miniature. Small-flowered blue-eyed Mary blooms around Easter, and its common name might refer to that loose association with the Virgin Mary; at the very least, it's a handy way to remember the approximate bloom time.

ID tips: Annual, 1–16 in. tall. Opposite leaves have rounded tips and edges that are usually rolled under. Tiny flowers bloom near stem tops, each with 2 white to pale lavender upper lobes and 3 blue lower lobes.

Locations: Common annual in moist soils across Oregon. Look for it at Camassia Natural Area, Canemah Bluff Nature Park, and Cooper Mountain Nature Park.

> "Faith" is a fine invention
> for Gentlemen who can *see* –
> but *Microscopes* are prudent
> In an Emergency.
> — Emily Dickinson

It's one of several rare larkspurs in the Willamette Valley.
Photo: Jeff Dillon

White Rock Larkspur (*Delphinium leucophaeum*)

Blooms: Early summer

Oh, the species we have lost and are losing; sometimes it takes your breath away. White rock larkspur is on Oregon's endangered list and is a federal species of concern. You have to go searching for it at one of its handful of known sites, but the quest is worth it—and may even inspire you to join efforts to conserve more habitat for species like this beauty.

If you strike gold and find white rock larkspur, for heaven's sake don't pick it or trample it (the same holds true for other wildflowers). What you can do is jump up and down on the trail and let confused passersby know about the value of protecting the remaining habitat for this rare species and others like it.

ID tips: Perennial, 8–24 in. tall, with lots of deeply dissected, palmately lobed (spreading like fingers from a palm) leaves on a long stem. The inflorescence has up to 30 whitish flowers with 2 blue inner petals.

Locations: Rare in loose, shallow soils, including on the edges of oak woodlands and moist meadows. Look for it at Cooper Mountain Nature Park and Canemah Bluff Nature Park.

Fuller's Teasel *(Dipsacus fullonum)*

Blooms: Summer

Fuller's teasel is a holdover from another era—or, really, many eras. The Roman author Pliny the Elder described teasel almost 2,000 years ago, and it was used in Europe long before Columbus and crew sailed west. Settlers in early America used its stiff, prickly flowerheads like scrub brushes to raise the nap on woolen threads that were spun into clothing. Teasel was also valued as a decoration for graveyards.

By at least 1900, Fuller's teasel had made its way to Portland, where it's no longer needed to fashion clothing, nor wanted as a graveside adornment. It's now a nuisance plant that stands tall as a reminder of pioneer days and the lasting change wrought by importing plants from afar.

A bumblebee feeding on the tiny flowers.
Photo: Tracy Aue

ID tips: Non-native biennial, 3–6 ft. tall. First year, there's a basal rosette of leaves. Second year, an upright, spiny stem grows. Flowering stems are topped by a cone-shaped, spiny flowerhead surrounded by long, thin bracts.

Locations: Locally common in moist meadows, wetlands, and disturbed areas, including lots of roadsides and ditches.

Vinca *(Vinca spp.)*

Blooms: Spring to early fall

Vinca is a groundcover that is—how to say this diplomatically?—very successful at what it does. That is, it really, really covers the ground. All of it. Every inch. Those other native plants that might have happily grown on that same patch of ground? Choked out. And that other patch of ground across the trail or sidewalk? Vinca might take that over too.

A pretty picture, but there's never just one vinca.
Photo: Tracy Aue

Portland has larger *(V. major)* and smaller *(V. minor)* vinca species that are also called periwinkles because of their pretty violet flowers. Their beauty might be why some people tolerate or even like having vinca in their yards. The plants do help prevent erosion, and might be slightly better ecologically than having a swath of non-native turf—but only slightly. It's a far better idea to plant native groundcovers like bunchberry, wild strawberries, kinnikinnick, and Oregon oxalis that aren't such bullies.

ID tips: Non-native perennial, up to 16 in. tall (typically 3–6 in.). *V. minor* leaves are about 1 in. long, narrow, and elliptic (*V. major* leaves are wider and up to 2 in. long). Both have glossy, leathery leaves with a milky, sticky sap that can irritate your skin. Always wash your hands and don't ingest any part.

Locations: Very common in Portland neighborhoods and natural areas such as Forest Park and Hoyt Arboretum.

COMPOSITES

Branching stems bear small leaves. Photo; Evelyn Sherr

Chicory *(Cichorium intybus)*

Blooms: Late summer

Chicory is one of the better-known weeds because its starchy taproots can be roasted, ground, and used as a coffee substitute or additive. That has made this wildflower extremely popular in years past, including for soldiers desperate for a coffee fix during both world wars and the Civil War.

Chicory's popularity eventually led to its introduction to the Portland area, where it's now a common, and rather attractive, roadside weed. If its pretty blue blooms pop up where you don't want them, you can try to dig up the plant, but you might have to do so more than once.

ID tips: Non-native perennial, 1–4 ft. tall. Long leaves (up to 1 ft. long) at the base are roughly like dandelion leaves. Sky-blue, aster-like flowerheads are 1–2 in. across, with each flower tip edged with 5 small teeth. Flowers bloom in the morning, follow the sun, and may close by noon on bright days.

Locations: Common in meadows, disturbed areas, and other places with full sun, including at Powell Butte Nature Park, Tryon Creek State Natural Area, and Fernhill Wetlands.

DID YOU KNOW?

Dandelion is another very common roadside weed. Its name comes from the French *dent de lion* ("lion's tooth"), which refers to its deeply toothed or serrated leaves. The Brits have other names for dandelion that refer to its diuretic effects, including wet-the-bed, tiddle beds, and old man's clock.

Douglas's Aster
(Symphyotrichum subspicatum)

Blooms: Summer to fall

If you can't tell an aster from a daisy, trust me: I feel your pain. One helpful guidepost is that asters like this one tend to bloom later than daisies. Also, daisies usually have dozens of petal-like ray flowers surrounding the yellow middle, while asters tend to have fewer and slightly broader rays.

This particular aster (the word means "star," as in "astronaut") is best known as a coastal species, but it grows in moist soils across Oregon. One way to help distinguish Douglas's aster from other asters is to look behind (or beneath) the flowerhead, where you'll see layer upon layer of overlapping bracts.

ID tips: Perennial, 1–4 ft. tall. Thin leaves are linear to lance-shaped (up to 6 in. long), with slightly toothed edges. In each flowerhead, 15–45 ray flowers surround a middle with 50–75 yellow disk flowers that turn reddish. Under the flowerheads, look for loosely overlapping green bracts (phyllaries) with yellow to brownish bases.

Locations: Here and there in moist and disturbed areas, including at Cooper Mountain Nature Park, Tryon Creek State Natural Area, and Hoyt Arboretum (in one large clump).

Asters usually have fewer and broader rays than daisies. Photo: Paul Slichter

Look under the flowerhead for loosely overlapping bracts. Photo: Paul Slichter

THE LANGUAGE OF COLOR

By noting the features of flowers, including their color, shape, and scent, you can learn a lot about the pollinators they're trying to attract.

- **Bees** are attracted to blue and yellow flowers but can't see red.
- **Butterflies** see red well but often ignore blue and violet flowers.
- **Flies** are attracted to the smell of decaying matter. Flowers that smell awful tend to attract flies and beetles.
- **Night-flying moths** are attracted by scents that some flowers produce only at night.

The big, broad leaves are distinctive.
Photo: LeeAnn Kriegh

Bitter Dock *(Rumex obtusifolius)*

Blooms: All summer

Bitter dock (aka broadleaf or butter dock) is a non-native weed found across the Portland area, although it does not spread like mad, outcompete many native plants, or otherwise rise to the level of more pernicious invasive species. You'll also see the similar curly dock (*R. crispus*) around town.

Bitter dock's big leaves have many uses. You can crush them and apply their juices to skin that's been irritated by stinging nettle. You can also use the leaves to wrap up and conserve butter, although these days refrigerators fill that role rather well. You can even eat the leaves in small quantities, either raw or cooked (they're not as bitter as their name suggests).

ID tips: Non-native perennial, 1.5–5 ft. tall. Large leaves (up to 30 in. long) have slightly wavy margins (curly dock has wavier, lance-shaped leaves). Tall flowering stems bear greenish flowers that are toothed. In late summer, maturing fruits turn red, then brown.

Locations: Locally common in fields and roadsides, including at Powell Butte Nature Park and Forest Park.

Do not pick this, or any, native wildflower.
Photo: Susan Berger

Checker Lily *(Fritillaria affinis)*

Blooms: Midspring

Some Native tribes used to eat and trade the tart, rice-like bulblets of checker lilies (aka chocolate lilies or mission bells). Today, nobody makes a meal of these rare treasures, which have lost most of their native habitat, especially oak woodlands.

You can still find checker lilies in several local natural areas, but you'll have to work for it, especially because their mottled petals blend in so well. Look for them in our remaining oak woodlands and in the Columbia River Gorge at Dog Mountain and Catherine Creek. You can also enjoy checker lilies in your own yard, although it takes a few years for them to bloom.

ID tips: Perennial, 4–48 in. tall. Near the bottom of the stem, narrow leaves (up to 6.5 in. long) are in 1–4 whorls of 2–8 leaves at each node. Flower stalks hold nodding flowers (up to 1.5 in. long) checkered with brown, yellow, green, and purple.

Locations: Rare in open woods and meadows, including at Tom McCall Nature Preserve and Cooper Mountain Nature Park.

The heart-shaped leaves have a distinctive notch. Photo: Kermit Williams

Wild Ginger *(Asarum caudatum)*

Blooms: Late spring to early summer

Yes, the leaves of wild ginger have a lemon-ginger smell when crushed. But no, wild ginger is not related to the culinary ginger *(Zingiber officinale)* in your spice rack. This and other plants in the *Asarum* genus are believed to contain carcinogens, so they're definitely best smelled and not eaten.

Caudatum means "with a tail" and refers to its tapering sepals. Photo: Kermit Williams

Wild ginger's glossy, heart-shaped leaves persist year-round, making this one of our prettiest native groundcovers. In early spring, lift the leaves to look for the unusual blooms hiding below. The purplish-brown sepals are unusual, with tails up to three inches long trailing from each.

ID tips: Perennial evergreen, 4–6 in. tall. Heart-shaped (cordate) to kidney-shaped (reniform) leaves are 2–5 in. wide, often spreading via rhizomes to form large mats. Maroon to brown bell-shaped flowers have long sepal tails (1–3 in.).

Locations: Common in moist, shady woodlands, including at Forest Park, Oxbow Regional Park, and Powell Butte Nature Park.

YUM!

Wild ginger's ground-hugging blooms invite pollination by ants and other insects that come out of the ground in spring and mistake the dark-colored flowers for rotting flesh.

It works as a houseplant because it can survive in low humidity. Photo: Evelyn Sherr

A little plantlet getting its start.
Photo: LeeAnn Kriegh

Piggyback Plant (*Tolmiea menziesii*)

Blooms: Late spring to early summer

Piggyback plant gets its various quirky names, also including pig-a-back and youth-on-age, from the small buds, or plantlets, that grow from the petiole at the base of some of the leaves. Those wannabe plants (which look like small leaves sitting atop the big leaves) sometimes take root when the stem falls over and they touch the soil.

Piggyback plant's scientific name refers to two famous people. William Fraser Tolmie was a surgeon, scientist, fur trader, explorer, and politician who spent much of his life in the Pacific Northwest. Archibald Menzies was a botanist and intrepid explorer whose name is associated with a few other local species, including Douglas-fir (*Pseudotsuga menziesii*).

ID tips: Perennial, 1–30 in. tall (can be trailing). Broad leaves are up to 3 in. long and heart-shaped, lobed, and coarsely toothed. Smaller leaves grow atop larger leaves as plantlets. The floral stalk (1–3 ft. tall) bears small purplish-brown flowers with 4 ribbon-like petals and long stamens sticking out.

Locations: Fairly abundant in moist, shady forests and some open areas. Look for it at Hoyt Arboretum, Jenkins Estate in Beaverton, Tryon Creek State Natural Area, and Forest Park.

ONE YARD AT A TIME

Backyard Habitat
Certification
Program

You've probably seen these signs poking out of yards around town, indicating the 6,000-plus homes that take part in the Backyard Habitat Certification Program. The program is brilliant in its simplicity: You pay a small fee, and they provide expert advice and discounts to help you transform your yard into a haven for native plants and animals. Learn more at backyardhabitats.org.

Stinging Nettle *(Urtica dioica)*

Blooms: Spring and summer

Is there a Portlander out there who hasn't had a close encounter of the unpleasant kind with stinging nettle? If your bare skin brushes past the leaves or stems, hollow hairs (trichomes) will break off and, like a hypodermic needle, inject a cocktail of super-not-fun toxins. Itchy white welts then form and burn for several hours.

The stinging hairs deter large mammals (us included), but insects don't mind them at all. Research by David James at Washington State University has shown that stinging nettle is a refuge for dozens of insect species, and host to five butterfly species in the Yakima Valley alone. It's also well-known for its many human uses, including as an edible plant (when cooked) and as material for making twine, clothing, and even paper.

Urtica is derived from the root uro, which means "to burn." Photo: Paul Slichter

If you get nettled, one traditional remedy is to crush up the leaves of dock and place its juices on the affected area. It's also possible that searching for bitter or curly dock leaves will simply pass the time and distract you from the pain inflicted by stinging nettle.

ID tips: Perennial, 3.5–10 ft. tall. Leaves (2–6 in. long) are lance-shaped to triangular. Look for 3 keys to identify the leaves: They're arranged opposite one another along the square stem, they're coarsely toothed along the margins, and most taper to an extended point. Stems and leaves may be covered in glandular hairs. Clusters of small flowers droop from the upper leaf axils (where the leaf attaches to the stem).

Locations: Here and there in area forests, meadows, and disturbed areas. Nettles are abundant in Forest Park and Tryon Creek State Natural Area, and found in patches at Mt. Tabor, Powell Butte Nature Park, and other parks and trails.

NATIVE PLANT SALES

Want to grow native plants in your yard or garden? Our native pollinators applaud your choice, which will also make your corner of the world more beautiful. As early as January, you can buy native plants at nurseries and from groups like these:

- **Audubon Society of Portland:** audubonportland.org
- **East Multnomah Soil and Water Conservation District:** emswcd.org
- **Hardy Plant Society of Oregon:** hardyplantsociety.org
- **Jackson Bottom Wetlands Preserve:** jacksonbottom.org
- **Tryon Creek Trillium Festival:** tryonfriends.org
- **Tualatin Hills Nature Park:** thprd.org
- **Washington County Small Woodlands Association:** new.wcswa.com

Photo: Tracy Aue

Photo: LeeAnn Kriegh

Photo: Tracy Aue

OTHER PLANTS

A better name for this chapter might be "Prolific Plants." Trees, shrubs, and wildflowers get more love and attention, but here you'll find plants and lichens (as you'll see, lichens are not considered plants) that don't fit into those better-known categories but cover much more ground—and trees, roofs, lawns, and sidewalks—across Portland and surrounding areas.

First up are ferns, the city's ever-present but often overlooked green backdrop. Then on to the lichens and mosses that cling to and droop from just about every surface: rocks, soil, dead trees, living trees, shrubs, the backs of beetles (really), and more.

Photo: M.A. Willson

Photo: Tracy Aue

Photo: Tracy Aue

Photo: LeeAnn Kriegh

Photo: Tracy Aue

Photo: Buddy Mays

The Pacific Northwest has about 1,000 lichen species and nearly that many mosses—a few too many to profile them all here, but at least we can get to know the basics of these ancient and essential life forms.

There's one more prolific group profiled in this odd-and-ends chapter: invasive plants. These are the don't-play-well-with-others bullies that wreak ecological and economic havoc, often outnumbering and outcompeting our native plants. Learn to identify invasives so you'll know what to yank out of your own yard and why it's important to support efforts to remove them from wild places.

Bracken can be up to nine feet tall.
Photo: M.A. Willson

It grows singly from the ground, not in bunches.
Photo: Tracy Aue

Bracken Fern *(Pteridium aquilinum)*

Bracken is the world's most widespread fern. Often reaching head height or above, it's a rugged, adaptable species that I imagine shading rats, cockroaches, and broken iPhones in a post-apocalyptic world.

While many plants are harmed by disturbance, these deep-rooted native ferns only get stronger, growing up to several inches a day to dominate landscapes that have been disrupted by logging, grazing, or fire. In an ironic twist, bracken isn't as prolific in Portland as it used to be, likely because it's sometimes outcompeted by Himalayan blackberry, a fellow lover of disturbed soil that can be even more tenacious.

As a sign of just how durable bracken is, it has survived for centuries even though its young curled leaves (fiddleheads) are a popular edible in Korea, Japan, and other countries. Beware, however: Bracken contains a known carcinogen and other chemicals designed to repel the many insect species that like to take a bite out of it.

ID tips: 1-9 ft. tall. Large, sturdy fronds (leafy blades plus their stalks) grow singly from the ground, not bunched like sword ferns. Each blade is triangular and usually hangs horizontally. Blades are 2–3 times pinnate and subleaflets are mostly opposite each other along the spine (stipe).

Locations: Common just about everywhere, including in Forest Park, Hoyt Arboretum, and Powell Butte Nature Park.

FUN FACT

Most ferns have pinnate leaves (from the Latin *pinna* for "feather"), which means their blades (the leafy part) have a single spine, with leaflets on each side. With me so far? When each leaflet is itself pinnately divided into subleaflets, the leaf shape is said to be double pinnately divided, two times pinnately compound, or bipinnate. And, yes, tripinnate—and even more complex pinnate leaf shapes—also exist.

Lady Fern *(Athyrium filix-femina)*

To be clear, lady fern is no more lady-like than any of our other ferns. A variety of reasons are given for the common name, including that it's a particularly tall and elegant fern, with spores concealed in a feminine manner under demure, eyelid-like coverings called indusia.

To identify lady fern, look for a fern that's growing in a clump (like sword ferns), with blades that are wider at the waist and thinner at the tip and base. Also check the underside of each leaflet for jellybean-shaped spore clusters (sori). Lady fern's long mint-green fronds make a beautiful addition to shade gardens.

Look for the wide waist. Photo: LeeAnn Kriegh

ID tips: Perennial, 1-6 ft. tall. Lacy fronds grow in clumps. Each long blade is widest in the middle (narrower at the base and tip) and 1-2 times pinnate. Look at the stalk below the blade for dark scales. Fronds die back with the first frost.

Locations: Here and there along streams and other wet places, including at Forest Park, Oxbow Regional Park, and Tryon Creek State Natural Area.

Licorice Fern *(Polypodium glycyrrhiza)*

Have you noticed fern fronds poking out horizontally from the moss on bigleaf maples, red alders, and other trees? Those are most likely licorice ferns. If it seems odd for a fern to sprout out the side of a tree, consider how moist and nutrient-rich moss is and how much less competition for sunlight there is up above the forest floor—it's a smart strategy.

Leaflets connect directly to the spine, like attached earlobes. Photo: Tracy Aue

Licorice ferns are prettiest in fall, when autumn rains trigger fresh fronds to sprout from tree trunks, as well as from branches, rocks, and logs. To understand where this fern got its name, scratch your fingernail along a rhizome and place a tiny bit on your tongue. The strong, bitter taste is a long way from Red Vines.

ID tips: Deciduous fern, 8-20 in. tall. Unlike sword fern, it doesn't grow in clumps, individual blades are smaller and softer, and leaflets connect directly to the spine (stipe). Fronds have yellow to brown sori (clusters of spores) underneath.

Locations: Grows on rocks and logs and out of the moss on tree trunks. Very common at Hoyt Arboretum, Forest Park, and other wild areas.

It grows directly out of moss. Photo: Alice Doggett

Adiantum, from the Greek for "unwetted," refers to how the leaflets repel water.
Photo: LeeAnn Kriegh

Maidenhair Fern (*Adiantum aleuticum*)

Sword and bracken ferns are the biggest, most common, and arguably the toughest ferns you'll see in Portland-area forests. By contrast, maidenhair fern is their soft, elegant cousin, a favorite among many for shade gardens.

Maidenhair ferns are less common in part because they grow only in continuously moist sites. Look for them on cliffsides and along soil-rich streamsides where the trees are tall and wildflowers such as wild ginger and western trillium grow.

When you find maidenhair fern, look under the scalloped side of a leaflet. Unlike many other ferns, maidenhairs don't have protective coverings (indusia) over their spores; instead, the edge of each leaflet rolls over to shelter its spores in what seems a maternal way.

ID tips: Perennial, 1–2.5 ft. tall. Each blade arises singly on a shiny black or dark-brown stipe and tends to hang horizontally. Stipes split into fan-like or palmate shapes (like hands with fingers). Each leaflet is deciduous and soft to the touch.

Locations: Here and there in moist, rich forests where they grow out of mossy stumps, rocks, and logs. Also look for them along streambanks and under waterfall sprays. Sites include Forest Park, Oxbow Regional Park, and Hoyt Arboretum.

They grow in clumps with arching fronds.
Photo: Evelyn Sherr

Sword Fern (*Polystichum munitum*)

Go for a walk in any moist forest in the Pacific Northwest and look down. Or to your right. Or left. In every season of the year, you'll see clumps of sword ferns in every direction. They're ubiquitous because they're hardy plants that tolerate full sun and resist drought. They're useful, too, stabilizing many a hillside with their deep roots.

In spring, sword ferns' tightly coiled new fronds rise up, eventually extending up to four feet from a central point. Florists have long used the fronds for funerals, and some Native tribes bundled and used them as mattresses. Individual fronds die back in a year or two, but the underground rhizomes of the sword ferns you see growing along Portland-area trails can be hundreds of years old.

ID tips: Perennial, 3–5 ft. tall. Upright to arching evergreen fronds are up to 4 ft. long, dark green, growing as a circular clump. Look for the boot-toe or thumbs-up projection at the base of each leaflet, pointing toward the tip of the frond.

Locations: All over forested areas, in shady and sunny areas, including at Hoyt Arboretum, Forest Park, and Powell Butte Nature Park.

Common Horsetail *(Equisetum arvense)*

If we traveled back in time a few hundred million years, we could walk through forests filled with horsetails, some as tall as trees. Nearly every member of that once-great order of plants died off long ago. The horsetails you see in Portland are members of the sole surviving genus.

Common horsetail is the species you'll see most often in moist areas of the city. It can grow a couple feet tall, rather short in comparison to another survivor, Mexican giant horsetail *(E. myriochaetum)*, which can reach heights of 20 feet or more in Central and South America.

Horsetails reproduce via spores, not seeds. In spring, the underground rhizome of common horsetail produces a pencil-shaped fertile shoot, topped by a cone-like structure (strobilus) that's full of spores eventually released to the wind. In summer, the rhizome produces a second, very different type of shoot. This sterile shoot has thin branches that stick out horizontally, making it look like a bottlebrush or the tail of a horse.

The branches tell you these are sterile shoots.
Photo: Evelyn Sherr

Why devote so much energy to producing sterile shoots? Because with the help of those green branches, the sterile shoots feed the rhizome through photosynthesis well into fall. That helps horsetails survive winter and send up fertile shoots again the following spring. It's been a successful strategy for millions of years.

Look for: Perennial, 1–2.5 ft. tall. Note the obvious joints, or nodes, where inconspicuous leaves occur in whorls. Fertile shoots tend to be brownish, topped by cones filled with spores. Sterile shoots are green and have thin branches.

Found: Horsetail adapts to a variety of conditions but is most common where there's both sunshine and moisture, including in Portland-area meadows and along streams.

OUR YOUTHFUL FERNS

The common story about ferns is that they're all ancient, spore-producing plants that were largely replaced when flowering plants came along. Except that's not exactly true. Yes, ancient, sometimes tree-sized fern species date back over 300 million years, more than a million years before flowering plants emerged. But the modern fern species we see in Portland? DNA studies show they evolved only after the rise of flowering plants, making them relative upstarts in the plant world.

LICHENS & MOSSES

Letharia vulpina is a fruticose lichen that grows on conifer trunks. Photo: M.A. Willson

Lichens (*Various*)

If there's one sure thing we remember from biology class, it's that "Freddy Fungus and Alice Alga took a lichen to each other," meaning that lichen is a union between a fungus and an alga (or cyanobacteria). The fungi provide the "house" (shelter, among other things) and microscopic algae or bacteria provide the "food" through photosynthesis.

There are two problems with that old saying. One is that those stereotypical gender roles are sexist as all get-out. Two is that sometimes yeast adds a third component to the famous relationship, which means we need to come up with a whole new saying to describe the more complex threesome.

What remains true is that the thousand or so lichen species in the Northwest do a lot of good in the world. Wild animals eat lichens, hide in them, and use them to build nests, and plants depend on lichens to fix nitrogen in the air, turning it into a soluble form that supports growth. People have also used lichens in many ways, including as antibiotics, natural dyes, and perfumes.

Lichens can withstand drought, freezing temperatures, and even radioactivity—there's a reason they've been around about a billion years. What they don't tolerate well is air pollution, which makes them, along with mosses, extremely helpful to scientists. If a given area lacks a diversity of healthy lichen species, it's likely an early sign of trouble for other species, including us.

This fruticose lichen in the Usnea genus is called old man's beard or beard lichen. Photo: Tracy Aue

ID tips: There are about 15,000 lichen species worldwide. They have no roots, stems, or leaves. The 4 basic types are crustose that grow like a crust or stain; foliose that are leaf-like; fruticose that are branched and can look like little shrubs; and squamulose that have scale-like lobes. Lichens can be yellow, brown, orange, or many other colors. They can resemble peeling paint or a leafy plant or a dusting of powder or many other things.

Locations: On tree branches and trunks, rocks, bare soil, and more. Look on the bark of cherry trees at Waterfront Park to see both gray, leaf-like *Parmelia* and orange, crusty *Xanthoria* lichens.

DID YOU KNOW?

Lichens are not plants. Because they're made up of a fungus and one or more symbiotic partners, they're considered composite organisms. Fungi aren't plants either. They're genetically more closely related to animals like you and me than they are to plants.

Mosses *(Various)*

Portland grows moss like Iowa grows corn, which makes it easy to overlook the jaw-dropping wonders of "the green stuff." First, a little perspective: When *Homo sapiens* arrived on the scene a few hundred thousand years ago, mosses had already been cushioning the Earth for about 450 million years. And while we're the only species of our kind, there are about 800 moss species in the Pacific Northwest alone. Heck, dozens of species can grow on a single tree!

Moss forms beds that support other life. Photo: Buddy Mays

Are you sufficiently humbled? The word "hardy" doesn't do mosses justice. During drought they simply go dormant for days or weeks—or decades. When rain returns (or when you dribble some water on them), they immediately spring back to life, absorbing up to 200 times their weight in water.

Now, it's true that mosses lack seeds, flowers, fruits, and internal plumbing to transport water and nutrients; they are, in fact, the most primitive land plants in the world. Yet these simple-seeming species play a critical role in area ecology: building and stabilizing soil, offering nesting sites for birds, and providing essential nutrients that many other plants depend on.

Mosses also trap pollutants, so they (and lichens) can be used to detect air pollution. Most of us learned about that several years ago, when studies of a moss called *Orthotrichum lyellii* identified unhealthy concentrations of cancer-causing metals in Portland's air.

A song sparrow perched on a moss-covered branch. Photo: Tracy Aue

ID tips: There are so many moss species that it's hard to boil it down to a simple description, but generally moss is green, grows in moist areas, and looks somewhat leafy. Look for a central stem with leaves coming off it in regular arrangements (lichens don't have true stems, leaves, or roots). Species identifications typically require a microscope—sometimes a compound one.

Locations: Anyplace with moisture. Moss grows on trees and rocks, in sidewalk cracks, on walls, and in lawns. Great examples can be seen at Lower Macleay Trail in Forest Park, Hoyt Arboretum, and Tryon Creek State Natural Area.

> Every chemical stupidity,
> every burned field, every better
> home & garden finally overrun
> by the green will, the green greenness
> of green things growing greener.
> — Tim Seibles, excerpt from the poem "Fearless"

Look for long, slender flower clusters.
Photo: © City of Portland

Butterfly Bush *(Buddleja davidii)*

Blooms: Spring to late summer

Let's not beat around the bush: Butterfly bush is beautiful. It resembles a lilac with its footlong clusters of fragrant, colorful flowers, and it's a magnet for butterflies and hummingbirds. So what's not to love? A lot, as it turns out.

Every one of those pretty flower clusters releases tens of thousands of seeds that can travel for miles, and butterfly bush also reproduces by rhizome fragments. As a result, this shrub spreads fast, outcompeting native plants everywhere it grows, from meadows to slopes to industrial yards to streambanks. Its name is a misnomer because though it attracts butterflies, it's not a host plant for caterpillars; plus, it prevents the growth of native plants that actually would benefit caterpillars.

To get rid of this pretender, cut it down and dig to remove the whole root crown. Then plant a similarly showy and far more controllable native shrub such as red-flowering currant, mock-orange, elderberry, or oceanspray. Local nurseries sell nearly seedless cultivars of butterfly bush, but going native is the best way to support native wildlife and avoid any unwanted spreading.

ID tips: Shrub, 3–15 ft. tall with arching stems. Lance-shaped leaves (6–10 in. long) are opposite each other on the stems and have velvety undersides. Flowers have purple, white, or pink petals fused into a tube with 4 distinct lobes. Flowers are bunched into long, slender clusters, like lilacs.

Locations: Unpleasantly common in backyards, riparian corridors, roadsides, and other disturbed areas.

NATIVES, WEEDS, AND NUISANCES

- **Native plants** are indigenous to, or grow naturally in, a given region and were documented as being in that region before Euro-American settlement (in Portland, that's typically considered the 1800s). Most of the wildflower chapter is devoted to Portland's native plants.

- **Non-native plants** include most crop and food plants, as well as showy ornamentals and other plants commonly used in landscaping. Many non-native plants have beneficial uses, but a few can harm the environment.

- **Weeds** are native or non-native plants that grow where people don't want them. Weeds can be annoying, but they don't necessarily cause widespread damage to our wild places.

- **Nuisance plants** are true troublemakers that harm human health, the environment, and the economy. Federal and state laws further parse nuisance plants as "noxious weeds" or "invasive," depending on a variety of factors. The invasive plants in this chapter are among those the City of Portland considers especially harmful.

There's a whole lot of gray area, so thankfully the city has laid out a full list of native and nuisance plants. Download the Portland Plant List at portlandoregon.gov/citycode/article/322280.

English Ivy (*Hedera* spp.)

Blooms: Fall

The British gave us Shakespeare, Monty Python, and taxation without representation. They also gave us English ivy and other invasive weeds that have run amok in our backyards, forests, and ... well, everywhere.

English ivy originated not in England but in southern Russia, where the harsh climate keeps it in check. But here in lush Portland, the former horticultural inmate has escaped to wreak havoc across the city and most of the Pacific Northwest, helped along by ill-advised recommendations to plant it to stabilize hillsides after flooding.

Ivy can indeed stabilize hillsides, but it doesn't stop there—it spreads aggressively and covers the ground so completely that no other plants can survive in the resulting "ivy deserts." As you can see in places like Forest Park, ivy also climbs trees, wrapping itself round and round until the added weight makes the trees susceptible to toppling and blowdowns.

Ivy climbs trees, sometimes leading to their death.
Photo: Tracy Aue

Most people I know call all the ivy in town English ivy, but technically that species, *H. helix* (and its various cultivars), is far outnumbered by Atlantic or Irish ivy (*H. hibernica*). Whatever you call them, they're bad news—the word "catastrophic" has been used to describe the damage they're doing to area forests. Instead of planting ivy, go with native groundcovers such as wild strawberries, wild ginger, and creeping Oregon grape.

Birds eat the blue-black berries and spread the seeds.
Photo: © City of Portland

ID tips: To the untrained eye, the two *Hedera* species are virtually identical woody vines. As juveniles, they form a thick mat of vines with alternate, waxy, 3-lobed leaves (about 3 in. wide). When mature, the vines climb trees, walls, and family pets, and produce diamond-shaped, unlobed leaves. Greenish-white flowers bloom in clusters. Purple-black berries are eaten by birds that disperse the seeds.

Locations: Just about everywhere life exists (gardens, median strips, walls, forests, etc.). Look for ivy wrapping its woody vines around trees in any area forest, including in Forest Park and along Hwy. 26.

NO IVY LEAGUE

Got some pent-up aggression? Pulling ivy with a like-minded group of weed warriors is a great way to let it out. Since 1994, the No Ivy League has been educating people about ivy and leading volunteer crews at events like the annual No Ivy Day. Look online for details on how to get involved.

Look for clusters of four-petaled white flowers.
Photo: © City of Portland

Garlic Mustard (*Alliaria petiolata*)

Blooms: Spring

Garlic mustard sounds tasty, doesn't it? Its culinary uses led to its arrival in the eastern U.S. in the mid-1800s. But by the 1980s, ecologists had begun to recognize the unsavory threat the plant poses to forest understories. In Portland, it's been considered a priority invasive species since 2004.

Like many weedy plants, garlic mustard grows easily in disturbed areas, such as along roads and trails. Unfortunately, it doesn't stop there—it keeps spreading right into healthy forests, outcompeting native tree seedlings and other plants.

To confirm garlic mustard's identity, crush the leaves and smell for the distinctive garlic aroma. To get rid of it, don't cut or mow. Instead, dig or pull up the entire plant (getting all the roots), bag it, and put it in the garbage. Contact city experts for help, especially since it's easy to confuse garlic mustard with other mustard species, including natives.

ID tips: Biennial herb or winter annual, 1–6 ft. tall. First-year plants are typically low-growing rosettes with kidney-shaped leaves (not hairy like native fringecup and piggyback plant). In spring of the first or second year, the plants bolt, developing long stalks with triangular leaves and clusters of 4-petaled white flowers.

Locations: Dense patches grow along roads and other disturbed areas, as well as along many trails, including at Forest Park, Oaks Bottom Wildlife Refuge, and Reed College canyon.

EXPERTS ON INVASIVES

Have no fear! You are not alone in wondering how to identify and remove invasive plants. These are among the experts who can help.

Four-County Cooperative Weed Management Area: 4countycwma.org

East Multnomah Soil & Water Conservation District: emswcd.org

West Multnomah Soil & Water Conservation District: wmswcd.org

Clackamas County Soil & Water Conservation District: conservationdistrict.org

Tualatin Soil & Water Conservation District: swcd.net

City of Portland Early Detection/Rapid Response: 503-823-2989

On the plus side, the berries are tasty. Photo: Buddy Mays

Himalayan Blackberry (*Rubus armeniacus*)

Blooms: Summer

You know what would be better than our native trailing blackberry, which shares space with other plants and offers tasty fruits in moderation? How about 12-foot-high impenetrable thickets that produce large fruits in exchange for state domination?

That's the deal with the devil that was made in the late 1800s, when Luther Burbank, a plant breeder and eugenics fan, burdened us with this master race of blackberries. Burbank, who also developed Shasta daisies and elephant garlic, imported blackberry seeds from Armenia and sold them to unwitting customers from California to British Columbia.

Look for five leaflets, not three as on trailing blackberry. Photo: Tracy Aue

What those early customers didn't know is that Himalayan blackberries grow roots up to 30 feet long and three feet deep, and produce stems that can grow 20 feet in a season. It's a late-summer tradition to pick the fruits, but don't let their abundance and tastiness lull you into complacency. Himalayan blackberry dominates critical streamside habitats, displaces native plants that many wildlife species depend on, and costs the city a lot of money in maintenance and restoration.

Removal isn't easy, but it can usually be done with hand tools and a whole lot of persistence (there's a reason this monster infests over 1.6 million acres statewide). Contact the experts for details on how best to remove it.

ID tips: Perennial bramble, up to 12 ft. tall, with thumbtack-like prickles on 5-angled stems. Compound leaves have 3–5 slightly oblong leaflets with coarsely toothed margins and whitish undersides. Flowers are white with 5 petals.

Locations: Forms dense thickets all over moist, disturbed areas (roadsides, ditches, meadows, forest edges, etc.), including at Forest Park and Sauvie Island.

> "In the wet months, blackberries spread so wildly, so rapidly that dogs and small children were sometimes engulfed and never heard from again. In the peak of the season, even adults dared not go berry picking without a military escort. Blackberry vines pushed up through solid concrete, forced their way into polite society, entwined the legs of virgins, and tried to loop themselves over passing clouds." — Tom Robbins, *Still Life with Woodpecker*

A small snapshot of the thickets formed by giant knotweed. Photo: © City of Portland

Knotweeds (*Fallopia* spp.)

Blooms: Late summer to early fall

Cue the *Jaws* theme song: Knotweed is so pretty (*dun-dun*), surely it won't burst like a hungry shark through concrete and brick to take over whole yards and streamsides (*dun-dun*), and anyway we can just dig it out if we need to. But wait, digging actually spreads it farther and faster, and now it's taking over the city!

Knotweeds—including Japanese, Himalayan, Bohemian, and giant—are listed among the world's hundred worst invasive species by the International Union for Conservation of Nature. They form dense thickets that are a nightmarish problem along Oregon waterways, where they crowd out native plants without replacing the helpful services they provide, like shade and erosion control. Removal is a pain in the aster, so call the experts for advice on dealing with the knotweed menace.

ID tips: Perennial (some would say eternal), up to 13 ft. tall in the case of giant knotweed (which is in the *Polygonum* genus). All have spreading rhizomes and tall, bamboo-like green-reddish stems. Leaves vary in shape (look online for photos and full descriptions). Plume-like clusters of creamy-white flowers bloom in late summer.

Locations: They colonize streamsides, roadsides, and other disturbed areas, and they're in natural areas like Tryon Creek State Natural Area, where control efforts continue.

It's a cheater that chokes out native plants. Photo: LeeAnn Kriegh

Lesser Celandine (*Ranunculus ficaria*)

Blooms: Late winter to early spring

The city's Environmental Services team is not subtle about lesser celandine, which they describe as "death on dirt" and the plant that "makes everyone want to scream." Why such antagonism toward this little buttercup lookalike?

For one thing, it cheats at the starting line, emerging in late winter to form dense mats that choke out natives. The double whammy is that lesser celandine dies back in early spring, leaving the ground prone to erosion.

It's easy to mistake this impostor for our native marsh marigold, which leads to misguided plantings around town. To get rid of it, dig it up over and over, placing excavated soil, tubers, and bulbils in the trash (not yard debris bins).

ID tips: Perennial, up to 1 ft. tall. Forms dense, low-lying mats. Mounded rosettes have succulent, shiny leaves (shapes vary). Flowers have 6–26 yellow petals that fade to whitish with age. Unlike lookalikes (marsh marigold, western buttercup, and creeping buttercup), there are 3 green sepals on the underside of each flower.

Locations: It has taken over many, many neighborhood yards and parking strips, and is a subject of eradication work at Hoyt Arboretum and other wild areas.

Old Man's Beard (*Clematis vitalba*)

Blooms: Summer

Old man's beard gives English ivy a run for its money in the competition for Portland's most invasive vine. English ivy is much more common, but old man's beard (aka traveler's joy) grows up to seven times faster—at least 30 feet per year.

Like ivy, old man's beard trails along forest floors, creating dense mats where nothing else can grow. Also like ivy, it climbs up and around trees, smothering them and eventually leading to their collapse. If you want a climbing vine in your yard, consider instead planting orange honeysuckle, western clematis, or one of the non-invasive garden varieties of clematis.

ID tips: Deciduous perennial climbing vine, easily 40 ft. long. Smooth to lobed leaves are arranged opposite one another on the stem. Leaves are compound, usually with 5 leaflets (native clematis usually has 3). White flowers bloom in summer (not spring like native clematis). In fall and winter, fruits and seeds have a puffy, beard-like appearance.

White flowers bloom in summer.
Photo: © City of Portland

Each plant can produce over 100,000 seeds.
Photo: Tracy Aue

Locations: Dense patches form on forest edges, along streams, in waste areas, and in wooded areas with partial sun, including in Forest Park, especially Lower Macleay Park, and along Hwy. 26 from the Vista Ridge Tunnel toward Sylvan Hill.

Perennial Morning Glory
(*Convolvulus arvensis*)

Blooms: Late spring to early fall

Morning glory annuals are attractive, innocuous vines. This perennial morning glory (aka field bindweed) is different: It's an uber-aggressive bully that sinks its roots nine feet deep, persists for up to 20 years, and can spread more than 10 feet in a single growing season. Little wonder it's considered one of the most noxious weeds in the world and one of the most difficult to control invasive plants in Oregon's agricultural areas and roadsides.

Proof that pretty things aren't always nice.
Photo: Evelyn Sherr

To rid your yard of this plant, you'll first need to quit your job and devote yourself full-time to the endeavor. Or at least accept that for several years you'll have to pull it up every few weeks in the growing season. Pulling these "glories" is a pain because the stems break easily—but there's nothing more satisfying than beating a bully.

ID tips: Perennial vine with deep roots and trailing stems 2-4 ft. long. Leaves alternate along the stem and are usually arrowhead-shaped. White, trumpet-shaped flowers (up to 1 in. across) have 5 fused petals, sometimes with pink streaks.

Locations: It's versatile, claiming roadsides, backyards, pastures, and more, including at Forest Park and Tryon Creek State Natural Area.

It looks a lot like edible parsley or dill. Photo: © City of Portland

Poison Hemlock (*Conium maculatum*)

Blooms: Early summer

When he was sentenced to death, the Greek philosopher Socrates chose a drink made of poison hemlock as his method. What was true back then remains true today: Poison hemlock kills. In fact, in the first five months of 2015, the Washington Poison Center treated 10 people—two a month!—for poisoning by this lethal plant.

Also known by the delightfully not-subtle names of beaver poison, devil's flower, woomlick, break-your-mother's-heart, and scabby hands, poison hemlock was introduced as an ornamental and now grows in disturbed sites across Portland. To remove it, put on gloves, pull it, bag it, and put it in the trash (not yard debris bins).

A final warning: Don't touch poison hemlock with your bare hands, don't inhale its scent, and don't eat any part of related plants in the wild carrot or parsley family if you can't identify this one. A mistake could be deadly to you or your pets.

ID tips: Biennial, 2–10 ft. tall. First-year rosette has glossy, fern-like leaves (5–12 in. long). In the second year, smooth, upright flowering stems have distinctive red-purple spots, streaks, or blotches. White flowers together form umbrella-shaped clusters.

Locations: Common in wet places, including ditches, backyards, vacant lots, pastures, and other disturbed areas. Look for it at Sauvie Island, Forest Park, and Tryon Creek State Natural Area.

BE A WEED WATCHER

It can be hard to tell invasive plants from natives. For details on how to identify and remove the offenders, attend a free Weed Watcher training provided every spring by local soil and water conservation districts.

Pokeweed *(Phytolacca americana)*

Blooms: Summer

Somewhere along the line, I was told that red berries are poisonous and blue and black berries are safe to eat. That's a dangerous myth, as proven by species like this one. Pokeweed's purple-black berries, and especially its roots, are toxic, so beware—and get to know any plant before you partake.

Pokeweed's berries cause a different problem for Portland's birds because they provide food in fall, when few native plants do. That tempts birds to stay in town longer, which throws off their migration patterns. To get rid of pokeweed, dig out the entire smelly plant (including roots), bag it, and throw it in the trash.

Don't eat these! Photo: © City of Portland

ID tips: Strong-smelling perennial, up to 10 ft. tall. Thick stems turn from green to dark pink by late summer. Look for huge (up to 1 ft. long), alternately arranged leaves with smooth edges and pointed tips. Flowers are usually white to pink, with 4–5 sepals. Long clusters of shiny berries mature to purple-black.

Locations: Forms dense patches in neighborhoods and disturbed areas, including along fence rows, power lines, pastures, and forest openings. Look for it at the Swan Island Lagoon and Columbia Slough.

Purple Loosestrife *(Lythrum salicaria)*

Blooms: Summer to early fall

It might surprise residents of rainy Portland that wetlands—which slow flooding, improve water quality, and provide essential habitat for plants and animals—now cover only about two percent of the state, making them a precious, and declining, resource.

Purple loosestrife clogs up and damages our remaining wetlands, crowding out native vegetation that would otherwise feed and provide cover for local wildlife. It spreads dangerously fast because each plant can produce numerous upright stalks that bear hundreds of flowers and millions of seeds.

Thickets grow in wet soil.
Photo: © City of Portland

From a distance, purple loosestrife resembles native fireweed, but fireweed usually doesn't grow in large thickets or in the same wet soils. If you want pretty blooms in moist areas, try Douglas spiraea, common camas, river lupine, or other native plants—they're gorgeous. And if you're stuck with this purple plague, contact the city on how best to remove it.

ID tips: Perennial, up to 5 ft. tall, often with fine gray hairs on stems. Lance-shaped leaves are opposite or whorled (2–5.5 in. long) with pointy tips. Long flower spikes are crowded with purple-pink flowers with long petals that look like crinkly crepe paper.

Locations: Fairly common along wetlands, streams, shallow ponds, rivers, and agricultural areas, including at Oaks Bottom Wildlife Refuge and Sauvie Island.

The scraggly shrubs are common along roads. Photo: Paul Slichter

*It's in the pea family, as suggested by the shape of its flowers.
Photo Evelyn Sherr*

Scotch Broom (*Cytisus scoparius*)

Blooms: Spring to summer

Scotch broom is reportedly so named because those industrious Scots used the long stems as brooms. Now, if only every Oregonian would do the same, perhaps we could sweep our roadsides and streambanks clear of this invader, which the Oregon Department of Agriculture estimates costs the state over $40 million per year, mostly in lost timber revenue.

In the 1930s and 1940s, Scotch broom was planted along the northern Oregon coast as an ornamental and to stabilize the dunes. An annual festival in Clatsop County even celebrated the plant and the golden hillsides it created. The problem is that Scotch broom is a fire hazard, forms dense patches that shade and crowd out native plants, and spreads fast with explosive seedpods that shoot seeds meters away—seeds that can remain viable for decades.

To remove Scotch broom, take loppers and cut the stems off just below the soil surface. With luck, there won't be much re-sprouting. You can also dig up the plants, crown and all, and pull seedlings when they're still small.

ID tips: Shrub, 3-10 ft. tall. Stems are stiff, upright, green, and often ribbed. Leaves are typically less than 1 in. long. Bright-yellow (sometimes reddish) flowers appear along stems in spring. Pea-like seedpods with fine white hairs appear in late summer.

Locations: Scotch broom prefers dry, sandy soils in full sun, so you'll frequently see it in clearcuts and along roads and dry riverbeds. It also grows well along waterways. Look for it along I-5 and other highways, and at Forest Park, Hayden Island, and Tualatin Hills Nature Park.

Stinky Bob *(Geranium robertianum)*

Blooms: All summer

Cultivated geraniums are pretty, hardy flowers that many gardeners enjoy. Unfortunately, some of those introduced geraniums—especially this one and the equally awful shiny geranium *(G. lucidum)*—have "hopped the fence," so to speak, and spread across local forests and other natural areas.

Stinky Bob (aka herb Robert) and shiny geranium are unwelcome because they take over entire swaths of the shady forest floor, crowding out the many native plants that should grow there. Once you recognize them, you'll see stinky and shiny geraniums in every area forest, and rightly come to resent their determined sprawl.

If you see "Bob" and his brethren in your backyard, try pulling them up before they go to seed. And plan to do so again and again for several years.

ID tips: Stinky Bob is an annual or biennial, 4–20 in. tall. Stems are usually reddish with soft hairs and a sticky feel. Parsley-like leaves (1-2 in. wide) are highly lobed to dissected, divided into 5 leaflets. Pink or reddish flowers have 5 petals and whitish veins. Shiny geranium is less stinky, with shiny leaves that are not as deeply lobed. Another small, weedy pink flower is filaree *(Erodium cicutarium)*, which has pinnate leaves (fern-like).

Locations: Abundant (often very abundant) in yards and open forests, meadows, and clearings at Hoyt Arboretum, Kelley Point Park, and many other natural areas.

Stinky Bob blooms are pretty, but stinky. Photo: Evelyn Sherr

This is shiny geranium (red, stressed leaves are typical). Photo: Tracy Aue

The Chinese name translates to "foul-smelling tree." Photo: © City of Portland

Tree-of-Heaven *(Ailanthus altissima)*

Blooms: Late spring and early summer

Betty Smith, author of the classic *A Tree Grows in Brooklyn*, wrote of tree-of-heaven that it's the "only tree that grows out of cement." Indeed, this urban-loving import from China sprouts right out of sidewalks, which it then fractures as its aggressive root system sprawls and the tree grows and grows—up to six feet a year.

Each ironically named tree-of-heaven produces up to 350,000 seeds each year, which spread the tree far and wide. Once rooted, it's tough to get rid of (contact the pros for details), and to make matters worse, it uses chemicals in its roots to kill neighboring plants. Oh, and the trees smell like rancid peanuts, cat urine, or sweaty socks, which pretty much seals the deal on this being the least welcome tree in tree-friendly Portland.

ID tips: Deciduous tree, up to 80 ft. tall. Bark is smooth and pale gray. Leaves can be up to 4 ft. long, with pointed leaflets (3-5 in. long). Yellow-green flower clusters appear in late spring or early summer. Female trees produce yellow to red seeds that develop into papery samaras.

Locations: Used to be planted as a street tree and is still seen in yards and parks and in disturbed and industrial areas, including along the Columbia Slough.

Yellow Flag Iris (*Iris pseudacorus*)

Blooms: Late spring or early summer

Yellow flag iris is a colorful and popular ornamental that you can easily buy online—but please don't. It's a nasty invasive that's damaging area lakes, wetlands, and irrigation ditches.

One reason yellow flag iris is so popular is that it's easy to grow: really, really easy to grow. Plant one, especially in standing water, and you could soon have dozens of five-foot-tall irises connected by a thick, dense mat of underground rhizomes. The plants also reproduce via huge and hardy seed capsules that house cork-like seeds and can float for miles, like from your pond to a nearby stream or wetland area.

Plenty of native plants are as pretty as this one and actually benefit the environment, including yellow monkeyflower, skunk cabbage, and some native irises like Oregon iris. Or, opt for a non-native ornamental that's not invasive, such as Japanese or Siberian iris.

ID tips: Perennial, up to 5 ft. tall. Leaves are thick, upright, and strap-like (up to 1 in. wide). Flowers have a typical iris form, with 3 upward-pointing arms and 3 large (up to 3 in. long), downward-facing, curved bright-yellow sepals, or "falls," often streaked with brown.

Locations: If you see a yellow iris growing in or along any Portland wetland area, it's almost certainly this one. Look for lots of them behind the main Hillsboro Library and on Sauvie Island.

Use gloves to pull the plant and rhizomes.
Photo: © City of Portland

Other native plants are as pretty and far less harmful.
Photo: Tracy Aue

THE INTERNET IS NOT FOR FLOWERS

If a popular plant like yellow flag iris is sold online, it must be okay to buy, right? Wrong. Online sources are notoriously untrustworthy for plants—you won't know until it blooms what you've actually purchased, and too often you'll end up with plants that are invasive in Portland. Shop sales at local native plant nurseries instead.

Photo: John Williams

Photo: Mark Lundgren

Photo: Buddy Mays

BIRDS

Getting to know the birds of Portland will change your life, simple as that. Bus stops will become bearable. The ride to work will not last long enough. You'll wear headphones less often, and podcasts will go unlistened to as you spend more time tuning in to the romance and drama taking place in the trees above.

You'll smile more, and struggle not to identify birds, unasked, to friends who now seem irrationally absorbed in the day-to-day of human experience. When stuck in traffic, you'll reach for your binoculars, because you will have binoculars, and you will stash your "binos" in your car precisely for moments like these. Eventually you'll buy a camera too, and immediately wish you had a longer lens.

Photo: Buddy Mays
Photo: Tracy Aue
Photo: John Williams
Photo: M.A. Willson

You'll spend more time looking at the sky, not to see the shapes of clouds, although there is always that, but to wonder if the warblers and swallows and cranes are back in town. Their singing, swerving, and soaring will make you feel a little wild and free yourself.

The seasons will matter in new ways. At holidays you'll watch less football and more flocks of geese. And spring—oh, spring!—will be so raucous with mating songs and migrant visitors that you'll show up late to work, if at all.

In short, getting to know the birds of Portland will open up a rich new dimension of color and sound, sights and stories, that will make you and the city feel less lonesome and more alive.

WATERFOWL

A large flock taking to the sky is one of Oregon's great wildlife spectacles. Photo: Tom Lawler

Snow Goose (Chen caerulescens)

Seen: Wintering (Oct.–April)

It's a heart-thumping experience to see thousands of snow geese dotting a waterway like snow, then blotting out the winter sky as they rise in a clatter. Sauvie Island's flocks number up to about 6,000, a quaint figure compared to the hundreds of thousands that pass through the Klamath Basin on their spring migration north.

As Mary Oliver recognized, another part of these birds' allure is their fleeting nature: "Oh, to love what is lovely and will not last!" she wrote in her poem "Snow Geese." After a few months, they depart Portland in March or early April, waving like white flags as they wing thousands of miles up through British Columbia and Alaska, often to Wrangel Island in the Arctic Ocean. The good news? They'll be back next fall.

> "It is warm behind the driftwood now, for the wind has gone with the geese. So would I—if I were the wind."
>
> —Aldo Leopold, *A Sand County Almanac*

ID tips: Stocky, medium-sized geese with a white body and black wingtips you can see in flight. Bill and legs are pink. Look for the grin patch, a black line that runs along the bill.

Locations: Thousands spend winter on Sauvie Island.

The smallest of four forms is one-fourth the size of the largest Canada geese. Photo: Phil Nosler

Cackling Goose (Branta hutchinsii)

Seen: Wintering (late Sept. through April)

In Starbucks speak, Canada geese are venti and cackling geese are grande or sometimes tall. Cacklers were once considered one of many subspecies of Canada geese, but now they're recognized as a species all their own—one with most of the same traits and habits as Canada geese, although cackling geese breed farther north and west.

In a recent Audubon Society of Portland Christmas Bird Count, participants spotted over 22,000 cackling geese—more than any other bird species. By comparison, only about 2,600 Canada geese were recorded, meaning that from late fall through early spring, those ubiquitous flocks of geese on lawns and natural areas are much more likely to be cackling geese than bigger and better-known Canada geese.

ID tips: Slightly larger than a mallard. Basically identical to Canada geese, only smaller and more compact, with a shorter bill, neck, and legs.

Locations: Look for flocks of 50 or more at sites including Sauvie Island, Vanport Wetlands, and Fernhill Wetlands.

Canada Goose *(Branta canadensis)*

Seen: Year-round

William Clark probably was not describing the endless honks of Canada geese when he wrote in 1806 that the birds near present-day Ridgefield National Wildlife Refuge "were emensely numerous, and their noise horid." That's because Canada geese used to stop over only for brief respites in the Portland area.

But now many grass-loving Canada geese have turned in their passports and opted to stay in the U.S. year-round, resulting in lots of honking and lots of goose droppings on lawns and sidewalks. Poop problems aside, these are interesting birds that do better than us when it comes to mating for life. Research shows that they divorce only about 15 percent of the time, often when one partner refuses to nest.

ID tips: A big bird with a black neck and a black head with white chinstrap. Bill, neck, and legs are longer than those of cackling geese.

Locations: Where the grass is (parks, golf courses, sports fields). Hotspots include Sauvie Island, Fernhill Wetlands, and Ridgefield and Tualatin River national wildlife refuges.

Goose, goose, duck. Photo: Tracy Aue

Tundra Swan *(Cygnus columbianus)*

Seen: Wintering (Nov.–April)

Like snow geese, tundra swans are big white birds that spend winter in a few less disturbed spots in Portland. You might argue that wintering in Portland is an odd choice: Don't they know summers here are better? And yet in spring tundra swans shun us for the remote Arctic, where they have to defend against wolves, golden eagles, and bears. Clearly there's no accounting for taste. Or instincts.

Females are pens, males are cobs, and their young are cygnets. Photo: Dave Rein

Tundra swans are the most common swan in North America. They resemble our much less common trumpeter swans, but tundra swans are smaller and many adults have a small yellow spot at the base of the bill. Also, trumpeter swans trumpet like

They fly with necks outstretched. Photo: Chuck Gates

a French horn, whereas tundra swans have a higher-pitched call. In flight, tundra swans' wings whistle, leading Meriwether Lewis to call them whistling swans.

ID tips: Large (bigger than snow geese), long-necked white swans. Bill and legs are black, and many have a bill with a yellow spot near the eyes. Often in flocks.

Locations: Agricultural fields and large bodies of water such as those at Sauvie Island, Jackson Bottom Wetlands Preserve, and Ridgefield National Wildlife Refuge.

The Idris Elba of ducks. Photo: Dave Rein

Breeding females are also easy on the eyes.
Photo: John Williams

Wood Duck *(Aix sponsa)*

Seen: Year-round

There's nothing subtle about wood ducks. They are, hands down, the most colorful ducks in North America, with a scientific name that translates as "waterfowl in bridal dress." During breeding season, males are ridiculously, overwhelmingly, almost comically handsome birds that appear to be wearing aerodynamic helmets from the Tour de France.

As their name suggests, wood ducks nest in trees, which creates an interesting challenge for their young. Less than two days after hatching, the tiny fluffballs have to make a giant leap for duckling kind, jumping or tumbling from their tree cavity into the water or onto the hard ground, where their mother awaits to lead them to food.

ID tips: Males have red eyes and a crested head with multicolored plumage, including a white flare down the neck. Females are mostly dark gray with a whitish throat and a pretty white teardrop around the eyes.

Locations: In park settings with large trees near water. Get an up-close view at Crystal Springs Rhododendron Garden, or look for them along the Columbia Slough or the slough along the Smith and Bybee Wetlands trail, and at the main Hillsboro Library.

HOW TO HELP BABY BIRDS

If you see a mother bird and her young crossing a road, you can help by stopping traffic—but don't interfere with the mother's work. Most ducklings and goslings have good, attentive moms, but if you spook them, they might be forced to leave their young behind. If a little one gets separated, let it peep to call its mom back. If you're certain it's truly orphaned, take it to the Portland Audubon Wildlife Care Center.

Breeding males have striking cinnamon bodies and red eyes. Photo: John Williams

Cinnamon Teal *(Anas cyanoptera)*

Seen: April through Oct.

Cinnamon teal have been living in Oregon since at least the last Ice Age. They're graceful swimmers and low, swift fliers, able to reach at least 60 miles per hour. They're also beautiful birds, with cinnamon-red bodies on males and powder-blue wing patches that both sexes show off in flight.

In late spring, scan the thick vegetation along pond edges to spot a group of cinnamon teal, also known as a seasoning. In the water, they can be seen swimming one behind the other, not to draft but to take advantage of food that's stirred up by the bird in front.

ID tips: Small ducks. Males have a cinnamon head and body, red eyes, and a light-blue patch with a white border on their upper wings. Females are warm brown with a long black bill and a similar light-blue wing patch.

Locations: In and near shallow ponds with grassy edges. Look for them at Sauvie Island, Fernhill Wetlands, Scappoose Bottoms, and Heron Lakes Golf Course.

Northern Shoveler *(Anas clypeata)*

Seen: Wintering (Sept.–May)

There are so many species of ducks! How can we possibly keep track of them all? One answer is patience and persistence. Another is to start with species like this one that make it easy: If you see a duck in Portland with an exceptionally long bill shaped like a spatula, you've got yourself a northern shoveler.

You can see why they used to be called spoonbills. Photo: Tracy Aue

Unlike other dabbling ducks, northern shovelers usually dip only their bills into the water to let food flow in (small projections on the edges of their bills serve as strainers). Groups of shovelers can sometimes be seen, bills down, swimming in circles like kids in a dizzy bat relay, a clever strategy they use to churn up food.

ID tips: The very, very long bill (wider at the tip) is a giveaway. They're medium-sized ducks with green heads, white chests, and rusty sides on males. Females are grayish-brown with a bill that's orange and olive-green.

Locations: Look for them at Fernhill Wetlands, Sauvie Island, Vanport Wetlands, and Smith and Bybee Wetlands.

Males have a black patch at the tail.
Photo: Phil Nosler

Gadwall *(Anas strepera)*

Seen: Year-round (less common in summer)

I'm a big fan of this underdog, or underduck, as it were. Other birds have cool nicknames, but this one? Its nickname is "gray duck." But surely its common and scientific names have interesting origins? Actually, no. Nobody even knows what "gadwall" means or where the name originated, and *Anas strepera* translates as "noisy duck" (which they're not).

Okay, but at least gadwalls are rare? No again. They have a wide range and have become pretty common in the Portland area, which I'd argue is a wonderful thing. Look closely, and you'll find that these gray ducks are handsome, subtly patterned birds. They're also strong swimmers with an interesting trick up their sleeves: One study found that gadwalls feign death when nabbed by red foxes.

ID tips: Slightly smaller than mallards. Males are gray-brown and intricately patterned, with a white wing patch and a black patch at the tail (no white patch, unlike wigeons and others). Females look like female mallards, but their bill is thinner and black with a strip of orange along the sides.

Locations: Look for them at Fernhill Wetlands, Jackson Bottom Wetlands Preserve, Koll Center Wetlands, and Smith and Bybee Wetlands.

Males have a green face patch. Females have brown bodies. Photo: Kim Elton

American Wigeon *(Anas americana)*

Seen: Wintering (Sept. through April)

When you see the butt of a duck sticking up in the air with feet dangling, you can bet you're looking at a dabbler (as opposed to a diving duck like a merganser or a perching duck like a wood duck). American wigeons are among our many dabblers, which means they—like mallards, gadwalls, cinnamon teal, and others—tip forward to feed on underwater vegetation.

The one big difference to note between these and other dabblers is that American wigeons have a shorter, sturdier bill that allows them to pluck vegetation from the ground. That's why you'll see them in and around golf course ponds, grazing in a most un-duck-like way.

ID tips: Medium-sized, stocky, short-billed ducks. Breeding males have a creamy-white forehead, iridescent-green face patch, and white shoulder patch on each wing. Females are mostly gray and brown. Both have pale bills with a black tip.

Locations: In and near golf courses and shallow ponds, and at natural areas including Fernhill Wetlands, Jackson Bottom Wetlands Preserve, and Commonwealth Lake Park in Beaverton.

A handsome male trailing a female. Photo: Tom Lawler

Mallard *(Anas platyrhynchos)*

Seen: Year-round

Robins are the best-known backyard bird, and mallards are surely the best-known waterfowl; at the very least, they're the most abundant and widespread. You'll see them on just about every local pond, where you'll also hear the female's familiar quack (the male makes a deeper, raspier noise).

As with other common birds, it's easy to overlook mallards or disparage them as pond pigeons. One of many reasons not to dismiss them is that research has shown that they play a valuable role in maintaining wetlands. Because of their ubiquity, as well as their specific foraging and

Mallards fly low, beating their wings like mad. Photo: Dave Rein

roosting habits, mallards spread a huge amount of plant seeds from one wetland to another, increasing plant biodiversity and fostering healthier wetlands that benefit all sorts of other species, including our own.

ID tips: Males have a glossy green head with a white ring around the neck, yellow bill, maroon breast, and pale body. Females are mostly mottled brown in color. Both sexes have white in the tail.

Locations: Portland's most common and widespread duck can be found just about anywhere with water, from ditches to ponds to rivers.

DID YOU KNOW?

Mallard males (drakes) and most other male ducks look different in different seasons of the year.

WINTER/SPRING: Most male ducks are at their most colorful and appealing (to hens and us) leading up to and during the spring breeding season.

SUMMER: Soon after mating, many ducks ditch their bright feathers in favor of understated "eclipse plumage." Mallards are among species that also molt their flight feathers, leaving them sitting ducks—flightless and vulnerable. This is why you won't see many drakes in late summer; they're here, but they're disguised as females.

FALL: By October, drakes molt again into the green-headed beauties we're accustomed to, while teal and some other ducks maintain their eclipse plumage a little longer.

A pointy-tailed female (left) and male. Photo: Mark Lundgren

Northern Pintail *(Anas acuta)*

Seen: Wintering (Sept.–April)

Northern pintails are common birds across much of North America, but that may be changing as their populations continue a steady decline. Males are especially handsome and in contention with wood ducks, hooded mergansers, and arguably a couple other species for the prize of best-looking duck in Portland.

The most distinctive features on northern pintails are their long necks and pointed tail feathers. They're also celebrated as phenomenally fast and agile fliers, earning them the nickname "greyhound of the air."

ID tips: A slender, medium-sized duck with a long, thin neck and pointed tail. Males have a white chest, white stripe up the neck, and brown head. Females are unique among dabblers for having a long neck and tan face (also note their pointed tail).

Locations: Look for them in shallow water at Smith and Bybee Wetlands and Jackson Bottom Wetlands Preserve. Washington County tallies some of North America's highest numbers of northern pintails in the annual Christmas Bird Count.

Look for a flashy green swoop through their eyes. Photo: Dave Rein

Green-winged Teal *(Anas crecca)*

Seen: Wintering (Sept.–early May)

Three teal species are common in North America: cinnamon teal and green-winged teal, both profiled here, and blue-winged teal that are less common in Portland. All are dabbling ducks known for being extremely fast in the air.

Green-winged teal are the smallest of the three teal species and the second smallest of all duck species in Portland (only buffleheads are smaller). During breeding season, males are particularly dashing birds, with a sparkly green swoop through each eye. To see thousands of green-winged teal, though not always in breeding plumage, take a scope with you to Smith and Bybee Wetlands.

ID tips: A very short, stocky dabbling duck. Small numbers breed in Portland, and during breeding season, males have a cinnamon head with a green swoop from the eye to the back of the neck. Also look for the vertical white stripe that runs from waterline to their shoulder. Females are brown and notably small and stocky.

Locations: Found around the edges of shallow wetlands at Jackson Bottom Wetlands Preserve, Koll Center Wetlands, and Smith and Bybee Wetlands. You can see them and cinnamon teal at Force Lake, at the entrance to Heron Lakes Golf Course.

Ring-necked Duck *(Aythya collaris)*

Seen: Wintering (Oct.–early May)

I don't know about you, but I think a bird called a ring-necked duck ought to have a ring around its neck—a prominent, eye-catching ring. Instead, this bird has a faint chestnut ring, sometimes, maybe, if the light is right and you're holding the duck in your lap. By rights, these birds ought to be called pointy-headed ducks because their heads are peaked, or maybe gray-billed ducks because of the color of their beaks.

There's a faint ring around the neck.
Photo: John Williams

Better yet, how about calling them ring-billed ducks, seeing as though both sexes have a whitish ring around their bill—one you can easily see. In a maddening twist, they used to be called exactly that, until some biologists in the 1800s looked at dead ducks (in their laps, no doubt) and decided that the dark ring around the dark neck was a better way to identify this diving duck.

Females are much lighter in color.
Photo: John Williams

ID tips: Look for a peaked head, white ring on the bill, and white patch in front of the flanks. Males have glossy heads and are black and gray. Females are brown and gray with a whitish eyering and gray bill with a white band.

Locations: Often in shallow wetlands and little ponds, including at Tualatin River National Wildlife Refuge, Fernhill Wetlands, Sauvie Island, and Koll Center Wetlands.

Lesser Scaup *(Aythya affinis)*

Seen: Wintering (Oct./Nov.–April)

What the heck is a scaup? It might be how someone once spelled their discordant call (*skawp! skawp!*), or it might be derived from "scalp," a Scottish term for a bed of shellfish where you might see these birds hunting.

Greater scaup prefer saltwater habitats and are only sometimes seen in the Portland area. In most years, smaller, freshwater-loving lesser scaup are more common. Lesser scaup are

A male (left) and female.
Photo: Tom Lawler

powerful divers, able to swim underwater for more than 60 feet at a time. Look for their slightly peaked heads and note the bluish bill that has led some to call them little bluebills.

ID tips: A medium-sized diving duck with a slight peak at the back of the head and a bluish bill with a small black tip. Males have a black head, chest, and rear end, with gray sides. Females have a dark-brown head and neck with a white area at the base of the bill.

Locations: Lesser scaup can be found at Broughton Beach, Fernhill Wetlands, and Ridgefield and Tualatin River national wildlife refuges. Greater scaup can be seen on the Columbia River.

The right light shows off a male's gorgeous purple-green head. Photo: John Williams

Bufflehead *(Bucephala albeola)*

Seen: Wintering (Oct./Nov.–April)

Like kingfishers, buffleheads are colorful birds with improbably large heads. The archaic word "buffle" means "buffalo" and refers to the supposed resemblance between buffleheads' puffy noggins and the massive furred dome of a buffalo.

Their heads may be big, but overall buffleheads are among the most diminutive of ducks, dwarfed, for instance, by mallards that can be twice their length. Buffleheads are diving ducks, not dabblers, so watch for several of these little birds to plunge as if on command, sometimes with a sentinel keeping watch above the water.

ID tips: A very small duck with an outsized head. Males have a white body, black back, and large white patch around the back of the head (hooded mergansers have a similar patch but they have chestnut flanks). Females are gray-brown ducks with a white cheek patch.

Locations: In and near ponds and other slow-moving waters deep enough for diving, including Fernhill Wetlands and Jackson Bottom Wetlands Preserve.

A male displays his black, white, chestnut, and gold colors. Photo: Dave Rein

Females have fluffy brown crests. Photo: John Williams

Hooded Merganser *(Lophodytes cucullatus)*

Seen: Every season except summer

As you might expect given their names, hooded mergansers are not so common as common mergansers. But they're similar in that both are "fish ducks" that dive to catch fish in their serrated beaks. When underwater, a transparent extra eyelid called a nictitating membrane protects their eyes, like a pair of built-in goggles.

I like to think of hooded mergansers as among the introverts of the bird world. They prefer quiet sites and small groups, and like wood ducks, they're wallflowers that tuck themselves in among vegetation at the edges of wetlands. The one time they get showy is during breeding season, when males call attention to their biggest asset by erecting their crests, flaring out the large white patches behind their eyes, and shaking their impressive heads.

ID tips: A small duck with a thin bill and crested, oversized head. Males have a black head and neck with a big white patch behind the eye, a white breast, and chestnut flanks. Look for the shaggy crest on gray-and-brown females. Males have golden eyes; females, dark eyes.

Locations: Along shorelines of rivers and ponds with fish (a few breed in the Portland area). You might be able to see them up close at Laurelhurst Park, or head to Fernhill Wetlands, Tualatin River National Wildlife Refuge, or Oaks Bottom Wildlife Refuge.

Common Merganser *(Mergus merganser)*

Seen: Every season except summer

Common mergansers are the most common merganser in Portland, found every season but summer on just about any waterway with fish. While most ducks eat plants and small invertebrates, mergansers are pescatarians that use the saw-like edges of their narrow bills to grip small fish.

A male in breeding season (note the red bill). Photo: Tom Lawler

Their name is based on the Latin *mergere* ("to plunge") and *anser* ("a goose"), and common mergansers are said to be the best of the diving ducks at their craft, descending up to 15 feet underwater to catch their prey. They're athletic and powerful enough to strike from the sky like an osprey, nabbing fish underwater and returning to the air with their meal.

Females have white chin patches and shaggy hairdos. Photo: Dave Rein

ID tips: A big, long-bodied duck with a narrow bill. During breeding season, males have a white body with greenish-black head. Wings are mostly white on the inner half and black on the outer half. As with most waterfowl, from July to October the sexes look alike; in this case, mostly gray with reddish-brown heads and white chins.

Locations: In and near most area rivers (where the fish are), including along the Columbia River shoreline at Broughton Beach. Also at Koll Center Wetlands and in large groups along the Willamette River in early spring.

Ruddy Duck *(Oxyura jamaicensis)*

Seen: Wintering (Oct./Nov.–May)

Ruddy ducks are awfully funny ducks, especially during breeding season, when blue-billed males with jacked-up tails court females by, of all things, stirring up bubbles in the water and belching a frog-like sound. In 1926, one grumpy naturalist described it as a "ludicrous courtship performance."

Males in summer plumage are worth searching for outside Portland. Photo: Dave Rein

It's too bad we miss out on the showy summer plumage of ruddy duck males, including their reddish ("ruddy") bodies as well as that quirky blue bill. By the time these odd ducks arrive in Portland for the winter, males have dull-gray bills and are best identified by their stiff tails and white cheeks.

ID tips: Small ducks that bob on the water. Look for the scooped bill and long tail that's often cocked

A male strikes the water to create bubbles as part of his mating display. Photo: Kris Kristovich

upward. In winter, males have a blackish cap, white cheeks, and a dull-gray bill. Females are brownish with a pale cheek patch with a stripe running through it.

Locations: They prefer marshy lakes and ponds, so look for them at Fernhill Wetlands, Vanport Wetlands, and Smith and Bybee Wetlands.

GREBES

A parent and its heavily "pied" chick. Photo: John Williams

Breeding adults have a black stripe on the bill. Photo: John Williams

Pied-billed Grebe
(Podilymbus podiceps)

Seen: Year-round

You don't have to read *The Beak of the Finch* to know that birds evolve different shapes and sizes of beaks to accomplish different tasks.

The distinctively thick, downturned beak of the pied-billed grebe is a prime example, as it's designed specifically to crush amphibians, fish, crustaceans, and other large and crunchy prey.

For my money, pied-billed grebes' best and funniest trick is being able to trap or expel air as needed from between their body and their feathers. That's so these blocky, almost tailless birds can shift quickly from bobbing on the water like a yellow ducky to sinking like a submarine to avoid predators.

ID tips: A little brown bird with a blocky head and short, thick bill that in summer turns whitish with a black band ("pied-billed"). Look for their black throat in spring and summer.

Locations: At Koll Center Wetlands, you can see nests and hear young calling. Look for these grebes among cattails and other vegetation at many other natural areas, including in large numbers at Smith and Bybee Wetlands (bring a scope).

> "As I whispered a bird's name after it,
> it became a small thing known in a world filled with many
> unknowns; and with each bird I was calling myself home."
> — Robyn Yzelman, *The Willowherb Review*

A pair "rushing," or running across the water. Photo: Tom Lawler

Western Grebe *(Podilymbus podiceps)*

Seen: All year except summer

Maybe you've seen or heard of the ballet-like mating ritual known as "rushing," in which two birds rise up and run side by side along the water with their long necks gracefully extended? It's a gorgeous display—and it might surprise you to learn that it's not performed by elegant swans but rather by swan-like western grebes.

To watch their iconic mating display—one of the must-see birdwatching experiences in Oregon—your best bet is to head to the Klamath Basin in spring. In Portland, western grebes can be seen in fall and winter on large lakes and the Columbia River, where their long black-and-white necks make them one of the area's most beautiful and distinctive waterbirds.

Note the black caps and red eyes. Photo: Dave Rein

ID tips: The biggest grebe in Oregon has a very long neck, white in front and black behind. Bills are long, thin, and dull greenish-yellow (similar Clark's grebes have bills that are bright orange-yellow). Unlike the Clark's grebe, their black cap extends around their red eyes.

Locations: Look for groups congregating on large bodies of water. The best viewing spot is Columbia Point near the east end of Hayden Island, where you can see a hundred or more in winter. The Columbia River shoreline at Broughton Beach is another good bet.

DOVES & PIGEONS

The city's surveillance team. Photo: Tracy Aue

Their necks often have iridescent green and purple feathers. Photo: John Williams

Rock Pigeon (*Columba livia*)

Seen: Year-round

People started domesticating cliff-dwelling rock pigeons about 6,000 years ago, developing homing pigeons and hundreds of other breeds, many with outrageous colors, feathers, and body shapes. Some of those domesticated pigeons escaped and interbred, resulting in the variously colored rock pigeons that now live in Portland.

Rock pigeons are derided as "rats with wings," a term coined in 1966 by the New York City parks commissioner, when fears ran high about pigeons being a health menace like rats. The truth is every animal, humans included, carries diseases, but pigeons aren't good disease vectors—they don't make us sick. Nonetheless, the catchy phrase stuck, and the old view of pigeons as beautiful and heroic birds (for carrying messages during both world wars) went out the window.

ID tips: Wild pigeons are pale-gray overall with two black bars on each wing. Domestic and feral pigeons come in all sorts of colors and patterns.

Locations: All over the city.

Look for the white mark on the back of their neck. Photo: Chuck Gates

Band-tailed Pigeon (*Patagioenas fasciata*)

Seen: Late March through Oct.

People tend to think very highly of doves (the symbol of peace) and very negatively about pigeons (the symbol of dirty urban streets), which is odd because they're similar birds.

Beautiful and sociable band-tailed pigeons certainly deserve some dove-like love. They are, of all things, pigeons of the forest, nesting in conifers and eating berries off native plants like salal. They form monogamous pairs, and females generally lay only one egg per nest, up to three times per year. That slow reproductive rate doesn't help their populations, which neared extinction in the early 1900s because of hunting and remain a concern today.

ID tips: Bigger, darker, and with shorter tails than mourning doves. They're blue-gray above and purplish-gray below, with a yellow bill and feet. Look for the white crescent on the back of their neck (not black like on collared-doves).

Locations: In open countryside, burned forests, and urban areas. Forest Park, Hagg Lake, and the Portland Audubon's Wildlife Sanctuary trails are hotspots. In spring, head to Mt. Tabor to see their courtship flights.

Eurasian Collared-Dove
(Streptopelia decaocto)

Seen: Year-round

It's hard to believe now, but in the mid-1900s, English aristocrats prized these birds as a rare and exotic species imported from the Middle East. But collared-doves didn't stay rare for long. They spread through Europe faster than any other bird on record, and more recently have done the same across the United States.

They have a black band around the back of the neck.
Photo: Kim Elton

By the 1980s, collared-doves had reached Florida and begun expanding across the Southeast. It took them just seven years, beginning in 2000, to spread all the way to Alaska. Collared-doves are not (yet) found all over Portland, but they're abundant on Sauvie Island and other agricultural areas near the city.

ID tips: A non-native, latte-colored bird, bigger and paler than a mourning dove but smaller than a pigeon. Note the black collar around the back of the neck. Tail is squared-off, not pointed like a mourning dove, but the *koo-koo-kook* call is similar.

Locations: Look for them in suburban agricultural areas and on Sauvie Island.

Mourning Dove *(Zenaida macroura)*

Seen: Year-round

Our other native dove, along with band-tailed pigeons, is one of the most common birds in North America, a welcome visitor to backyards that serenades us with gentle, owl-like laments *(coo-ah, coo, coo, coo)*. By human standards, mourning doves are wonderful family birds that are monogamous, share chores, and take turns incubating (males get the dayshift). Both parents even produce the crop milk that they feed to their young.

They have dark spots on their wings and the sides of their neck. Photo: M.A. Willson

In one of my favorite studies, a researcher placed mourning doves on a treadmill (because why not?). Oddly, they stopped head-bobbing and started walking like "normal" birds. It turns out their usual walking style, where they thrust their heads forward and then let their bodies catch up, is necessary because they process visual input slowly and need to hold their heads still for a moment to absorb their surroundings. On a treadmill, the scenery never changes, so the birds' heads don't bob.

ID tips: Look for a wee head atop a plump body. They're smaller than collared-doves and have black spots on the wings and side of the neck (not a ring around the neck). Also look for their long tail that tapers to a point.

Locations: Not common in Portland. They prefer open habitat in a variety of areas, from forests to neighborhoods.

> **"I will show you my pigeons! Which are the greatest treat, in my opinion, that can be offered to a human being."**
> — Charles Darwin, in a letter to Charles Lyell

SWIFTS

September is the best time to watch the swifts at Chapman Elementary. Photo: Tracy Aue

Vaux's Swift *(Chaetura vauxi)*

Seen: April through Sept.

One of the quintessential Portland birding experiences—and outdoor experiences, period—is to head to Chapman Elementary School in Northwest Portland in fall to watch thousands of Vaux's swifts swirl around and around in the evening sky, before spiraling like a tornado into the school's chimney. In 2019, more than 168,000 of the birds stopped by the school on their way south to Central America.

Since there are few large trees, dead or alive, to sleep and nest in, Vaux's (rhymes with "boxes") use old chimneys like the one at Chapman as a stand-in. Inside the chimneys, they sleep like upright bats, clinging to the walls with their toenails and huddling together to stay warm.

Their legs are too weak for perching, so Vaux's swifts spend most of their lives on the wing, eating, drinking, and even mating in midair. "They fly wild," writes author Katherine Rundell, "and they fly like a stroke of luck incarnate."

ID tips: The smallest swift in North America is dark gray to dark brown overall, with long, pointed wings swept back to create a crescent shape in flight. Bill is short and tail is square. Stiff, fast wingbeats contrast with the gliding wingbeats of swallows.

Locations: September is prime time, and Chapman Elementary is the go-to place. You can also view swifts entering dozens of other chimneys across Oregon and all along the West Coast.

BEST BIRDING BY SEASON

These are among the best Portland-area birding experiences for every season of the year:

 SPRING: Head up to Mt. Tabor Park to look for migrating songbirds.

 SUMMER: Visit Sandy River Delta Park to see lazuli buntings, yellow-breasted chats, Swainson's thrushes, and more.

 FALL: Join the crowds at Chapman Elementary in Northwest Portland to watch thousands of Vaux's swifts swirl into the chimney at sunset.

 WINTER: You can't beat Sauvie Island for snow geese, sandhill cranes, swans, raptors, and sparrows.

HUMMINGBIRDS

Males have reddish-pink feathers on their heads. Photo: Nagi Aboulenein

Anna's Hummingbird (Calypte anna)

Seen: Year-round

At just over four inches, Anna's are the "big" hummer in these parts, tipping the scales at an impressive two sticks of gum. A fairly recent arrival (first recorded in Oregon in 1944), Anna's are now the only hummingbird that toughs it out year-round in Portland, likely aided by climate change and a whole lot of backyard feeders.

Females have a small patch of pink on their throats. Photo: Chuck Gates

In winter and early spring, keep an eye and ear out for their amazing mating displays. Males climb about a hundred feet in the air and zoom downward at 385 body lengths per second—by body length, that's twice as fast as a peregrine falcon. At the last moment, males pull upward and generate a high-pitched chirp as air rushes through their flared tail feathers. Keep watching, because if the female swipes left, the male may try again ... and again.

ID tips: A big hummer with a green body and dingy-colored belly. Males have a fuchsia helmet; females have a spot of the same color on their throat. Their bodies aren't reddish like rufous hummingbirds. Males sing a complex song that our ears can barely detect as a dry, scratchy buzz.

Locations: At backyard feeders and in suburban areas. Look for them along the Willamette River and Springwater Corridor.

SECOND TO NONE

In the span of a single second, a hummingbird can:

- Beat its wings 80 times.
- Beat its heart about 20 times.
- Shake its body 55 times to shed dirt and pollen.
- Dart its tongue in and out of a flower about 20 times.

That deep-orange throat patch is called a gorget.
Photo: Chuck Gates

Rufous Hummingbird (*Selasphorus rufus*)

Seen: March–Sept.

While Anna's are the biggest hummingbirds you'll see in Portland, rufous hummers are the feistiest—not only in Portland but across the continent. They aggressively buzz, chatter, and chip, chasing off Anna's, as well as just about any other bird, squirrel, or other animal with the audacity to enter their territory.

Rufous hummingbirds migrate from Mexico to as far north as Alaska, one of the longest migratory journeys of any bird by body size (three inches). And they know where they're going: Year after year, they'll return to the same exact spot, such as a feeder or red-flowering currant in your yard.

The reason they value feeders and flowers so much is that they need to drink large amounts of sugar water (nectar) to power their turbocharged metabolism. According to researcher Kenneth C. Welch Jr., if hummers were the size of adult men, they'd need to drink the sugar content of a Coke can every minute of every day.

Females have greenish-gold heads and backs.
Photo: Kim Elton

ID tips: "Rufous" (meaning reddish-brown) is the key word: Males have an iridescent red throat and bright orange on the back and belly. Females have reddish flanks and often an orange spot on the throat.

Locations: Look for them at backyard feeders in spring (March, April) and late summer (August and September), and natural areas such as Sandy River Delta Park through the summer. Compared to Anna's, rufous hummers prefer more rural and upland areas.

HOW TO HELP HUMMERS

- **Grow native flowering plants** that bloom from early spring through fall.
- **Avoid pesticides** since hummingbirds depend on insects and spiders for food.
- **Provide a water source** in your yard.
- **Hang nectar feeders** and keep them warm during the winter (the Audubon Society of Portland has details).

Virginia Rail (*Rallus limicola*)

Seen: Year-round

When Mark Twain coined the phrase "thin as a rail," he was referring to a fence post, but he could have been describing thin-bodied birds in the rail family, including Virginia rail and sora.

Rails are shy and difficult to spot, in part because of their lateral compression (meaning they look narrow-bodied when seen head-on but like typical birds when seen from the side). Their leanness enables them to weave undetected among thick wetland vegetation. Of all Northwest rails, Virginia rails are the easiest to find, but you'll have to work for it by scouting marshland edges and listening for calls that include a pig-like grunt.

Note the large bill and upturned tail.
Photo: Tom Lawler

ID tips: Marshbird with a long, heavy bill and short, upturned tail. Bill and legs are reddish, and body is rusty overall with a gray face and dark streaking down the back.

Locations: Fernhill Wetlands is the go-to spot. Also look at Jackson Bottom Wetlands Preserve and Killin Wetlands.

American Coot (*Fulica americana*)

Seen: Wintering (Aug.–May)

If you've ever been bullied or shamed for being different, do I have a bird for you. American coots are pudgy birds disparaged by many as "mudhens." They're common, taste bad, and raise funny-looking chicks (cooties?). They also struggle to fly, requiring an embarrassing running start made possible by their laughably large, crab-like feet.

Look for the white bill.
Photo: Chuck Gates

On the other hand, they mate for life and form synchronized units with fellow coots to evade predators like bald eagles. They're also pugnacious and powerful, duking it out with each other (those big feet come in handy) and sometimes picking on their young. But they'll also defend those cooties, as John Kemper describes in *Southern Oregon's Bird Life*.

At Yellowstone, Kemper watched as two trumpeter swans attacked a group of coot chicks. In zoomed an angry old coot that rammed into the side of one of the swans, then backed away to have another go, while a second coot swept in to bash the other swan. After a wild melee, the bullies retreated and one of the adult coots floated off triumphantly with the surviving chicks.

ID tips: Like plump chickens floating on water. They're dark gray to black, with a pointed white bill, red forehead patch, and yellow-green legs with huge feet.

Locations: Most wetland areas, including Koll Center Wetlands, Sauvie Island, Lake Oswego (the lake), and Smith and Bybee Wetlands.

CRANES

In Japan, cranes are called "marsh gods." Photo: Dave Rein

Look and listen for them in fields on Sauvie Island. Photo: Rick Derevan

A crane performing its mating dance; they mate for life. Photo: Chuck Gates

Sandhill Crane *(Antigone canadensis)*

Seen: Wintering (Sept.–April)

A friend says she can never live anywhere else but Sauvie Island. Why? Because on winter mornings she wakes to the sound of sandhill cranes bugling in the skies above and chattering among themselves in the field behind her house. Eavesdropping on these prehistoric birds and watching their graceful mating dances is somehow reassuring: Yes, wildness remains. Yes, nature persists.

Sandhills are the world's most abundant crane, and several thousand spend fall, winter, and spring on Sauvie Island. Visit the island to see them flying overhead, cavorting in fields, and feeding at Sturgeon Lake.

ID tips: Big-bodied, tall, long-necked birds with broad wings and slate-gray bodies. Their legs and bill are black, and their rump has a bustle of downturned feathers. Adults have a whitish cheek and red crown. Great blue herons have a black instead of red crown and fly with a curved neck (sandhills fly with a straight neck).

Locations: Sauvie Island is the go-to spot for seeing hundreds or even thousands of these cranes.

"If the Emperor Napoleon, when on the road to Moscow with his army in 1811, had condescended to observe the flights of storks and cranes passing over his fated battalions, subsequent events in the politics of Europe might have been very different. These storks and cranes knew of the coming on of a great and terrible winter; the birds hastened toward the south, Napoleon and his army toward the north."

— Frank Buckland in *The Life of Frank Buckland*

SHOREBIRDS

Killdeer *(Charadrius vociferus)*

Seen: Year-round (less common in winter)

A runner's legs, black bands, long tail. Yep, that's a killdeer. Photo: Dave Rein

Killdeer are quirky little birds. They're shorebirds that don't bother limiting themselves to shores, so you'll see them on golf courses, in arid climates, in the Steens Mountain Wilderness— pretty much any open habitat will do. Wherever they are, you can be sure they'll be making lots of noise. Chicks start peeping before they hatch and keep going their whole lives, announcing themselves day and night with their piercing *kill-dee* and *dee-dee-dee* calls.

Killdeer are famous for their broken-wing display, an act they and other species put on to draw predators away from their nests. But that's not killdeers' only theatrical performance: When large animals like cows or deer walk toward their nests, these birds have been known to charge the enormous beasts. A writer in the 1800s recalled watching a tiny killdeer protect its nest by bravely parting a stampeding herd of bison.

ID tips: Medium-sized, with two black breast bands, a red eyering, and a white collar. In flight, look for long white stripes on their wings and a reddish-orange rump.

Locations: Near slow-moving rivers and ponds with gravel, including Vanport Wetlands, Smith and Bybee Wetlands, and Broughton Beach.

Western Sandpiper *(Calidris mauri)*

Seen: Late summer and fall

Note the black legs and droopy bill. Photo: Tom Lawler

Sandpipers are a varied group of beach-loving shorebirds with long bodies and legs. Some species, like this one, are helpfully called sandpipers, while others go by curlew, snipe, dowitcher, and other names.

Western sandpipers have long been known as the Pacific Northwest's most abundant shorebird, famously forming flocks of tens of thousands all along the Pacific coast, from San Francisco in the south to the Copper River Delta in Alaska. Today, western sandpipers are seen in much smaller numbers. Some migrate through Portland-area wetlands, but head to Bandon for your best chance of seeing large numbers in Oregon.

ID tips: Small, chubby shorebird with black legs (least sandpipers have yellow legs) and a thin-tipped black bill that droops a bit. Their backs are gray-brown and their chests are mostly white.

Locations: When mudflats are showing, they can be seen at Sturgeon Lake on Sauvie Island and at Smith and Bybee Wetlands, Vanport Wetlands, Broughton Beach, and other wetlands.

Breeding adults have rust colors on their head and back. Photo: Chuck Gates

Look for them on the shores of lakes, streams, and rivers. Photo: Dave Rein

Spotted Sandpiper *(Actitis macularius)*

Seen: Mainly May–Oct.

What if female birds were larger and more aggressive, arriving first at breeding grounds to fight over territory? And what if, after mating, females ditched males, forcing them to incubate and raise their chicks alone, while females quickly moved on to mate with other males?

That is, in brief, what spotted sandpipers do, and have done successfully, for generations. In their courtship displays, it's the females that swoop through the air and strut along shorelines. And it's the females that mate with as many as four males in a breeding season. Researchers don't yet know why this reversal of traditional sex roles occurs, but it's plenty fun to speculate.

ID tips: A short-necked, long-tailed shorebird with a pot belly. Their bodies are brown above and white below. In breeding season, they have orange bills and dark spots on white breasts. They fly low, with stuttering wingbeats followed by a glide.

Locations: They're widespread in wetland areas (and nesting along rivers) but not abundant in any one spot. Look for them at Smith and Bybee and Fernhill wetlands, and along the Columbia Slough.

Note the especially long bill and yellow legs. Photo: Dave Rein

Greater Yellowlegs *(Tringa melanoleuca)*

Seen: Spring and fall migrant

If you see a shorebird with long, eye-catching orange-yellow legs, you're probably looking at a yellowlegs—either this one or its smaller and less common relative, the lesser yellowlegs.

A few stay the winter, but most yellowlegs pass through Portland in spring and fall, on their way to and from their breeding grounds in Alaska and Canada. They're tough to tell apart unless they're standing side by side, but the greater yellowlegs has a larger body, a longer and thicker bill that typically has a slightly upturned tip, and a louder call that usually has more syllables.

ID tips: A fairly large shorebird with long yellow legs, a long neck and bill, and a white rump. Their bill is much longer than their head (more so than with the lesser).

Locations: When mudflats are showing, look for them at Sturgeon Lake on Sauvie Island and at Smith and Bybee Wetlands, Vanport Wetlands, and Force Lake.

SHAKE A LEG

Mallards have orange legs, great blue herons have pale-gray legs, western sandpipers have black legs, and greater yellowlegs have … well, you know. Why the variation? Researchers wonder the same thing. Dark legs might help species sneak up on prey, while brightly colored legs might have evolved to stir up prey, attract mates, or help others of their kind identify them in a crowd.

California Gull *(Larus californicus)*

Seen: July–April

California gulls aren't limited to the Golden State, or even to the West Coast. They breed as far inland as western Minnesota, then migrate west for winter. Which leads us to the story of how these gulls became the state bird of ... Utah.

Their bills have both a red spot and black marks.
Photo: Chuck Gates

The popular story—the "Miracle of the Gulls"—is that in 1848 thousands of Mormon settlers were at risk of starvation because a plague of insects was eating their crops. In swept a heroic horde of California gulls to eat the crickets and save the people. The outlines of this legend are true, but don't be too "gullible." It wasn't so much a miracle as it was nature at work, as these gulls routinely feed on insects as they migrate through Utah and other inland areas.

ID tips: A medium-sized gull with a round head. Wings are long and pointed in flight. Black primary feathers have white tips. Adults have dark eyes, yellow-green legs, and a yellow bill with black and red spots on the lower mandible.

Locations: Broughton Beach is the go-to place to see all sorts of gulls.

Glaucous-winged Gull *(Larus glaucescens)*

Seen: All seasons but summer (abundant in winter)

What do you call a seagull that flies over a bay? A bagel, of course! That painful pun may help you remember that both "seagull" and "bagel" are bogus terms for birds. Many gulls live near the sea, but there are exceptions—which is why you'll see gulls (not "seagulls") cruising Portland neighborhoods and parking lots.

Their wingtips are the same color as their back.
Photo: Chuck Gates

The gulls of Portland—and there are many more than highlighted here—are tough to tell apart. Glaucous-winged gulls are so named because their wingtips are grayish, not black or white. From there the story gets much more complicated because gulls look different during their pre-adult years and often hybridize with other gull species.

ID tips: A large gull with grayish wingtips. Head and underparts are white during breeding with pale-gray upperparts. Heads are mottled in winter. Legs are pink; bill is thick and heavy. Plumage changes over first 4 years (see a field guide for details).

Locations: Look at Broughton Beach and in sports fields and other open areas.

> **"If you give [gulls] a little time and devote your attention to them you will see this great intelligence behind that eye and this caginess, and this generalist sensibility that I think is very relatable to a human. Because it's kind of the same way we go through the world."**
> — Dr. Sarah J. Courchesne in *The New York Times*

Note the dark wingtips. Photo: Nagi Aboulenein

They're the world's largest species of tern.
Photo: Dave Rein

Look for the orange patch on their bill.
Photo: Nagi Aboulenein

They typically eat small fish. Photo: Sue Anderson

Caspian Tern *(Hydroprogne caspia)*

Seen: Mostly in spring and fall

Terns are related to gulls, but they're smaller and "sharper" overall, with slighter bodies, narrower wings, and a sharply pointed bill.

The world's largest breeding population of Caspian terns lives on East Sand Island, at the mouth of the Columbia River. That's where things get political because Caspian terns have a fish-based diet that includes juvenile salmon. With salmon runs declining, it's tempting to point the finger at terns and fellow fish eaters like cormorants. After all, removing birds seems easier than addressing broader issues like dams and habitat loss. One promising compromise involves using decoys to draw terns away from the mouth of the Columbia to other nesting areas, but it's unclear if that will work.

ID tips: Large bird with a white body, black cap, and huge red bill (sometimes with black tip) that points downward when they're foraging over water. Wingtips are dark on the underside. Call *(kaarrr!)* is harsh and loud.

Locations: Not abundant but can be seen along the Columbia River waterfront.

Double-crested Cormorant
(Phalacrocorax auritus)

Seen: Mainly overwintering (Aug.–April)

Look at a pretty little hummingbird in your backyard and you might ask yourself: Are birds really dinosaurs? Then you see a double-crested cormorant standing on a dock with its bony black wings outstretched, and you question no more.

Oregon has three cormorants, but only the double-crested mixes with white pelicans and other species on inland waters—you can see them along Marine Drive near the airport. They really stand out when they stretch their wettable wings four feet wide to air-dry them before making their next dive.

ID tips: A big brown-black waterbird with a small head atop an S-curved neck. Look for the orange patch at the base of the bill, which is hooked at the tip.

Locations: On and near deep water. Watch for them along the Columbia River.

At nine feet, their wingspan is as wide as a California condor's. Photo: Dave Rein

American White Pelican (*Pelecanus erythrorhynchos*)

Seen: April–Oct.

The American white pelican has the longest wingspan and largest bill of any bird in Oregon. Seeing a flock of these huge white birds sailing in unison over the Willamette is a startling experience—so much so that they've been mistaken for UFOs.

Pelicans weigh up to nearly 20 pounds, and raising each chick requires a total of about 150 pounds of food. Early on, parents feed their chicks via regurgitation. When the chicks grow a little bigger, they clamber into the pouch of the parent to help themselves to the seafood buffet.

A knob, or keel, grows on the bill before breeding season. Photo: Dave Rein

ID tips: Huge, snowy-white waterbird with broad wings and a long neck, short tail, and massive bill that could carry a baby within. Look for black flight feathers when wings are spread. Bill and legs are yellow-orange.

Locations: September is peak season for flocks at Sauvie Island and Ridgefield National Wildlife Refuge. They're also found at Smith and Bybee Wetlands (a recent phenomenon) and at Fernhill Wetlands in Forest Grove.

AVIAN GIANTS

The largest birds that ever lived were the so-called "elephant birds" of Madagascar, *Vorombe titan*, which were 10 feet tall and a svelte 1,700 pounds. By comparison, the heaviest bird alive today is the ostrich, which weighs up to about 350 pounds. Elephant birds were nocturnal, couldn't fly, and went extinct in the 1600s, in part because people stole and ate their massive eggs.

HERONS

Look for their S-curved neck in flight. Photo: John Williams

They're up to four feet tall and weigh less than six pounds. Photo: Buddy Mays

Great Blue Heron (*Ardea herodias*)

Seen: Year-round

Great blue herons became the official bird of Portland in 1986, thanks in part to the enthusiasm of Mayor Bud Clark, who reportedly issued one of his famous "Whoop, whoop!" responses when local naturalist Mike Houck proposed the idea to him. But even without the proclamation—and the city's efforts to restore, manage, and protect heron habitat—the great blue heron would belong to Portland.

Portland-area streets, buildings, music festivals, and of course BridgePort's Blue Heron Ale are all named after these outrageously photogenic birds. You can also celebrate Great Blue Heron Week each spring and, best of all, you can easily view these birds in their natural habitat.

Hundreds of great blue herons nest in and near Portland, making them by far the most common of the five herons that spend at least part of the year here (the others are green herons, great egrets, and, rarely, black-crowned night-herons and American bitterns).

Great blues are long-legged beauties that perform a sort of walking meditation as they wade mindfully along water edges, carefully placing one foot forward, then pausing for half a lifetime before placing the next. It's a quiet joy to watch them hunt for fish and rodents in their ancient way.

Some of their meals are larger than others. Photo: Dave Rein

In late May and early June, look up high in the cottonwoods that line area waterways to spy great blue heron rookeries. You can watch as young herons flap their wings vigorously to build up the strength and courage to step off the edge and launch the first of a lifetime of flights.

ID tips: They're up to 4 ft. tall and mostly bluish-gray. Their crown is black (not red like on sandhill cranes). They fly with an S-curved neck.

Locations: All over Portland. Look for rookeries along the Columbia Slough and at Jackson Bottom Wetlands Preserve, Ross Island near Oaks Bottom Wildlife Refuge, Sauvie Island, and Smith and Bybee Wetlands.

They frequently prowl water edges.
Photo: John Williams

CHRISTMAS BIRD COUNT

One way Portlanders show their love for birds is through the National Audubon Society's Christmas Bird Count. Every winter, volunteers led by the local Audubon chapter record how many species they see in the field and at feeders on one day (not actually Christmas). The first Portland count was in 1926, and today more than 350 Portlanders routinely turn out to report on over 100 species, making it one of the two most popular counts in North America.

An egret with prey in hand ... er, bill.
Photo: Dave Rein

Their long black legs trail behind them in flight.
Photo: Tracy Aue

Great Egret *(Ardea alba)*

Seen: Year-round

The great egret is the symbol of the National Audubon Society, the best known and one of the oldest organizations devoted to protecting birds and their habitats. You couldn't hope for a more elegant emblem for bird conservation than this striking white bird that's nearly as big as a great blue heron ("egret" comes from the French *aigrette*, meaning "little heron").

Oregon is home to three egret species, of which the great egret is the largest. Second largest (half the size of the great egret) is the rarely seen snowy egret, which has a black instead of yellow bill. Smallest is the cattle egret, named for its association with livestock. The great egret is by far the most commonly seen egret in Portland, and the only one you can spot year-round.

ID tips: An all-white, long-legged wading bird, a little smaller than a great blue heron. Look for the big yellowish-orange bill and black legs.

Locations: The greatest numbers (and a nesting colony) are at Smith and Bybee Wetlands, where populations peak in late summer and fall. You can also see them at Fernhill Wetlands and on the agricultural fields on Sauvie Island where they hunt for rodents.

FASHION-FORWARD CONSERVATION

Fashionable women in the late 1800s wore hats with feathered plumes taken from snowy egrets, great blue herons, and other birds. About five million birds were killed each year to feed the avian fashion craze, driving some species to the brink of extinction.

Near the turn of the century, Harriet Hemenway and her cousin Minna Hall dared to ruffle the feathers of their fellow Boston socialites by convincing them to stop wearing feathered hats. They eventually rallied 900 women supporters, helped found the Massachusetts Audubon Society, and pushed their state to pass the first law banning the feather trade.

Green Heron (*Butorides virescens*)

Seen: April–Sept. (a few in winter)

Great blue herons are much more common and better known, but Portland is also home to shorter, stockier, and equally beautiful green herons. Despite their name, these herons aren't very green, and they're harder to spot than great blues because of their smaller size and more reclusive habits.

Keep an eye out for grumpy-looking green herons perching on low-hanging tree limbs that line area waterways. Like their taller brethren, they spend hours slowly prowling the water edge hunting for fish, reptiles, rodents, and other delicacies.

Green herons can also be seen doing something truly astounding and more often associated with notoriously intelligent crows and magpies: They use tools. If you're lucky, you might see one of these feathered anglers purposefully dragging an item they've collected (such as an insect, feather, flower, twig, or earthworm) along the surface of the water to entice fish.

ID tips: Much smaller than great blue herons, with a dark body, rounded wings, and yellow legs. In good light, you can see their velvet-green back and chestnut breast and neck. They sometimes raise their dark cap in a crest.

Locations: Look for them at Commonwealth Lake Park in Beaverton and Crystal Springs Rhododendron Garden near Reed College.

They often tuck their neck and hunch over.
Photo: Dave Rein

When alarmed, they twitch their tail and raise their crest. Photo: Phil Nosler

> "I am not just a stone skipping over the surface, clattering along, but actually feel connection to the plants and animals that I see. I notice small things: small smells, small sounds and it's a sense of awareness and mindfulness and presence. It's wonderful therapy for these discouraging times that we're in. It's like going into a library or listening to a concert—it's puzzles: a hundred daily miracles."
> — Prof. Nathaniel Wheelwright in *The Bowdoin Orient*

A mug only a mother could love. Photo: Buddy Mays

*They teeter in flight.
Photo: Dave Rein*

*Nature's cleanser, waiting to be
of service. Photo: Kim Elton*

Turkey Vulture (*Cathartes aura*)

Seen: Mid-March–mid-Oct.

At the Audubon Society of Portland's annual Wild Arts Festival one year, an admiring crowd formed around the great horned owl, while a few feet away the turkey vulture and its handler stood quietly, like wallflowers at the dance. Such is the plight of this redhead that even the great naturalist Charles Darwin called a "disgusting bird" with a head "formed to wallow in putridity."

It's true, turkey vultures eat cadavers. They also defecate on their feet to cool them off and kill bacteria. And when disturbed or harassed, they vomit, either as a generous food offering for their enemies or in an attempt to reduce their body weight so they can fly off faster. So, yes, disgusting. But aesthetics aside, turkey vultures fill a vital role as nature's cleanser. Who or what else is going to rid the world of all those rotting carcasses and the diseases they breed?

Vultures are remarkably efficient fliers (like "large dark lazy butterflies," wrote Mary Oliver) that ride warm air flows called thermals up to 10,000 feet or more, then spiral slowly down for hours until they catch the next ride up. Nearly all of their daylight hours are spent this way: not looking for carcasses but smelling for them, circling like bloodhounds to home in on their next dead meal.

ID tips: A large, dark bird with a featherless red head and wings ending in long "fingers." In flight, their wings form a "V" and the birds teeter from side to side.

Locations: Look up—way up. They're most commonly seen soaring over greenspaces, lost hikers, and the Willamette and Columbia rivers.

They're also called fish eagles or fish hawks. Photo: John Williams

Osprey *(Pandion haliaetus)*

Seen: Late March–mid-Oct.

Bald eagles are the best-known victims of DDT poisoning, but osprey and many other species suffered too. By 1976 only 13 pairs of ospreys nested between Portland and Eugene.

Thanks to the eventual banning of DDT, as well as years of restoration efforts,

They add to their nests each year. Photo: Kim Elton

these white-bellied raptors are again a common sight along Oregon waterways. Their ever-growing stick nests are common on channel markers, utility poles, standing dead trees, and other tall structures across Portland.

Ospreys, which were named Oregon's state raptor in 2017, are recognized as among the best anglers in the avian world. Pack a picnic and watch as they patrol back and forth above area waterways scanning for supper. When they spot a fish, they dive hard and fast, sometimes descending several feet underwater before fighting their way up with their catch. As they fly back to their nests, osprey carry fish headfirst to minimize wind drag, hanging onto their wet and squirmy prey with specialized barbules on their feet.

ID tips: A large bird with a dark strip along the eyes and down the side of the face. They have white underbellies and a unique crook in their wings when in flight.

Locations: Near rivers, lakes, and other waterways, including along the Columbia and Willamette rivers. Look for nests at Jackson Bottom Wetlands Preserve, Oxbow Regional Park, Smith and Bybee Wetlands, and Sauvie Island.

They listen for prey, then swoop in for the kill.
Photo: Tom Lawler

Long tail, long wings, gliding low.
Photo: Jim Anderson

Northern Harrier *(Circus cyaneus)*

Seen: Winter and in migration

If you see a slender, long-tailed brown hawk gliding low over a marsh, with a white spot on its rump and its wings forming a shallow "V," you're looking at a northern harrier. The sexes differ in looks (males are gray above; females are brown), but that white rump and low glide are true of both.

Northern harriers are unusual raptors with flat, owl-like faces and owl-like hearing to go with it. As they course along just above open fields, they're looking for prey—and listening for it. Stiff feathers on their face help direct even the slightest of sounds, like the rustle of a mouse, to their ears.

ID tips: Long-tailed, long-winged hawks. Males are "gray ghosts" with whitish undersides and black, finger-like wingtips. Females are mostly brown with streaked bellies; both sexes have a white rump patch.

Locations: Seen flying low over fields and marshes in places such as Sauvie Island and Smith and Bybee Wetlands. A pair has nested recently in Sandy River Delta Park.

Sharp-shinned Hawk *(Accipiter striatus)*

Seen: Winter and in migration

Sharp-shinned hawks are built for speed and agility. The smallest hawks in Canada and the U.S., they have short wings and long tails that help them pursue equally fleet-flying songbirds.

Even good birders bicker over whether a bird seen at a distance is a sharpie or a Cooper's hawk, both of which are in the *Accipiter* genus that also includes many other birds of prey. To avoid conflict, you might want to memorize the helpful phrase, "It's an *Accipiter* of some sort."

Note the small, rounded head.
Photo: Kris Kristovich

If you really want to figure out which species it is, note that robin-sized sharpies are up to six inches smaller than crow-sized Cooper's hawks. But females of both species are larger than males, so a big female sharpie can be almost as large as a small male Cooper's (see, it's not easy!). Sharpies have small, rounded heads that don't project far beyond their wings in flight, whereas Cooper's have bigger, blockier heads that stick out. Also, sharpies usually have a square-tipped tail, not rounded like a Cooper's tail.

ID tips: Nearly identical to a Cooper's hawk. Adults have a dark-gray back and wings, and reddish-orange barring on the breast. Kestrels are smaller, with more colorful faces.

Locations: All over Portland where there are small birds to eat, including at your backyard feeder.

Cooper's Hawk *(Accipiter cooperii)*

Seen: Year-round

There are a couple telltale signs that a Cooper's hawk is in the vicinity. One is a pile of pretty feathers littering the ground. Another is the sudden silence of still-living songbirds that are hoping to avoid the notice of this remarkably fast and agile hunter.

Cooper's hawks are crow-sized bird ambushers that are small enough to tear through obstacle-filled forests in pursuit of their prey, yet large enough to take down medium-sized birds like doves, jays, and robins. They kill their hapless prey by squeezing them to death with their talons, or sometimes by drowning them. So, no, there probably won't be any Disney movies made about Cooper's hawks, but they are phenomenal at what they do.

ID tips: A crow-sized bird with rounded wings, long and rounded tail, and long yellow legs. They flap their wings slowly a few times, then glide.

Locations: A pair has been nesting at Mt. Tabor in recent years. They're also relatively common in Forest Park and Tualatin Hills Nature Park, and in fall they can be seen above Chapman Elementary picking off Vaux's swifts as they try to enter the chimney. They might stake out your backyard feeder for similar reasons.

The flattened head is key to identifying Cooper's hawks. Photo: Chuck Gates

Juveniles have yellow eyes and brown streaking on the breast. Photo: Chuck Gates

BY THE NUMBERS	
400 BILLION	Approximate number of individual birds worldwide—about 50 per person
10,500	Approximate number of bird species worldwide
537	Number of species on the Oregon Bird Records Committee's state list as of 2018
356	Number of species on the all-time list for Multnomah County developed by East Cascades Audubon Society
200+	Number of bird species that spend at least part of the year in Portland

An eagle scooping up its next meal. Photo: Rick Derevan

The "bald" head indicates that this eagle is at least five years old. Photo: Kim Elton

Bald Eagle *(Haliaeetus leucocephalus)*

Seen: Year-round

It might be a fading memory for some (and news to younger people), but bald eagles nearly went extinct in the 1970s due to hunting and pesticide poisoning. Even as late as 1990, there were only a few nesting pairs in the Portland area. But eventually their Endangered Species listing (removed in 2007) and a massive recovery effort paid off, and bald eagles again became a common sight near many Portland-area wetlands.

As is often mentioned, the bird that symbolizes our great nation steals food from osprey and other birds and scavenges garbage and carcasses. (Baldies have been described as "vultures with good hair and press agents.") But, hey, bald eagles are big and heavy with wingspans of up to eight feet—if they had to expend energy catching all their prey, they might not survive.

ID tips: A very big bird with a big head. Adults have unmistakable white heads (feathered, not bald) and tails, and dark-brown bodies and wings. Their legs and bill are bright yellow.

Locations: Look for huge nests—with sticks added year after year—at large wetlands, including Tualatin River National Wildlife Refuge, Ross Island, Jackson Bottom Wetlands Preserve, and Smith and Bybee Wetlands. Sauvie Island is a particularly good place to see bald eagles and their nests.

DID BEN FRANKLIN REALLY PREFER THE TURKEY?

You've probably heard the story of Benjamin Franklin arguing that the turkey ("a bird of courage"), not the bald eagle, should be our national symbol. Franklin wrote to his daughter that the bald eagle "is a Bird of bad moral Character" that "does not get his Living honestly."

The truth of what Franklin was up to isn't so simple. In his letter to his daughter, he was criticizing the bald eagle image on a medal for war veterans, not on the Great Seal. Also, his letter was private—he never publicly expressed an anti-eagle agenda—and was probably tongue-in-cheek. The great statesman might get a good laugh at how seriously later readers have taken his letter.

Red-tailed Hawk (*Buteo jamaicensis*)

Blooms: Year-round

Red-tailed hawks are the most widespread raptors on the continent, as you might suspect when you drive to open areas outside the city and see them perched on every other utility pole. You'll also see them flying above Portland-area agricultural fields in pursuit of squirrels, rats, snakes, and other prey.

The red-tailed hawk's call—*kee-eeeee-arr*—is the classic cry that people associate with both hawks and eagles, but only the red-tailed hawk actually makes the sound. If you remember the opening to "The Colbert Report," the image was of a bald eagle, but the searing cry was the red-tailed's. Same goes for many a classic Western movie.

In spring, look up when you hear that famous call, and you might be fortunate enough to witness a "sky dance" in which the male performs a series of roller-coaster climbs and dives, then approaches the female from above and briefly touches or grasps her with his talons. Sometimes the female then flips over, and they clasp each other's beaks or talons and spiral toward the ground before letting go.

ID tips: If you see a raptor, it's probably a red-tailed hawk. When they're perched, look for a dark band of feathers across the belly and white shoulder streaks. When they're soaring, look for the dark leading edge of the wings (most adults also have reddish tails).

Locations: Anywhere around Portland. They've nested on Mt. Tabor and, famously, on the Mark O. Hatfield Federal Courthouse in downtown Portland. Powell Butte Nature Park, Sauvie Island, the Portland airport, and Marine Drive are other good places to look.

*Note the dark band across the belly.
Photo: Kim Elton*

Taking to flight. Photo: John Williams

> **"... when the little boy discovered, at four, the same thing Mr. Smith had learned earlier—that only birds and airplanes could fly—he lost all interest in himself. To have to live without that single gift saddened him and left his imagination so bereft that he appeared dull even to the women who did not hate his mother."**
>
> — Toni Morrison, *Song of Solomon*

A kestrel with snack in hand. Photo: Kim Elton

*One of the real beauties of the raptor world.
Photo: Kim Elton*

American Kestrel *(Falco sparverius)*

Blooms: Year-round

Peregrines get a lot more press, especially in Portland, but kestrels are another falcon worth celebrating. They're richly colored raptors with a beautiful mix of chestnut, blue-gray, black, and other colors, all stitched together with dots and a bold vertical streak down the face. Recent DNA tests have found that colorful kestrels and other falcons are more closely related to parrots (yes, parrots) than they are to hawks and eagles.

Kestrels are the smallest falcon on the continent, about the size of a mourning dove. As such, they're preyed upon by lots of bigger birds, including red-tailed hawks and barn owls. Look for this so-called "freeway falcon" perched on roadside power lines or hovering over open fields in the Portland area.

ID tips: Males have blue-gray on their head and wings, a whitish breast, and a reddish-orange back and tail. Females have tan to rufous backs and wings with black markings. On both, look for their erect posture and the vertical black stripe on their faces. In flight, look for pale undersides and pointed, swept-back wings.

Locations: They can be seen hovering over open areas at Powell Butte Nature Park and Sauvie Island. Their numbers are dropping fast in the eastern U.S., and they're declining here too, but they're still common just outside the urban growth boundary in Washington County. In winter, look for them perched on power lines along country roads.

DID YOU KNOW?

Like most non-human animals, kestrels can see ultraviolet light. That enables them to track rodents by following their fluorescent trails of urine. When kestrels catch a surplus of rodents or other prey, they think ahead—storing their kills in shrubs and other hiding spots so they'll have a food source during lean times.

Peregrine Falcon *(Falco peregrinus)*

Seen: Year-round (fewer in summer)

There's no denying that cities pave over habitat and displace many species, but the plight of Portland's peregrine falcons shows that sometimes a city and its devoted citizens can actually create habitat and restore populations.

Peregrines were one of the victims of DDT poisoning, and by 1970 there were no known nests in Oregon and only a handful across the West. In 1973, the species was listed under the Endangered Species Act, leading to new protections and programs to raise and release captive peregrines in the Columbia River Gorge and elsewhere.

Their long, pointy wings help them descend at over 200 mph.
Photo: John Williams

Fast-forward two decades, and a pair of falcons was found nesting on the Fremont Bridge, and the local Peregrine Watch was organized to monitor and protect them. Soon another pair was nesting on the St. John's Bridge, then more falcons were spotted on other bridges across the Willamette and Columbia rivers.

Today, peregrines have been removed from the Endangered Species List, and the world's fastest birds—like a "crossbow flinging through the air," wrote J.A. Baker—continue to thrive on their urban pseudo-cliffs. In fact, New York City now has the world's highest density of peregrines, followed by London.

ID tips: Their dark head and facial feathers resemble a helmet, with a contrasting light-colored neck and breast. Look for dark barring on the lower breast and a slate-gray back.

Their black head feathers resemble a helmet. Photo: Buddy Mays

Locations: Near shallow lakes and shorelines. They breed on bridges, and in migration are found wherever there are tasty shorebirds and pigeons around.

OWLS

Their asymmetrical ears give them extremely acute hearing. Photo: Kim Elton

They're nearly silent in flight. Photo: John Williams

Barn Owl (*Tyto alba*)

Seen: Year-round

If you've ever been startled on a cold, dark evening by the pale face or harsh scream of a barn owl, you understand why they have such an ethereal and even sinister reputation. Instead of hooting, they hiss like the angriest cat you've ever met, and the ghostly juveniles happen to start screaming like banshees right around Halloween.

Adding to their spookiness, barn owls—which I should add are splendid mouse eaters and not scary in any serious way—are nocturnal, can see in the dark, fly without making a noise, and have better hearing than perhaps any other bird. Not that they'd use those skills to sneak up behind you on some misty autumn night ...

ID tips: Slender, medium-sized owl with a whitish face, chest, and belly (at night they can look all white). Eyes are large and dark; head, back, and upper wings are gray or tawny brown. Heads are rounded with no ear tufts.

Locations: Uncommon, but found where there are abandoned buildings to nest in and open ground with rodents to hunt. They nest and roost in barns on Sauvie Island and can be seen in North Portland industrial areas.

Western Screech-Owl (*Megascops kennicottii*)

Seen: Year-round

The western screech-owl is woefully misnamed. To find one, don't listen for a fingernails-on-chalkboard screech but rather for a series of short whistles, or toots, followed by a long, descending trill.

Although these diminutive owls are fairly common in forested parks and neighborhoods, they're challenging to spot because they hunt at night and spend most of the day blending into the tree bark they've evolved to resemble. They also might be getting pushed out (i.e., eaten) by barred and great horned owls.

ID tips: A small owl with a stocky body. Listen for their toots and look for ear tufts, yellow eyes, and a pale breast and belly with black streaks.

Locations: They're in most parks with mixed woodlands, including Mt. Tabor, Reed College canyon, Hagg Lake, and Oaks Bottom Wildlife Refuge.

Great Horned Owl *(Bubo virginianus)*

Seen: Year-round

Barred owls and screech-owls are the most commonly seen owls in Portland. But in rural areas of the state, you're more likely to encounter the long ear tufts, yellow eyes, and deep-throated *who-hoo-hoo-oo* call of great horned owls.

Appropriately nicknamed the feathered or winged tiger, great horned owls are among the world's fiercest birds. Sure, they'll eat the usual mice and voles. But they also punch well above their weight, using specialized talons to take down skunks, rats, porcupines, and frankly anything else they set their minds to.

The ear tufts are feathers, not horns. Photo: Chuck Gates

On the softer side, they're tender caregivers and deeply protective of their families. Oregon naturalist Jim Anderson tells of a mother covering her owlets to shield them from two hungry ravens. When one raven hopped onto the female's back and pecked at her head, her mate swooped in "like an F-16" and slammed into the raven, eventually killing it to save his mate and their young.

ID tips: A large, thick-bodied owl with two big head tufts (they're feathers, not horns or ears).

Pity the mice in this neighborhood. Photo: Tom Lawler

They're a mottled gray-brown color overall with reddish-brown faces and yellow eyes.

Locations: Sites include Sauvie Island and Ridgefield National Wildlife Refuge. A pair regularly nests on Mt. Tabor.

Barred Owl *(Strix varia)*

Seen: Year-round

Barred owls were first spotted in Oregon in the early 1970s, in the Blue Mountains. From there, they kept moving west, eventually settling in as year-round residents of Portland, where their distinctive call *(Who cooks for you? Who cooks for you-allll?)* can be heard in forested areas.

The spread of barred owls is bad news for endangered northern spotted owls because barred owls—which eat a more-varied diet and nest in a wider range of habitats, including younger forests—dilute the gene pool by mating with spotted owls. They're also aggressive and will kill spotted owls.

Note the streaks, or bars, on the breast. Photo: Kim Elton

ID tips: A grayish-brown owl with no ear tufts, distinctive horizontal bars across the throat and upper breast, and vertical brown streaks on the lower breast and abdomen.

Locations: Mostly in forested areas. They're regularly seen at Marquam Nature Park, Forest Park, Portland Audubon's Wildlife Sanctuary, River View Natural Area, and Tryon Creek State Natural Area.

KINGFISHERS

A female smacking her prey against a branch. Photo: Rick Derevan

You can tell this squawker is a female by the reddish-brown band. Photo: John Williams

Belted Kingfisher *(Megaceryle alcyon)*

Seen: Year-round

Belted kingfishers are popular and colorful birds, always dressed for a night on the town with their flashy blue suits and spiky pompadours.

To see one of these big-headed birds, sit for a spell at a place like Smith and Bybee Wetlands. You might spy one perched on a bare branch above the water or hear their distinctive rattling call as they defend their territory and patrol for fish, insects, and other prey (when paired in spring, couples defend half-mile territories).

When kingfishers spot small fish in the water, they'll take your breath away with their sudden dives. If they snag a fish in their long bills, they fly back to their perches, and—there's no gentle way to say this—bash the fish to death against a branch, before swallowing it headfirst. For the fish, that's the best-case scenario because kingfishers with young in the nest will sometimes beat the fish only until it's almost dead, then throw it back into the water so the youngsters can learn to fish for themselves.

ID tips: A big-headed bird with a shaggy crest and long, thick bill. Back and wings are slate blue, and chest is white with a blue band. Females are more colorful than males, with an additional reddish-brown band across the lower chest.

Locations: Where the fish are, so near rivers and lakes at places like Fernhill Wetlands, Smith and Bybee Wetlands, Reed College canyon, and Oaks Bottom Wildlife Refuge.

> **"Look up. No, look down. Just—trust me—keep looking.**
> **This is the secret to happiness."** — Charlotte Mendelson

WOODPECKERS

Acorn Woodpecker *(Melanerpes formicivorus)*

Seen: Year-round

You might share the acorn woodpecker's wide-eyed look of surprise when you learn about their fascinating lives.

Their name comes from their autumn obsession with collecting acorns from oak trees and storing them in the sides of "granary trees." They bore holes into the trees and insert the nuts to eat through winter. Granary trees can be used for generations—one had 50,000 holes in it! If acorns were stored in piles, they'd rot and get moldy; only in trees, utility poles, and other woody sites do they dry out properly for later consumption.

Look for the red cap and white on the face.
Photo: Travis Chaney.

You can imagine how prized those granary trees are, and acorn woodpeckers have a unique system for defending them: Instead of pairing up, they're one of about three percent of bird species that engage in cooperative breeding, with a dozen or more "helper" birds working together to incubate eggs, feed the young, collect acorns and other nuts, and defend their treasured granary trees.

ID tips: A medium-sized woodpecker with a red crown. Males are dark overall, with a colorful face (white face, black patch around the bill, yellow eyes). Females have a smaller red crown. Note the small white patch on folded wings.

Locations: Not seen in Multnomah County, but look for them in native oak groves in Washington and Yamhill counties, including near the main Hillsboro Library and at Rogers Park in Forest Grove.

Red-breasted Sapsucker *(Sphyrapicus ruber)*

Seen: Year-round

Want a fun birding goal? See if you can spot all six of the Portland area's woodpecker species in one calendar year (the toughest one is the acorn woodpecker, above).

To find red-breasted sapsuckers, look for the cribbage boards they drill into the sides of tree trunks. Those orderly, pea-sized holes are ingenious "sap wells" that invite fungus into the tree but also allow sapsuckers to rid the tree of insect pests. The birds return again and again to the holes, both to drink the sap and to eat the beetles and other insects that are drawn to it.

Note the red breast. Photo: John Williams

ID tips: A medium-sized woodpecker with a red head and breast (no other woodpeckers have red on the breast). A vertical white patch is usually visible on each folded wing.

Locations: Most parks, including Cedar Mill Wetlands, Hagg Lake, Mt. Tabor, Washington Park, and Forest Park.

Both downy and hairy woodpeckers have a white stripe down their backs. Photo: John Williams

Males have a red head patch. Photo: Tracy Aue

Downy Woodpecker *(Picoides pubescens)*

Seen: Year-round

If you spot a black-and-white woodpecker in or near Portland, odds are it's a downy woodpecker. At under seven inches, they're the smallest woodpeckers on the continent, and one of the more fun to watch as they scurry up, down, and across tree trunks and thin branches in their quest for insects and other food.

Like their lookalike, the hairy woodpecker, downies prefer to nest in dead trees or dead parts of living trees. You can help out these and other headbangers by leaving snags (standing dead trees) in your yard that they can drill into. The holes they create are used as nests by many other birds and small animals.

ID tips: A small woodpecker with a short bill, black-and-white face, black wings spotted with white, and a white stripe down the back. Males have a red patch on the back of the head. Listen for a whinnying call that descends in pitch ("down" for downy).

Locations: All over, especially places with riparian (waterside) vegetation, including Mt. Tabor, Oaks Bottom Wildlife Refuge, and Smith and Bybee Wetlands.

WOODPECKER TONGUES

Apropos of nothing, Leonardo da Vinci wrote this reminder to himself in his notebook: "Describe the tongue of the woodpecker." Leo got distracted by a few other projects, so let's provide the description for him.

Woodpeckers have sticky, often barbed tongues that they can extend well beyond their bills to catch insects. When not in use, their tongues are coiled all the way around the back of their head to the front of their eyes. When thus stored, their long tongues help cushion woodpecker brains from the repeated shock of hammering at tree trunks.

Hairy Woodpecker *(Picoides villosus)*

Seen: Year-round

It's easy to confuse downy and hairy woodpeckers. If only they'd cooperate and perch next to one another, you'd see that hairy woodpeckers are about one-third larger, but usually you have to look at the bill of whichever woodpecker you see. It's evident even from a distance that the hairy has a much longer bill—as long as its head, compared to the downy's stubby bill.

To remember which of these woodpeckers is which, the common refrain is "downy is dinky and hairy is huge." Hairy woodpeckers also differ in that they generally eschew urban areas for forests, especially burned-over forests with lots of beetle larvae, ants, and other insects.

ID tips: A medium-sized woodpecker with a long, straight bill about the same length as the head. Both sexes have black-and-white heads and a white stripe down the back; males have a red patch on the back of the head.

They have longer bills than downies.
Photo: John Williams

Locations: In forests with lots of conifers, including Forest Park.

Northern Flicker *(Colaptes auratus)*

Seen: Year-round

Northern flickers are the most commonly seen and heard woodpeckers in Portland. I know, I know—we'll talk about how often they're heard—but first let's focus on a couple reasons to appreciate our urban neighbor.

Flickers eat more ants than any other North American bird species: One flicker belly had 5,000 ants in it! So if you don't like being overrun by our six-legged friends, you've got to love flickers. They're also prolific drillers that leave some tree holes to be used as nests by wood ducks and other native birds.

Listen for wick-a, wick-a, wick-a in spring. Photo: John Williams

Now, about that noise: Flickers have a loud springtime call that resembles maniacal laughter, and a piercing one-note call that sounds like they're about to shock someone's heart: *Clear!* In spring, males drum like mad on any metal surface they can find, including metal roofs, gutters, and chimney flashing. They're usually not trying to drill holes, so the main damage is to your eardrums, but consult the Audubon, Backyard Birds, or other pros to learn how to encourage flickers to practice their percussion elsewhere.

ID tips: A colorful, footlong bird that forages on the ground for ants and beetles. They have a black bib, a red mustache on males, and black spots and dashes everywhere. Watch for their roller-coaster flight pattern and white rump in flight.

Locations: Common all over, from urban neighborhoods to dense forests.

The red cheek stripe identifies this one as a male.
Photo: Mark Lundgren

Pileated Woodpecker (*Dryocopus pileatus*)

Seen: Year-round

Portland has lots of attractive birds but only a few that will take your breath away—this is one. The pileated woodpecker is the sixth largest woodpecker on the planet, the so-called "King o' the Woods" that brightens old-growth forests with its shock of flame-red feathers.

Like northern flickers, pileateds are ant lovers that forage on the ground and, most famously, excavate footlong rectangular holes in trees to uncover tunnels made by carpenter ants and other insects. Because they help control beetle populations and create tree cavities used by other birds and mammals, these woodpeckers are considered a keystone species, meaning they play an especially important role in forest ecosystems.

Pileateds prefer to nest in dead trees and fallen logs in forests, but they occasionally nest in cities. Look for them and their telltale excavations wherever there are enough large old trees around to support them.

ID tips: Nearly as large as a crow, with a dark body, triangular red crest, and bill almost as long as the head. They have a white stripe on their face and neck; males also have a red cheek stripe.

Locations: Uncommon but seen in a few places like Forest Park, Smith and Bybee Wetlands, Tryon Creek State Natural Area, and Sandy River Delta Park.

SCHOOL OF HARD KNOCKS

Let's not dance around the fact that woodpeckers spend a fair chunk of their lives bashing their faces into trees. Their head strikes occur:

- At about 15 miles per hour
- Up to 20 times per second
- At 1,200 G's, meaning 1,200 times the acceleration of gravity (fighter pilots pass out at about 7 G's)

Olive-sided Flycatcher *(Contopus cooperi)*

Seen: May–Sept.

Some people quickly catch on to bird sounds, recognizing first a handful, then a dozen or two, on up into the hundreds. Alas, I am not one of those people. I have to hear the same call about 427 times before it begins to sink in—more if the bird dares to vary the notes. All of which is why I look forward to the spring arrival of olive-sided flycatchers and their clear, loud, and easily translated call: *Quick, three beers!*

Looking dapper in an unbuttoned vest.
Photo: Kim Elton

Olive-sided flycatchers are world travelers that winter in Panama and South America, then migrate up to the Pacific Northwest by May. Once here, they belly up to the forest bar all day long, issuing their distinctive call again and again. Their populations are declining, but you can still hear them every spring. You can also see them near treetops where they perch on exposed branches, dart out to catch insects, then quickly return to the branch to order up another few beers.

ID tips: Flycatchers are difficult to tell apart. These are heftier and more bull-headed than western wood-pewees. They're olive-gray overall, with a whitish stripe down the middle of their breast and belly. Also look for white patches between their wings and lower back.

Locations: They breed in Forest Park, can be seen in migration at Mt. Tabor, and are found along Germantown Road.

They perch on branches near treetops.
Photo: Mark Lundgren

LIGHTS OUT PORTLAND

Lights Out Portland is part of a nationwide effort to convince people to turn off their lights at night, especially during spring and fall migrations (March 15 to June 7 and Aug. 25 to Nov. 15). Most songbirds migrate at night, using the moon and stars to navigate, so urban lights can confuse them and lead to window collisions.

They have good posture and a peaked crown. Photo: Mark Lundgren

Western Wood-Pewee *(Contopus sordidulus)*

Seen: May–mid-Sept.

One sign that spring has sprung is the sound of a western wood-pewee—one of our more common flycatchers—singing at least the first part of its name (*peeee* or *peeee-er*) from the tip of an exposed branch.

Flycatchers are tough to tell apart, and this one makes it harder by not only resembling the olive-sided flycatcher but also performing a similar yo-yo flight, darting out from a branch to catch insects, then hustling right back. Listen for the western wood-pewee's call on warm afternoons, when other flycatchers are quiet.

ID tips: A medium-sized flycatcher with a peaked crown and upright posture. They're grayish-brown overall with two pale wingbars. Underparts are whitish with gray smudges on breast and sides. They don't have an eyering.

Locations: Look for them perched on bare branches, particularly of deciduous trees, at Sauvie Island, Sandy River Delta Park, Mt. Tabor, and Smith and Bybee Wetlands.

Note the absence of an eyering. Photo: Kris Kristovich

Willow Flycatcher *(Empidonax traillii)*

Seen: Late May–mid-Sept.

If you hear a cute sneeze (*FITZ-bew!*) issuing from willows and shrubs at an area wetland, it's likely this bird, which arrives in Portland later in spring than most other migrants.

Willow flycatchers don't learn their distinctive songs from their parents. Even when raised with no exposure to adults of their own species—and repeated exposure to the song of another species—they grow up to sing *FITZ-bew* over and over, suggesting they're born knowing their sneezy song.

ID tips: A small, slender flycatcher, brownish-olive overall with a yellowish belly. Their throat is white and there are two whitish wingbars. They have shorter wings and tails than wood-pewees, and their head isn't peaked. They stand out in the *Empidonax* genus for what they don't have: an eyering.

Locations: Willow flycatchers flit around large, less disturbed wetland areas that have patches of willows or other shrubs. Sandy River Delta Park is the best place to look, or try Smith and Bybee Wetlands.

BIRDSONG WALKS

Mt. Tabor is one of the best places to see and hear migrating songbirds, which is great—if you know what you're looking and listening for. To help you out, the Audubon Society of Portland offers fun, low-key birdsong walks at Mt. Tabor and other hotspots. Look them up online for details.

Hammond's Flycatcher
(*Empidonax hammondii*)

Seen: April through Sept.

Don't underestimate Hammond's flycatchers, diminutive dynamos known to tangle so intensely over their territories that they'll lock bills in midair and fall to the ground in a tangled mess. That behavior is unique to males, but both sexes are ruthless hunters. Granted, their insect prey is small, but the fact that they pull the wings off moths before gobbling up their bodies is rather spine-chilling.

Look for the tiny bill and white eyering and wingbars. Photo: Chuck Gates

Small flycatchers in the *Empidonax* genus (from the Greek for "gnat master") are easily confused, and that's especially true of Hammond's and dusky flycatchers, although the latter is much less common in Portland. Even experienced birders record many sightings as "*Empidonax* sp.*" Don't feel bad if you do the same—for most of us, it's enough to know we've spotted a flycatcher in action.

ID tips: Small, grayish flycatcher with a prominent white eyering, white wingbars, and a tiny bill. Head is slightly peaked and their lower belly sometimes has a pale-yellow wash.

A very similar dusky flycatcher. Photo: Mark Lundgren

Locations: Hammond's are more likely than other "Empids" to be found near conifers. They're common during spring migration (mid-April through May) at eastside buttes like Mt. Tabor and Powell Butte Nature Park.

Pacific-slope Flycatcher (*Empidonax difficilis*)

Seen: Mid-April–mid-Sept.

It's appropriate that this flycatcher has the species name *difficilis*. During migration, Pacific-slopes are the most commonly seen bird in the *Empidonax* genus, and the only one that nests in the city's forested areas. Yet it's still challenging to spot them, in part because they're greenish birds that live in mature, shady—and green—forests.

They have teardrop-shaped eyerings and yellowish undersides. Photo: Chuck Gates

Your best bet is to listen for their *pseeeet* call or their squeaky, three-part song (*ps-SEET, ptsick, seet!*). But even that can be *difficilis*, as their vocalizations sound a lot like those of Hammond's and dusky flycatchers.

ID tips: A small flycatcher with an olive-colored back and yellowish underparts. Look for the pale eyering shaped like a teardrop.

Locations: They're common at Mt. Tabor in spring and fall; Forest Park is the best place to look overall.

Their bill's thicker than a kinglet's.
Photo: Chuck Gates

Hutton's Vireo *(Vireo huttoni)*

Seen: Year-round

What the heck is a vireo? The word is Latin for "to be green" and was first used to describe a green migratory bird. Now the term is applied to a family of vaguely greenish passerines found in what's commonly called the New World. (A passerine is a perching bird, more casually referred to as a songbird, and the New World is the traditional, Euro-centric term for the Americas, from Canada to Argentina, as opposed to the Old World of Europe, Asia, and Africa.)

Now that we're oriented, the Hutton's vireo is Oregon's only year-round vireo, a quiet songbird found in mixed forests and particularly near our remaining populations of oak trees. It's easily confused with the more common ruby-crowned kinglet, but go on a birding trip to Cooper Mountain Nature Park, and you'll start to appreciate the differences.

ID tips: Small songbird that's greenish-gray above and below, with a whitish eyering that's broken above the eye. Look for two whitish wingbars. Similar to ruby-crowned kinglets, but with a thicker and slightly hooked bill, less prominent eyering, and wings that aren't as dark.

Locations: They can be found in Forest Park but prefer dense vegetation with a variety of deciduous trees. Cooper Mountain Nature Park is the best place to look.

They have a small bill and dark line through the eye.
Photo: Tom Lawler

Warbling Vireo *(Vireo gilvus)*

Seen: Mid-April–mid-Sept.

Warbling vireos won't overwhelm you with their flashy good looks (the word "drab" comes up a lot in descriptions), but they make up for it with the bird equivalent of a great personality—a pretty, memorable, and persistently repeated song.

Males warble rapidly for a few seconds, usually ending on a high-pitched note that makes it sound like they're asking a question. Writer Pete Dunne says they sound "like a happy drunk making a conversational point at a party." Listen for their cheerful warble coming from high above in deciduous trees like alders and aspens.

ID tips: Small, chunky songbird with gray-olive upperparts, whitish underparts, and a little bill. Look for a dark line through the eye and a pale eyebrow.

Locations: Most often found among deciduous trees. Look for them at Mt. Tabor and Sandy River Delta Park in spring and fall.

JAYS & CROWS

Steller's Jay *(Cyanocitta stelleri)*

Seen: Year-round

If you've spent much time in local natural areas, you might be inured to the beauty of Steller's jays. But the initial response of East Coast visitors—"What's that gorgeous bird with a mohawk?"—is a reminder of how stunning these azure-bodied birds really are.

Steller's jays are the only crested jay in the West and one of the more skilled mimics in the bird world. They can imitate the scream of red-tailed hawks and, less often, they've been known to reproduce the sounds of cats, dogs, chickens, and squirrels. They also sing sweet "whisper songs" to one another for up to several minutes at a time.

They were voted British Columbia's official bird (beating out peregrines). Photo: Kim Elton

The sound you're most likely to hear from Steller's jays is their loud, raspy call, which is a common background noise in campgrounds, picnic areas, and tree-filled backyards, where these attractive jays are also known for bullying and killing smaller birds.

ID tips: A large songbird with a black head and shoulders, transitioning to deep-blue wings, tail, and belly. Their big head is topped by a spiky black crest.

Locations: They prefer coniferous forests. Forest Park is the best spot, along with Mt. Tabor. They're also common in residential areas of Northwest and Southwest Portland where there are lots of conifers.

They're big, handsome, raucous birds.
Photo: Sue Dougherty

JAY VS. CROW SWORD FIGHT

As described in Jennifer Ackerman's book *The Genius of Birds*, ornithologist Russell Balda once saw a Steller's jay dive-bomb a crow at a feeding platform.

The crow held its ground, so the jay flew into a nearby tree, broke off a twig, sharpened one end with its beak, and flew back to spear the crow. When the jay dropped the twig, the crow picked it up and tried to stab the jay (fair is fair). That's the first documented instance of a bird using an object as a weapon against another bird. It's also a terrific reminder of the ingenuity of jays, crows, and other corvids.

They work hard at keeping other birds away from backyard feeders. Photo: Kim Elton

A scrub-jay in Central Oregon perched atop a juniper. Photo: Kris Kristovich

California Scrub-Jay
(Aphelocoma californica)

Seen: Year-round

There is an actual blue jay that lives in the eastern and central U.S. But when people on the West Coast say they've seen a "blue jay," they're usually referring to a Steller's jay or to this jay that frequents urban areas and forest edges.

Like Steller's jays, scrub-jays are sometimes maligned for their loud, raspy calls and their penchant for stalking and killing the nestlings of chickadees and other songbirds. Also like Steller's jays, there's a lot more to appreciate about the cleverness of these birds.

Scrub-jays cache hundreds of nuts, insects, worms, and other foods—and they remember where and when they stored each type of food so they can retrieve the more perishable items first (nobody wants to eat a moldy worm). It was once thought only humans had this ability to mentally travel back in time to recall what, where, and when we did something. Turns out we're not so unique after all.

ID tips: A jay with deep-blue coloring on the head, neck, wings, and tail, and a blue band across the breast. Their backs are brownish-gray and their underparts are pale gray. Their stout bill is hooked for hammering open acorns.

Locations: Common along forest edges and all over urban parks and neighborhoods.

MOST COMMON RESIDENT BIRDS

It depends on where you live, time of year, and other factors, but these are 10 of the most commonly seen native birds that live year-round in Portland. Can you identify them all by sight and sound?

- American crow
- American robin
- Anna's hummingbird
- Black-capped chickadee
- California scrub-jay
- House finch
- Northern flicker
- Song sparrow
- Spotted towhee
- Steller's jay

American Crow *(Corvus brachyrhynchos)*

Seen: Year-round

My non-bird-loving friend swears there are only two bird species in Portland: crows and chickens. That is not technically true, although in close-in neighborhoods and under their downtown roost in winter, you might be excused for thinking she's at least half right—there are an awful lot of crows.

They're smaller than ravens, with a tail that opens like a fan. Photo: Chuck Gates

Crows are famously intelligent animals that can count, solve puzzles, make and use tools, and recognize human faces (even holding grudges against the mean ones). Mostly we notice their simple *caw-caw* sounds, but crows can mimic human speech as effectively as parrots, along with the sounds of ducks, dogs, cats, and even machinery. Each crow has a call all its own; if a mate disappears, researchers have documented the remaining crow copying the other's call in an apparent attempt to summon it home.

Crows are also playful: One woman shared with me the story of a crow that, entirely of its own accord, pulled a baby's favorite blanket just out of reach; every time the baby reached for the blanket, the crow tugged again. It's difficult not to share such stories of individual crows—because they are individuals. Portland's most famous crow, Havoc, was found in downtown Portland, where he drank from the Benson Bubblers and barked at blonde women. Havoc was apparently raised as a pet, but he loathed captivity and eventually had the good fortune of being released into the wild.

Crows are among the most common and least shy birds in the city. Photo: Tracy Aue

ID tips: A large bird (15–20 in.), coal-black in color. In flight, they don't soar or glide; they flap their wings slowly.

Locations: Look outside.

THE CROW YEAR

To bolster your crow love, especially on particularly noisy mornings (*caw, caw!*), watch how crow behavior changes by season:

- **Spring:** In late April and May, crows build large stick nests in the crotches of tall trees. They incubate 3–6 eggs for 18 days, then feed their young in the nest for about a month. Parents and last year's offspring care for the youngsters.

- **Summer:** May through July, keep an eye out for fledglings with light-blue or gray eyes walking around. They're learning to fly, so give them space.

- **Fall and winter:** Crows spend the night at communal roosts downtown and elsewhere, where up to thousands gather for protection. As the light comes up, they disperse in a morning commute to their favored neighborhoods.

Note the thick, extremely strong beak. Photo: Tom Lawler

Raven, crow, or hawk? That diamond-shaped tail is a giveaway. Photo: John Williams

Common Raven *(Corvus corax)*

Seen: Year-round

If you're not sure whether the black birds you're seeing in Portland are crows or ravens, suffice to say they're probably crows. Think of ravens as crows' less urban and much larger (hawk-sized) cousins. They have a deeper, croak-like voice (*cr-r-ruck*); a distinctly wedge-shaped tail; and a much heftier, built-for-eating-pigeons bill.

Ravens, or "apes in feathers," may be one of the few species even smarter than crows. They can solve intricate problems on the first try and will work together to overcome new challenges. They also display what's tough not to call a sense of humor—teasing each other, humans, and other animals.

On land, raven-owning Charles Dickens wrote of a raven moving "not in a hop, or walk, or run, but in a pace like that of a very particular gentleman with exceedingly tight boots on, trying to walk fast over loose pebbles." In flight, ravens are vastly different from city-slicker crows, soaring with ease and even performing aerial somersaults and wing-tucked dives. Seeing a raven fly upside down, seemingly for the pure joy of it, was one of the thrills of my nascent birdwatching life.

ID tips: A much bigger version of a crow (up to 26 in. tall). They weigh about 2.5 pounds, similar to a red-tailed hawk, and have much thicker bills than crows. Of their color, Oregon poet Elizabeth Woody writes, "They are not true black / but all blacks / fired into one another."

Locations: In Portland, they're far less common than crows, but you might see them in Forest Park and along the ridge south of Sandy River Delta Park.

> "Ravens are the birds I'll miss most when I die. If only the darkness into which we must look were composed of the black light of their limber intelligence. If only we did not have to die at all. Instead, become ravens."
>
> — Louise Erdrich, *The Painted Drum*

Note the yellowish throat, black bib, and "horns." Photo: Randall Moore

Streaked Horned Lark *(Eremophila alpestris strigata)*

Seen: Year-round

We don't usually think of cities as hotspots for wild animals in general or at-risk species in particular. But that's exactly what Portland is for the streaked horned lark, a brightly plumed subspecies of the horned lark that's listed as threatened under the Endangered Species Act.

Horned larks are ground-dwelling birds found across the Northern Hemisphere, where they're known for their distinctive black "horns" (feather tufts). Like other species that depend on grasslands, horned lark populations are in steep decline overall, and the entire population of the streaked horned lark subspecies is estimated to be under 2,000.

Multiple local groups are working to restore grasslands on Sauvie Island and elsewhere that will support and sustain streaked horned lark populations, as well as populations of many other grassland-dependent species.

ID tips: A small songbird, brownish above and pale below. They're the warblers of the horned lark world, saturated in yellow. Males have a yellowish throat, a curving black facial mask, and black feather tufts on either side of the head. Females are paler but with similar head and breast patterns.

Locations: In place of disappearing grasslands, they nest on grass seed farms and undeveloped industrial sites. You can spot them at Broughton Beach, Portland International Airport, and the few remaining undeveloped plots within the Rivergate Industrial Area.

SWALLOWS

The world's largest swallow.
Photo: Chuck Gates

Purple Martin *(Progne subis)*

Seen: April–Sept.

Lots of birds are said to herald spring, from robins to bluebirds, but the unique color of the purple martin and its boisterous singing at dawn make it a particularly apt symbol of spring renewal.

Purple martins need open country with lots of flying insects, and they don't compete well for nesting sites against non-native European starlings and house sparrows. You see where this is leading: Their populations have been declining across North America for half a century. That's why you'll see gourds hanging in backyards and from trees on Sauvie Island and elsewhere, a practice that appears to be helping their populations recover in the Portland area.

ID tips: A large swallow with tapered wings, a forked tail, and a smoother flight pattern than European starlings. Males are iridescent blue-purple overall with duller wings and tails. Females and immature birds are dusky-gray overall with some glossy purple on their crown and back.

Locations: They nest along rivers and where people have put up nesting boxes and gourds, including at Sauvie Island, Fernhill Wetlands, and Sandy River Delta Park.

In flight, look for white underparts and short tails.
Photo: Alice Doggett

Tree Swallow *(Tachycineta bicolor)*

Seen: Feb.–Sept.

Tree swallows require just a few things: water, food, and a place to nest. Water is notably easy to find in and around Portland. In spring and summer, the city also provides plenty of food in the form of flying insects, which tree swallows gobble up at the rate of 2,000 per day during the summer breeding season.

The third and most challenging piece of the puzzle is a nesting site. Snags (standing dead trees) with woodpecker-excavated holes are a hot commodity, especially with non-native starlings and house sparrows occupying many. That makes survival challenging for tree swallows and other species known as obligate secondary cavity nesters. They need to nest in holes (the obligate part), yet they can't make the holes themselves (the secondary part). As with purple martins, people are helping tree swallows by constructing nest boxes.

ID tips: Small, stocky, tuxedo-wearing birds that are blue-green above with snowy white underparts. Their short tails are squared off or slightly notched. They're often in large flocks, and they glide more than other swallows, in a flap-flap-glide flight pattern.

Locations: Most area wetlands have nest boxes to help populations. Look for them in rural, open areas like those at Fernhill Wetlands, Sauvie Island, and Smith and Bybee Wetlands.

Violet-green Swallow
(*Tachycineta thalassina*)

Seen: Mid-March–Oct.

Violet-green swallows are absolutely gorgeous birds, if only they'd hold still long enough for us to appreciate their iridescent colors. Watch their acrobatics above area waterways and you'll understand what poet Cornelius Eady meant when he wrote, "If an arrow could think / These are the handsome moves / it would choose for itself."

One of Oregon's most colorful birds.
Photo: Jim Anderson

Like our other swallows, violet-greens are social birds that winter in Mexico and Central America, then migrate up to Portland each spring. In the 18th century, famed scientist Carl Linnaeus was among many who doubted that tiny swallows could fly thousands of miles, back and forth, twice a year. Instead, they assumed the birds spent winter hibernating at the bottom of lakes. That seems silly now (the lack of gills would be a problem), but it's only in these modern times that we take birds' extravagant feats of trans-hemispheric travel for granted.

ID tips: Small, sleek swallows with pointed tails, greenish-bronze backs, and a violet rump. Their underparts are white, and white patches extend up the sides of their rump. Males have white cheek patches extending past the eye.

Locations: Anywhere near woods, including Forest Park, Smith and Bybee Wetlands (in summer), and Mt. Tabor. Also in urban and residential areas with nesting sites and sufficient insects.

Cliff Swallow (*Petrochelidon pyrrhonota*)

Seen: April–Sept.

In some other parts of Oregon, you can watch cliff swallows zip and zoom around the cliffs after which they're named—Smith Rock State Park is one famous site. In Portland, the "cliffs" where these swallows build their nests are often the undersides of bridges, but the viewing experience is still impressive.

Look for the headlamp. Photo: John Williams

Grab some binoculars to watch cliff swallows fly through the air—you might see them open their jaws nearly 180 degrees to scoop in insects. You can also watch as they swoop repeatedly into and out of their nesting sites, where they construct distinctive, jug-shaped nests. It's estimated that they carry a thousand or more mud pellets, one beakful at a time, to build each nest.

ID tips: Look for a cleanly bordered dark throat, white underparts, a cream forehead (headlamp), and a square tail. They have a pumpkin-colored rump.

Locations: In open country where they can find water for drinking and cliffs for nesting, including Tualatin River National Wildlife Refuge, Sauvie Island, Smith and Bybee Wetlands, Koll Center Wetlands, and Oaks Bottom Wildlife Refuge.

Presumably the parent's head was not swallowed whole. Photo: John Williams

*They have cinnamon underparts.
Photo: Tom Lawler*

*They sometimes fan out their forked tail
when in flight. Photo: John Williams*

Barn Swallow *(Hirundo rustica)*

Seen: April–Oct.

Some birds nest in forests, but barn swallows have adapted to human-made structures, taking advantage of the eaves under your house and other spots along the perimeter of natural habitats. Its adaptability may help explain why this fork-tailed swallow is the most abundant and widely distributed swallow species in the world, with populations spread across five continents.

It was the humble barn swallow—not the more famous great egret—that indirectly led to the founding of the bird conservation movement in the United States. George Bird Grinnell, prompted by the killing of barn swallows to decorate women's hats, wrote an editorial in *Forest and Stream* in 1886 that eventually led to establishment of the first Audubon Society.

ID tips: Slender, with a glossy blue-black head, back, wings, and tail, and rufous to tawny underparts. Forehead and chin are cinnamon-orange. Look for their deeply forked tail.

Locations: All over urban and suburban open areas (parks and agricultural fields), usually where there's water nearby and structures like barns, sheds, or bridges available for nesting.

DID YOU KNOW?

Legend has it that the barn swallow—a bird long known for living near humans—got its forked tail when it stole fire from the gods to bring to people. A wrathful deity hurled a fireball at the traitor, but the fleet-flying barn swallow avoided a direct hit, losing only its middle tail feathers.

CHICKADEES & BUSHTITS

Black-capped Chickadee *(Poecile atricapillus)*

Seen: Year-round

What's the one word you'd use to describe chickadees? My money is on "cute"—which is certainly true. But don't underestimate these ever-present little birds. After years of research on bird intelligence, writer Jennifer Ackerman concluded that the two most impressive species were New Caledonian crows and ... chickadees.

Ornithologist Edward H. Forbush calls them "a bird masterpiece beyond all praise." Photo: Chuck Gates

Their various songs and calls add up to what Ackerman describes as "one of the most sophisticated and exacting systems of communication of any land animal." One study found that they tack on a different number of *dee*'s to their *chick-a-dee* call depending on the size and type of danger perching nearby. A big but slow hawk warrants only a couple *dee*'s, while a nimble, dangerous pygmy-owl can earn a dozen *dee*'s.

Another sound associated with chickadees is their two-toned *fee-bee,* but they almost never sing that song in the Willamette Valley. Their regional variation involves a series of up to about five monotone whistles of roughly the same pitch.

ID tips: A small bird with a gray back and wings, buff-white underparts, and a black cap with white cheeks.

Locations: All over the place, probably including your neighborhood. Forest Park, Mt. Tabor, and other city parks are good places to look.

Chestnut-backed Chickadee *(Poecile rufescens)*

Seen: Year-round

If the chickadee you're looking at has a chestnut back, guess what? You're looking at a chestnut-backed chickadee. Black-capped chickadees are found across much of the U.S. and Canada, whereas chestnut-backed chickadees live only in a thin strip running up the West Coast.

Chickadees are noted for their curiosity. Photo: Mark Lundgren

Finding enough food is serious business for all chickadees, especially in spring, when parents need to feed their young every few minutes. It's said they need up to 9,000 caterpillars to raise a single clutch of young. You can help them out by putting up nest boxes and feeders, and by growing native plants. One study on Carolina chickadees found that they nest and forage more often in yards with native trees, which host far more insect larvae.

ID tips: A tiny bird with a big head, small bill, and long tail. Their head resembles that of other chickadees, but their chestnut back and flanks are unique.

Locations: Anyplace with conifers will do, including Forest Park and Mt. Tabor. They tend to stay higher in trees than black-capped chickadees.

This bundle of fluff has a pale eye, so we know she's female. Photo: John Williams

Bushtit (*Psaltriparus minimus*)

Seen: Year-round

Even professionals who study bushtits use terms like "cute" and "adorable" to describe them. That's not anthropomorphizing; it's stating facts. Bushtits are an inch shy of a Twinkie in length, and in every season but spring you can see and hear dozens of them flitting about shrubs, twittering to one another like tiny gossips.

In spring, bushtits pair off and start stitching together their distinctive nests, which look like dangling tube socks. It takes a month for couples to construct the footlong marvels out of spider webs, mosses, lichens, and prayers. Some pairs have "helpers" (siblings and other nonbreeding bushtits) that help incubate and feed the young. At night, all the wee family members—parents, helpers, young—pile into their tube sock to sleep together.

ID tips: Take a ping-pong ball, attach feathers, add a head (don't bother with a neck), and append a long tail. Voilá! They're gray birds, smaller than a chickadee. Males have dark eyes; females have pale eyes.

Locations: All over the place, in a variety of habitats. Look for them near any area stream.

NUTHATCHES & CREEPERS

Look for white eyebrows and reddish underparts. Photo: Mark Lundgren

Red-breasted Nuthatch (*Sitta canadensis*)

Seen: Year-round

The red-breasted nuthatch's distinctive *yank, yank* is one of the easier bird calls to learn, a loud, nasally sound you'll hear often in forested areas and backyards. You can also watch these gravity-defying birds as they wind around and around tree trunks to hunt for insects and seeds.

It's a common misconception that humans and primates are the only species that use tools. Many birds do too, including not only famously intelligent crows and ravens but also red-breasted nuthatches that use pieces of bark as spatulas to apply sap around the entrances to their tree cavities. The sap is believed to prevent insects and other unwanteds from entering.

ID tips: A barrel-chested bird with a long bill, short tail, and almost no neck. Their white eyebrows, black cap, and reddish breast differentiate them from other nuthatches.

Locations: In a variety of forest types, including at Forest Park and Mt. Tabor.

White-breasted Nuthatch *(Sitta carolinensis)*

Seen: Year-round

At an elephantine five inches long, white-breasted nuthatches are North America's largest nuthatch. They share the usual nuthatch traits of flitting around trees, walking placidly down trunks, and calling loudly (their call is similar to the red-breasted nuthatch's, but less nasally). But they're unusual in that pairs typically stay together all year, despite the male's annoying habit of pushing his mate away from feeders.

A typical gravity-defying nuthatch.
Photo: Mark Lundgren

One of many reasons our remaining oak trees are so important is that they provide food and habitat for birds like this one. It's insects, not acorns, that serve as the primary food for white-breasted nuthatches, and old oaks and other native trees support gobs of them.

ID tips: A small bird with a large head, no neck, a short tail, and a long bill. They're gray-blue on the back, with a dark cap, white face, and white underparts.

Locations: They prefer areas with oaks and other deciduous trees, including Sauvie Island and Cooper Mountain Nature Park. They also frequent stands of mature cottonwoods, such as at Sandy River Delta Park, Kelley Point Park, and Oaks Bottom Wildlife Refuge.

Brown Creeper *(Certhia americana)*

Seen: Year-round

No other bird appreciates trees quite like the diminutive brown creeper, which forages on trees, is camouflaged like a tree trunk, flutters to the ground like a leaf, and sings a soft song that sounds like *trees, trees, beau-ti-ful trees.* They also build their unique nests between a loose piece of bark and the trunk, using insect cocoons and spider egg cases to plaster it together.

They use their long, downturned bill to probe for insects in tree bark. Photo: Mark Lundgren

Their bark-like camo makes brown creepers tough to spot, but listen for that song and their high-pitched calls. Then watch as they scamper up and around the trunks of large conifers, maples, cottonwoods, and other trees with craggy bark, searching for insects to snatch up with their downwardly curved bills. Once brown creepers get near the top of a tree, they'll flit down to the base of the next, or same, tree and do it all over again.

ID tips: A tiny songbird with a downturned bill. Their bodies are white below and brown above (not gray like on white-breasted nuthatches). They use their long tails to prop themselves along tree trunks.

A creeper on the way up. Photo: Mark Lundgren

Locations: Common in coniferous forests like Forest Park but also in deciduous stands at Sandy River Delta Park, Mt. Tabor, and Smith and Bybee Wetlands.

WRENS

Listen for them where oaks grow.
Photo: Mark Lundgren

House Wren *(Troglodytes aedon)*

Seen: April through Sept.

Wrens are small, easily overlooked birds that produce some wonderfully high-spirited songs. It's not easy to put the house wren's melody into words, but in spring go to Oak Island on Sauvie Island and listen for a loud, long, bubbling cascade of birdsong—that's the one.

You can spot house wrens flitting through shrubs and low in trees. They're aggressive nesters known to fight for their right to reside in just about any cavity, from old woodpecker holes to the pocket of a coat.

ID tips: Plain brown bird with a flat head, curved bill (yellow at base), and dark bars on wings. Longish tail is often noticeably cocked or drooping. Underparts are darker than those of Bewick's wrens.

Locations: Rare within Portland city limits, but commonly seen in oak-rich areas of Sauvie Island and Sandy River Delta Park.

Small wren, big voice. Photo: Tom Lawler

Pacific Wren *(Troglodytes pacificus)*

Seen: Year-round

All our wrens are worth listening to, but Pacific wrens are a notch above, offering up one of the most beautiful songs of all the birds in North America. Watch as they bust out one of their complex, tumbling songs, and you'll see that they throw their whole body into it: head tilted back, stubby tail cocked stiffly upright, tiny body reverberating with the sound.

Pacific wrens are unique among wrens in their association with forests, and mature or old-growth forests in particular. Living trees, standing dead trees (snags), downed trees, thick shrubbery beneath trees—this wren needs them all for foraging and nesting.

ID tips: Very small (even for a wren), with a stubby tail often held upright. They're brown overall with dark barring on their wings, tail, and belly. There's a slight pale mark over each eyebrow.

Locations: Anywhere with dense, coniferous woods. They're likely the most abundant bird in the interior of Forest Park.

> "The robin is often pensive, and sings ... as though he sympathized with us. But the wren never sings except to say that it is the best of all possible worlds."
> — Robert Wilson Lynd, *Solomon in All His Glory*

Marsh Wren (*Cistothorus palustris*)

Seen: Year-round (quiet in winter)

If Pacific wrens win the wren version of "The Voice," I have to tell you the marsh wren comes in last, at least to my ear, with a repetitive rattle aptly compared to that of a sewing machine.

As you'd expect, you'll see and hear them around marshes. Photo: John Williams

Distinguishing marsh wrens from other Oregon wrens isn't too hard because they're the only wrens that nest over water. Males use grasses and other vegetation to weave football-shaped nests that resemble wasp nests. They typically build more than one nest so females have plenty to choose from, and possibly so predators won't know which home is active.

ID tips: A little brown bird with a dark cap, whitish eyeline, and bold black-and-white streaks on the back that help differentiate them from Pacific wrens. They have whitish chests and buff flanks.

Locations: They nest in small numbers in marshy areas, including at Sauvie Island, Smith and Bybee Wetlands, Vanport Wetlands, Fernhill Wetlands, and Jackson Bottom Wetlands Preserve.

Bewick's Wren (*Thryomanes bewickii*)

Seen: Year-round

Writer Tim Dee describes wrens as energetic walnuts, and hyperactive Bewick's wrens certainly fit the bill. Look for these busy birds foraging at head height and below, catching insects on the wing, hanging upside down to glean insects from trees, and—after an apparently tasty meal—wiping their bills back and forth on branches up to a hundred times.

Note the long tail and long eyebrow. Photo: Tracy Aue

It's easy to confuse the sound of a Bewick's wren with that of a song sparrow, but the Bewick's song has a stronger, louder, and richer tone, with a ringing trill. Young males learn their complex songs from neighboring males and add their own twists, eventually developing a repertoire of up to 22 songs.

ID tips: Medium-sized wren with a long, slightly downcurved bill and noticeably longer tail than that of other common wrens. They have dull-brown backs and light-gray fronts, with a bold white stripe over each eye. Their long tail has black bars and is often held upright.

House wrens destroy eggs in Bewick's wren nests. Photo: Mark Lundgren

Locations: All over the city, including residential areas. They nest at Mt. Tabor and are common there all year, as well as at Smith and Bybee Wetlands.

KINGLETS

Note the golden crown patch.
Photo: Chuck Gates

They rarely stay still long enough for photos.
Photo: Mark Lundgren

Golden-crowned Kinglet *(Regulus satrapa)*

Seen: Year-round

Golden-crowned kinglets are beautiful, boldly marked birds with colorful crown patches. Anyone can see these birds, but only some can hear them because their song is so high-pitched that it's the first to be lost by many people with upper-register hearing loss ("I'm losing my kinglets" is a common lament among birders).

It's challenging to get a good look at golden-crowned kinglets because they flit around so much and spend most of their time high up in the dense foliage of Douglas-firs and other conifers. They're worth the search, though. As nature photographer Nick Saunders wrote, "On a freezing day, seeing that orange-yellow glow almost makes you feel warm."

ID tips: Tiny, stocky songbird that's gray below and pale-olive above. They have a much bolder face pattern than do ruby-crowned kinglets, with a black-and-white striped face and a unique yellow-orange crown patch.

Locations: Anywhere with conifers, including Forest Park and Mt. Tabor.

Ruby-crowned Kinglet *(Regulus calendula)*

Seen: Wintering (Sept.–May)

Don't you dare overlook these winter gems. Ruby-crowned kinglets are one of the smallest songbirds on the continent, but they compensate for their size with a high-pitched, complex song that they practically bellow. Unfortunately, we only get to see ruby-crowned kinglets in winter, when the sound you're most likely to hear is a scolding *jit-jit-jit-jit-jit*.

Their tiny red crowns can be tough to see.
Photo: Kris Kristovich

To spot these high-energy birds, watch for their constant wing flicking, a trait that's helpful in distinguishing them from other twitterers like Hutton's vireos. Ruby-crowned kinglets fly around at eye level, so they're not hard to find, but taking a photo that's not blurry is a whole other matter.

ID tips: A tiny, chubby songbird that's olive-green overall with a pale-white eyering. Note the white wingbar with a black bar below it. The male's small ruby-red crown is occasionally visible.

Locations: All over the city in winter, often with chickadee flocks. Watch for them at Forest Park and Mt. Tabor, before they head north and east to high-mountain breeding sites.

THRUSHES

Western Bluebird (*Sialia mexicana*)

Seen: March–May

The soft *kew, kew* call of a bluebird is one of the most welcome, cheerful, and increasingly rare bird sounds in Portland. Western bluebirds are found on both sides of the Cascades, but populations on the west side have dwindled precipitously.

Bluebirds face several difficulties. One is that they depend on a decreasing supply of standing dead trees, or snags, for nesting. They also need northern flickers and other species to excavate holes for them. Even when that happens, bluebirds are often beaten out by introduced species like European starlings and house sparrows.

Thoreau wrote that "the bluebird carries the sky on his back." Photo: Mark Lundgren

ID tips: Males have a blue throat and upper parts, russet chest and flanks, and white belly. Females are a paler and duskier version of males. The older the bird, the more and brighter the blue and russet colors.

Locations: Rare, but you might get lucky and see one in February or March. Cooper Mountain Nature Park and Powell Butte Nature Park are good places to look.

Swainson's Thrush (*Catharus ustulatus*)

Seen: May through Sept.

The large thrush family includes lots of plump songbirds like this one that typically inhabit wooded areas and feed on the ground. Even good birders have a hard time spotting Swainson's thrushes, but you can learn to recognize their flute-like songs that spiral upward in pitch and their quirky calls that sound like water dripping from a faucet.

Look for the buffy eyering. Photo: Chuck Gates

During migration, especially in early May and September, you also might hear Swainson's giving calls as they fly at night. They're by far the most vocal of the species that migrate at night in the Portland area. Like many other songbirds, they take to the air after the sun goes down to avoid predators, conserve energy, and navigate more easily.

ID tips: A slim songbird with a buff wash and spotted upper chest, buff ring around each eye, and russet-colored back. A dark-brown stripe borders their whitish throat.

Locations: They're found at larger natural areas such as Sandy River Delta Park, Mt. Tabor, Cooper Mountain Nature Park, and Smith and Bybee Wetlands.

TAKE HEART AND TAKE ACTION

In the 1970s, Hubert Prescott started putting up nest boxes in the Willamette Valley because he'd seen bluebird populations declining for decades. Seventy years later, the all-volunteer Prescott Bluebird Recovery Project continues his work, monitoring hundreds of nest boxes and supporting the fledging of thousands of bluebirds each year.
Maybe you'd like to join them? www.prescottbluebird.com

Look for the reddish tail. Photo: Chuck Gates

Hermit Thrush *(Catharus guttatus)*

Seen: Wintering (mid-Sept.–May)

One excuse for leaving your yard a little messy is to attract insects that will then attract ground-foraging birds like this one. Hermit thrushes have a variety of methods for stirring up their insect prey, including hopping around on the ground, picking up leaf litter in their bills, and using their feet to shake the grass.

I'm sorry to say we mainly get to see hermit thrushes in fall and winter, when they're not singing the ethereal, flute-like song (*oh, holy holy, ah, purity purity eeh, sweetly sweetly*) for which they're famous. If it's any consolation (and it's really not), you might hear their *chuck* call when they spy some berries in the underbrush.

ID tips: Chunky birds that blend well with the forest understory. Portland has a brown-backed subspecies with spots on the breast, thin eyerings (not connected into glasses), and a reddish tail that distinguishes them from other thrushes.

Locations: They're found in Forest Park in fall and winter. Mt. Tabor is a good place to spot them in migration.

Somebody's been waking up early.
Photo: Tracy Aue

They raise up to three broods a year.
Photo: Phil Nosler

American Robin *(Turdus migratorius)*

Seen: Year-round

Is there any bird more American than the upright and industrious American robin? Just about everyone recognizes these famously orange-breasted birds, even if we don't always pay much attention to them as they talk in the trees above and walk among us with such serious purpose.

Robins are exceptionally common in Portland and across North America because we've planted so many earthworm carpets (i.e., lawns) and fruiting trees. In spring, they wake us up with repetitive pre-dawn songs (*cheerily, cheer up, cheer up, cheerily, cheer up*). In winter, many head out to open places and form flocks of up to 5,000 (up to a quarter-million in other regions). When spring rolls around again, rising temps and longer days lead them to break up their huge flocks and return to sing outside our windows.

ID tips: A large songbird that's "yam-breasted," as Toni Morrison put it. Head is dark on males and paler on females. In flight, look for a white patch on the lower belly and under the tail.

Locations: All over, especially in city parks and backyards. In winter, large flocks gather wherever they can find berries (mostly in suburban neighborhoods).

Varied Thrush *(Ixoreus naevius)*

Seen: Wintering (Oct.–April)

What a beauty the varied thrush is—some say the most beautiful of all Portland's birds. Who can help but admire those bold splashes of orange and the contrasting dark band across the breast? Their call is attractive too. It's not complex, just a long and rather somber sound that repeats at different pitches.

Varied thrushes are short-distance migrants. Not for them the epic thousand-mile migrations of many other birds; instead, some live year-round at the coast, while those in Portland breed in the Cascades. When snow arrives and covers the leaf litter they depend on for insects, they fly back to Portland for our winter viewing pleasure.

Females like this one are paler in color than males.
Photo: Chuck Gates

ID tips: A robin-sized bird with a plump belly. Look for the dark band across the breast and rich orange on the breast and head.

Locations: In forested areas and urban yards with leaf litter to provide food. Forest Park, Mt. Tabor, and suburban yards are among the hotspots.

STARLINGS

European Starling *(Sturnus vulgaris)*

Seen: Year-round

I'm going to go out on a limb and say there's no such thing as a bad bird species. Birds are just birds, living their bird lives and doing what they've evolved to do. The problem with the European starling isn't the bird itself but rather that it was yanked out of its home in Europe, where it's a much-loved native species, and brought to the United States.

They're invasive, harmful, and dazzling.
Photo: Kim Elton

Now all of North America is stuck with a bird that kicks native birds out of their nests and generally doesn't play well with others. Starlings arrived in Portland in 1947 (after a failed introduction at the turn of the century) and are now one of our most abundant birds, although the city's populations have dropped recently.

It's too bad starlings don't blend in well because they're wonderful in several ways, including their ability to mimic the sound of everything from barking dogs to croaking frogs and squeaking doors. Mozart's pet starling sang bars of his owner's music, and was buried by the grieving maestro in a ceremony attended by dozens.

ID tips: A stocky, short-tailed bird. In spring, they're glossy black all over with iridescent layers that glow different colors, depending on the light. By winter, they've added new feathers with white spots.

Locations: Flocks can be seen all over, but especially in farm country and suburbs.

WAXWINGS

Look for hipster hairdos and listen for their high-pitched call. Photo: John Williams

Cedar Waxwing (Bombycilla cedrorum)

Seen: May–Nov.

Ever wonder where all the berries on your cherries, crabapples, and hawthorns go in summer, or your rosehips in autumn? Look no further.

Cedar waxwings are one of the most striking birds in Portland, and they're famous frugivores (fruit eaters) that arrange their lives around their favorite food source. Listen for repeated whistles and high-pitched *bzeee* calls that signal when a flock of these masked bandits is about to devour the fruit in your trees and shrubs.

ID tips: A medium-sized songbird with a distinctive head crest, black mask and chin, and yellow wash across the belly. Their tail looks like it was dipped in yellow paint, and their gray wings have waxy red spots.

Locations: Wherever there are fruit-laden trees and shrubs, including backyards, parks, and natural areas such as Smith and Bybee Wetlands and Mt. Tabor.

FINCHES

Males have a pale bill and a yellow stripe over each eye. Photo: Chuck Gates

Evening Grosbeak
(Coccothraustes vespertinus)

Seen: Spring and fall migrant

How boring it'd be if we knew exactly which birds would be where on any given day. We can come close with some species, but not with famously irruptive evening grosbeaks. They'll show up when they want, where they want, in any numbers, and whatever they do this year will not necessarily predict what they'll do next year.

Listen for evening grosbeaks flying overhead during migration (they sound like a kid shooting a pretend laser gun: *tchoo, tchoo*). If you happen to spot them partaking of your backyard feeder or perched atop a conifer, you'll see that they're built like avian linebackers, with stout chests and a massive bill for cracking open seeds.

ID tips: A big finch with a conical bill. Males have a prominent white patch on the wings, a yellow stripe over the eye, and a pale-ivory bill. Females are mostly gray with black-and-white wings and a greenish-yellow tinge on their necks and sides.

Locations: Tough to predict, but look for them in residential areas outside summer months. In spring and fall, they're in Forest Park and Mt. Tabor.

House Finch *(Haemorhous mexicanus)*

Seen: Year-round

One of the more famous house finches is the female that landed on Bernie Sanders's lectern at a campaign rally at the Moda Center in 2016 (#BirdieSanders). House finches like that left-leaning one didn't arrive in the Willamette Valley until the 1940s, but they're now extremely common here and across the continent, with population estimates ranging from the hundreds of millions to over a billion.

This colorful male is likely popular with the opposite sex. Photo: Alice Doggett

Since they're so omnipresent and talkative, these are good birds to learn to identify by ear. Males sing loud and long, combining a number of short notes into a jumble that ends with an upward or downward slur *(zeee)*. It's one of the more common birdsongs in Portland neighborhoods.

Look for red coloring on males that comes from the seeds, buds, and fruit they eat during molt— the more pigment in their diet, the redder they get. Female house finches prefer to mate with the reddest male available, possibly because he's more likely to be a strong forager who can provide for their young.

ID tips: A medium-sized finch with a big head. Males have a reddish forehead, throat, eyebrow, and rump, with red in the breast. Females are grayish-brown overall, with streaks but no red.

Females are grayish-brown—completely different than males. Photo: Kris Kristovich

Locations: Extremely common in all sorts of wild areas as well as neighborhoods, where they're frequent visitors to backyard feeders.

SWEET SERENADES

Learning these common birdsongs and calls will then help you distinguish rarer ones. Even recognizing a few will liven up every walk you take in and near the city.

- **American robin** *(cheerily, cheer up, cheer up)*
- **Anna's hummingbird** (10 seconds or more of buzzing, whistles, and chips)
- **Black-capped chickadee** (series of 3–5 same-pitch notes, unique to our region)
- **House finch** (a few warbling notes, often ending in a distinctive *zeeee*)
- **House sparrow** (the classic bird sound: *cheep, cheep)*
- **Lesser goldfinch** (descending *tee-yer)*
- **Song sparrow** (several well-spaced notes, followed by a buzz or trill)

Males are more raspberry-red than purple.
Photo: Mark Lundgren

Females have a whitish stripe above the eye.
Photo: Mark Lundgren

Purple Finch *(Haemorhous purpureus)*

Seen: Mostly spring to fall

Purple finches aren't really purple. The ornithologist Roger Tory Peterson described them more accurately as a "sparrow dipped in raspberry juice." They can be difficult to distinguish from house finches, but house finches are far, far more common and purple finches have a deeply notched tail.

In the eastern U.S., house finches aren't native and they appear to be pushing out purple finches. Here, both finch species are native, and especially as purple finch numbers decline, the colorful looks of males and the warbling songs of both males and females are welcome year-round.

ID tips: Bigger and chunkier than similar forest birds. Males have pinkish-red heads and breasts, with brown on the back and white on the belly. Females and first-year males have no red; they're streaked below and have a whitish eyebrow.

Locations: At backyard feeders with sunflower seeds and at wild places including Cooper Mountain Nature Park, Sandy River Delta Park, and Tualatin River National Wildlife Refuge.

Red Crossbill *(Loxia curvirostra)*

Seen: Year-round

As their name suggests, red crossbills have crossed bills. But don't worry—no orthodontic work is needed. Their oddly shaped bills are perfectly designed to spread apart the scales of woody cones, so the crossbills can then use their tongues to withdraw the seeds.

That funky bill is perfect for opening seeds.
Photo: Kris Kristovich

Like the evening grosbeak, the red crossbill is a nomadic species seen irregularly in the Portland area. When local Douglas-firs and other conifers produce plenty of cones, you can expect to see red crossbills, but when cone production is low, they'll typically head elsewhere in hopes of finding the food they need. Continued logging is believed to be one reason their populations are dropping across the Pacific Northwest.

ID tips: Males have deep-red to reddish-yellow or greenish heads and bodies. Females are olive or grayish, with a greenish to greenish-yellow chest and rump.

Females should be called yellow or greenish-yellow crossbills. Photo: Tom Lawler

Locations: Look for flocks near the tops of conifers at tree-rich places like Forest Park, but mostly they're seen briefly as they fly overhead.

Pine Siskin (*Spinus pinus*)

Seen: Sporadic, but often Oct.–May

One year your feeder might be mobbed by deeply striped pine siskins, and the next you might see none at all. That's the nature of these nomadic birds, which have narrower bills than most finches and like to eat lightweight thistle seeds, as well as insects, pine nuts, alder catkins, and tree buds. When they're around, you'll know it because they form noisy flocks that buzz around calling *zreeeeeeet* and *zzzst, zzzst*.

Note the bright yellow on the wing.
Photo: Kim Elton

Pine siskins might be pint-sized, but they're tough enough to survive extremely cold temperatures. On subzero nights, they can crank up their metabolic rates much higher than most songbirds. They also put on more winter fat than relatives like the American goldfinch, and they can store up to 10 percent of their body mass in the area of their esophagus known as the crop—enough food to get them through even the coldest of nights.

ID tips: A very small songbird streaked with brown and white, with yellow markings at the base of the tail and on inner flight feathers. Listen for the nonstop, buzzy twittering of flocks. In flight, they flap and glide in an undulating pattern.

Locations: Generally in coniferous forests but impossible to predict from one year to another. They're drawn to the South Park Blocks to feed on the seeds of American elms.

Lesser Goldfinch (*Spinus psaltria*)

Seen: Year-round

The lesser goldfinch is the lesser in size and looks compared to the American goldfinch, but for reasons that aren't yet clear, the lesser has become the more common and widespread species in Portland in both winter and spring.

You'll see lesser goldfinches traveling in flocks all around the city, bouncing along in their never-ending search for the seeds and buds of trees like alders, willows, and oaks. Once you learn their call—a high *tee* followed by a lower *yer*—you'll hear these birds everywhere you go.

A male with a typical dark cap.
Photo: Mark Lundgren

In spring, listen for their much longer, prettier breeding songs. Once in a while, you might catch them embellishing their rambling songs with snippets of other birds' calls, including those of chickadees, northern flickers, and evening grosbeaks.

ID tips: The smallest goldfinch (not much larger than a hummingbird), with a pointy bill and short, notched tail. Males have a bright-yellow front and glossy-black cap all year long. Wings are black and white, and tail is black with white corners. Females have olive backs and dull-yellow underparts.

Locations: In all habitats, all over the city. They nest at Mt. Tabor and are frequent visitors at backyard feeders.

You can see why they've been called wild canaries. Photo: John Williams

A molting adult. Photo: Chuck Gates

American Goldfinch (*Spinus tristis*)

Seen: Year-round

Male American goldfinches are rather drab birds in winter, but come spring, they transform Clark Kent-like into golden beauties that flock to backyard feeders. I haven't taken a poll, but my hunch is that their vibrant breeding plumage and musical calls make them one of the more popular birds in Portland.

American goldfinches are different from most other birds in that they enjoy eating insects about as much as most people do. They prefer seeds—almost nothing but seeds. It's believed that's why they're one of the last Oregon birds to nest, waiting as late as August for plants like thistles and alders to produce the seeds they need to feed their young.

ID tips: Breeding males are bright yellow with a black forehead and wings, and white marks on the wings and tail (no black cap like lesser goldfinches). Females are duller yellow beneath and olive above. In flight, listen for their calls and watch for their undulating flight pattern, like many woodpeckers.

Locations: They prefer open to forested habitats. Look for them at Smith and Bybee Wetlands, as well as near other waterways and backyard feeders.

TOWHEES & SPARROWS

Plant shrubs to attract these beauties. Photo: Kim Elton

Spotted Towhee (*Pipilo maculatus*)

Seen: Year-round

Spotted towhees are one of the more common and vocal birds west of the Cascades. If you hear what sounds like a cat with a bad cold meowing from a shrub, there's a good chance it's a spotted towhee. Continuing with the feline connection, ground-dwelling birds like towhees are especially vulnerable to predation by housecats, so it's best to keep cats indoors or in enclosed outdoor spaces ("catios").

Towhees are striking birds when you spot them, and they make it easier to do that in spring, when males sing their hearts out from atop shrubs in city parks. Through the rest of the year, spotted towhees blend in with the leaf litter as they hop and scratch about for insects.

ID tips: A big, colorful, very common sparrow. Males have red eyes and a black hood over the head and upper breast. Females have a slate-brown hood. On both, look for a long tail and white spots on the wings. Sides are reddish and belly is white.

Locations: All over, especially in brushy areas (they love blackberry thickets). Look for them in your backyard and just about any wild place.

Savannah Sparrow *(Passerculus sandwichensis)*

Seen: Mid-March–Oct. (occasional in winter)

If you want to see vibrant colors, Savannah sparrows probably aren't the birds for you, but you might come to appreciate their elegant striping and the dashing splash of yellow by their eyes. They're common in farm fields, meadows, and grasslands across the continent, where they blend in as they forage for spiders and beetles, grasshoppers, and other insects.

The Savannah sparrow's common name refers to the city in Georgia, where one of the first U.S. specimens was found. The strange species name

Look for the yellow patch in front of their eyes.
Photo: Chuck Gates

of *sandwichensis* does not refer to a predilection for BLTs but rather to Sandwich Bay in the Aleutian Islands, where the first subspecies was described.

ID tips: Medium-sized, streaked sparrows with a distinctive yellow patch in front of each eye. They're brown above and white below, with streaks all over. Tails are short and crown feathers sometimes form a small peak. Song sparrows lack the yellow, have longer tails, and are darker overall.

Locations: Most common in agricultural fields and pastures. Look for them at Sandy River Delta Park and Oak Island on Sauvie Island.

Fox Sparrow *(Passerella iliaca)*

Seen: Winter and in migration

Quite a few sparrow species live in and fly through Portland. Song sparrows are the most abundant, but there are also fox sparrows, Lincoln's sparrows, and other species that are tough to distinguish between because they share a similar body shape and gray-brown coloring.

Fox sparrows are especially challenging to identify because there are four main groups and multiple subspecies—a field guide can help you sort them all out. In Portland, you're most likely to see the sooty subspecies foraging under your

A sooty fox sparrow with a chocolate-brown back.
Photo: Chuck Gates

birdfeeder in winter or kicking leaves around to stir up insects. The more native shrubs and brush piles you have, the more alive your yard will be with these and other birds that are seeking both shelter and food.

ID tips: Big, chunky sparrows of varying plumage, usually with brownish splotches on the flanks and chest. Similar to song sparrows but fox sparrows aren't common in summer and are slightly bigger, with an unstreaked head and a yellow lower mandible. In Portland, most are "sooty," with a chocolate-brown back and dark front.

Locations: Common but often overlooked at backyard feeders and in hedgerows, shrubs, and blackberry thickets at sites including Sauvie Island and Oaks Bottom Wildlife Refuge.

Note the long tail and heavy streaking. Photo: Kris Kristovich

Song Sparrow *(Melospiza melodia)*

Seen: Year-round

By the fourth month of Portland's winter, or surely by the fifth, you might find yourself lonely and adrift on a sodden raft of existential ennui. Out the door you'll trudge, head down, joints rusty, the late-winter rain drip-dripping straight into your soul. Then you'll

A lighter-colored song sparrow living up to its name. Photo: Phil Nosler

hear it: a song sparrow tilting his head back and singing, long and loud, perched just out of reach as he offers up a dose of hope on the dreariest of winter days.

In the late 1920s, these common and cheerful backyard birds caught the eye of Margaret Morse Nice, one of the first female ornithologists. She found that existing information on song sparrows was "meager ... and all of it wrong." So, over eight years, while raising four daughters and mourning the death of a fifth, she banded more than 870 song sparrows and studied every aspect of their lives, including counting the 2,305 songs one male sang in a single day. Nice's two-volume study earned worldwide recognition as a breakthrough in the study of animal behavior.

ID tips: Streaky overall, with brown marks on the breast converging to a central spot. Northwest birds tend to be darker than elsewhere. In flight, watch for the pumping action of their long tail. Each bird knows multiple songs, all variations on a theme translated as *Madge-Madge-Madge, put-on-your-tea-kettle-ettle-ettle.*

Locations: Extremely common bird in neighborhoods and brushy habitat near wetland areas. Go ahead and try visiting places like Forest Park, Mt. Tabor, and Smith and Bybee Wetlands without seeing or hearing a song sparrow—it won't be easy.

> **"... and when he throws up his head and sings the sweet song that gives him his name, you feel sure the world is worth living in."**
>
> — Florence Merriam Bailey, *Birds Through an Opera Glass*

White-crowned Sparrow
(Zonotrichia leucophrys)

Seen: Year-round

When famed ornithologist John J. Audubon first saw a white-crowned sparrow in 1817, he "thought it the handsomest bird of its kind." Look at those boldly striped heads and you'll be hard-pressed to disagree. The birds' plaintive songs, especially the long and melancholy opening note, are also delightful.

Early ornithologists called them "old skunkheads."
Photo: Kim Elton

Some white-crowned sparrows migrate, but you can see and hear them year-round in Portland-area fields, backyards, and parking lots. They're one of the best-studied of all songbirds, largely because they're abundant across the continent and easy to spot on the ground. One interesting discovery is that they have regional dialects. In Portland, for instance, their song endings are more clipped than in other Oregon cities.

ID tips: A large sparrow with a long tail, gray throat and breast, and boldly striped head. Adults have bold black-and-white head stripes. Immature birds have reddish head stripes and mix with adults during fall migration.

They have reddish head stripes during their first winter. Photo: Mark Lundgren

Locations: They're in clearcuts and natural areas like Sauvie Island. They can be seen foraging on the ground all over urban areas, including in the parking lot of your neighborhood Fred Meyer.

HIT THE SPARROW GRAND SLAM

A juvenile Harris's sparrow. Photo: Mark Lundgren

A friend once told me she had hit the "Sparrow Grand Slam" on Sauvie Island. What in the world? Turns out it's a birding game you can play. In the classic version, you have to find these four species in one day, ideally in one location (the last two species are too uncommon to make it into this book):

- White-crowned sparrow
- Golden-crowned sparrow
- White-throated sparrow
- Harris's sparrow

Their white outer tail feathers flash in flight.
Photo: Chuck Gates

Dark-eyed Junco *(Junco hyemalis)*

Seen: Year-round

Juncos are one of the most common birds on the continent, including in Portland. Almost all the juncos you'll see in town are a regional form known as the Oregon junco, which has a more reddish-brown back than the slate-colored junco that's rare here but common in the eastern U.S.

A decade or two ago, few juncos of any kind bred in Portland parks and neighborhoods, but these days they're widespread and frequently spotted under backyard feeders. Because they forage on the ground, you've no doubt stirred them into flight while walking along area parks and trails. To confirm whether you've flushed a junco, watch for the flash of their distinctive white outer tail feathers as they dart toward cover.

ID tips: A medium-sized sparrow with a long tail. They have a dark hood, rusty-brown or gray back, pink bill, whitish underparts, and white outer tail feathers that flash in flight.

Locations: All over just about any city park and at backyard feeders.

Males' black throat patches expand with age. Photo: Alice Doggett

House Sparrow *(Passer domesticus)*

Seen: Year-round

House sparrows are one of the world's most widespread birds, having trailed humans from Eurasia to shrubs across Portland, where you can now hear these so-called "McSparrows" cheeping and chattering nonstop. The adaptations that enabled house (aka English) sparrows to follow humans around the world include a large beak, a stout skull, and the ability to digest the many starchy grains that people produce, from field corn to Hot Lips pizza.

House sparrows' population success story is changing, as their numbers are declining in the U.S. and in many other countries. That could benefit other species because house sparrows evict native birds from their nest holes and have been known to kill even large birds like woodpeckers (and their young) to steal their nest cavities. On the other hand, the biggest problems for all species are large-scale habitat loss, pesticide use, and climate change, none of which are caused by house sparrows.

ID tips: Look and listen for flocks of chunky, chirping birds across the city and at backyard feeders. Males have a gray crown and black bib on the throat. On females, look for a buff eye stripe.

Locations: All over urban areas.

Females have a buff strip at each eye. Photo: Tom Lawler

In summer, their crowns are black and gold. Photo: Tom Lawler

Golden-crowned Sparrow *(Zonotrichia atricapilla)*

Seen: Wintering (Sept.–early May)

From fall through spring, Portland has a whole lot of golden-crowned sparrows—about 10 times more than white-crowned sparrows, according to the Audubon Society's Christmas Bird Counts. They're eye-catching birds, especially if you see them in early spring when they develop a more pronounced golden cap with crisp black borders.

According to John Burroughs, a member of the 1899 Harriman Alaska expedition that also included John Muir, miners in the Yukon Territory referred to golden-crowned sparrows as "Weary Willie" because of their plaintive three-note song, which has been translated as *I'm so tired* or *oh, dear me.*

*In winter, you'll see many juveniles like this one.
Photo: Tom Lawler*

Burroughs wrote that other miners translated the golden-crowned's song as *no gold here*, and resented the bird for repeatedly making its often-accurate prediction.

ID tips: A big, stocky sparrow with a long tail, smooth gray chest, and eye-catching yellow patch on the forehead. They're in Portland in winter when their colors are duller than in the summer breeding season, but they still have the yellow patch (no white like on white-crowned sparrows).

Locations: All over brushy areas in winter, including at Sauvie Island, Smith and Bybee Wetlands, and Mt. Tabor.

CHATS & BLACKBIRDS

They're not shy about voicing their opinions.
Photo: Chuck Gates

A meadowlark outside the showy breeding season.
Photo: Kim Elton

Western Meadowlark
(Sturnella neglecta)

Seen: Winter and in migration

Western meadowlarks aren't very common and don't nest in Portland anymore. But it wouldn't be right to leave out our state songbird, which also happens to be one of the most beautiful and musical birds in Oregon.

Not so long ago, you would've had a chance to enjoy many more melodious meadowlarks in Portland, but since the 1990s their populations have declined markedly across the Willamette Valley as more native grasslands have been converted to agriculture. They're now an Oregon Conservation Strategy species and are much easier to find in Central and Eastern Oregon, where their song carries far and wide over grasslands and sagebrush country.

In 2017, the Oregon Senate proposed dropping the meadowlark as state bird, in part, one legislator argued, because "many, if not most, Oregonians have never seen a live example." That cynical proposal was voted down, and the meadowlark remains our state songbird, with the osprey added as state raptor. To see a "live example" of our state bird, head east and south to open fields and unbroken wildness. It's worth the trip—and you'll see our state raptor there too.

ID tips: A robin-sized bird with a yellow belly and V-shaped black band across the chest. Upperparts are streaked tan and white. Males and females have similar markings.

Locations: Uncommon in Portland, but they can be seen in winter on Sauvie Island and near the Portland airport. Also be sure to listen for their loud, cheerful songs at Powell Butte Nature Park.

FUN FACT

Western meadowlarks and some other blackbirds have an unusual way of eating called "gaping." They bury their beaks in the ground and use their powerful jaw muscles to open wide, creating a hole for accessing insects that other birds can't reach.

Yellow-breasted Chat *(Icteria virens)*

Seen: May–Sept.

Chats are songbirds known for their chattering notes. According to the Cornell Lab of Ornithology, the yellow-breasted chat's especially chatty habits include a seemingly endless repertoire of songs "made up of whistles, cackles, mews, catcalls, caw notes, chuckles, rattles, squawks, gurgles, and pops."

When males arrive in spring, they sing their songs loud and long, day and night, both while flying and while hidden in dense thickets of blackberries and other brush. The Oregon Department of Fish and Wildlife describes the spring appearance of these birds as subtle as the "arrival of a brass band"—which is not to say they're easy to see (they're not).

They're chatty, colorful, and about seven inches tall.
Photo: Tom Lawler

ID tips: A colorful bird with a large head and long tail. They're olive-green above with a bright-yellow breast, gray face, and connected eyerings that look like glasses. Common yellowthroats are similar but much smaller, and male yellowthroats have a dark mask, not gray and white.

Locations: Uncommon (they're a Conservation Strategy Species in Oregon) but found in small numbers in low, thick brush at Tualatin River National Wildlife Refuge and Sandy River Delta Park.

Bullock's Oriole *(Icterus bullockii)*

Seen: Late April–Sept.

Thanks to the baseball team that shares their name, Baltimore orioles are better known than their western counterpart, the Bullock's oriole. For a while, the two species were lumped together, but it turns out they're not very closely related, despite their somewhat similar appearances.

The Bullock's (named after a bird collector) is the only oriole you'll see in Portland, and you'll have to work for it. They sometimes steal drinks from backyard hummingbird feeders, and you can search along area waterways for their pouch-like nests hanging from tall shrubs and from cottonwoods, maples, and other deciduous trees.

Listen for their whistles, buzzes, and rattles in trees
along waterways. Photo: Rick Derevan

ID tips: Look for the orange. Males are bright orange with a black back, black line through the eye, and white wing patch. Females and immatures are similar, but with lighter coloring.

Locations: Tough to find anywhere but in the trees at Sauvie Island and Sandy River Delta Park.

Listen for their loud and oft-repeated calls.
Photo: Tracy Aue

Red-winged Blackbird (Agelaius phoeniceus)

Seen: Year-round

Conk-la-ree! If you hear that exuberant—and piercing—song, it means winter's nearly over, and one of the continent's most abundant birds is announcing it's time to get down to the business of claiming territory and mating.

When that song hits your ears, look for the singer. He'll probably be perched nearby with his feathers puffed out and his brilliant-red shoulder patches, or epaulets, flashing. During territorial disputes, you might see another tough-guy pose where males and females stretch out their necks, point their bills upward, and sleek down their feathers. These birds are so bold that they'll attack humans, eagles, crows, and anyone else foolish enough to come close to their nests.

ID tips: Males are glossy black with red-and-yellow shoulder patches. Females are quite different: dark brownish overall, with streaks all over and a paler throat.

Locations: They're found across the city and nest in cattails and other marshy vegetation at Fernhill, Vanport, and other wetlands.

Females lay eggs in the nests of over 200 other bird species. Photo: Kim Elton

Brown-headed Cowbird (Molothrus ater)

Seen: March–Sept.

You know how you kind of appreciated Walter White, even as he built his meth empire on "Breaking Bad"? A similar affection for the antihero is necessary to admire brown-headed cowbirds, because what they do is both awful and masterful.

Females sneak into other birds' nests, lay an egg in about a minute, then fly off. What's a little sparrow, towhee, or warbler to do? If they puncture or toss out the offending egg, the "cowbird mafia" might return to destroy their nest. Yellow warblers have been known to suffocate cowbird eggs under nesting material, but that destroys their own clutch.

Most species don't recognize cowbird eggs, so they incubate them. Then instincts drive parents to feed large cowbird chicks at the expense of their own young. Worst of all, the antihero takes advantage of this largess and flies off to repeat the drama with other hapless victims. It might seem cruel, but the strategy works: Since they don't have to incubate and raise their young, females can lay up to 40 eggs a summer.

ID tips: Small for a blackbird. Males are glossy black except for their brown head. Females are brown (lightest on head), with mottling on the belly.

Locations: Most common in spring, especially in agricultural areas and on Sauvie Island. Seen far less often in summer and only occasionally in winter in flocks with other blackbirds.

Brewer's Blackbird *(Euphagus cyanocephalus)*

Seen: Year-round

Can we get some love for the handsome and helpful Brewer's blackbird? When the sun shines on males, you'll see they aren't simply black but rather a glossy amalgamation of black, midnight blue, and metallic green. If you've heard they're crop-eating pests, let's correct the record: They eat some grain, but their main diet is insects, including cutworms and tent caterpillars, so they're a farmer's friend.

A glossy male. Photo: Kim Elton

In 1967, Portland's Christmas Bird Count tallied a record 5,814 Brewer's blackbirds. These days, their populations are declining overall and in Portland, where Christmas counts have been hovering around a hundred. It's not only this species: nearly 30 percent of all wild birds in North America have vanished since 1970.

ID tips: Males are glossy black with some green and blue iridescence. Look for their bright-yellow eye. Females are brown with a dark eye. Brewer's have longer tails and stouter beaks than starlings.

Females are brown all over. Photo: Chuck Gates

Locations: Common in urban areas. Look for them around parking lots, in city parks, and walking along sidewalks.

WARBLERS

Orange-crowned Warbler
(Oreothlypis celata)

Seen: March through Sept. (rare in winter)

If you see a songbird in spring that's about five inches long with some yellow on it and it's not a goldfinch, you're looking at a warbler. In spring, orange-crowned warblers are one of the first warbler species to arrive in Oregon, and they're one of the city's more abundant visitors.

Looking for a bright-orange crown? Sorry. Photo: Mark Lundgren

Their name is a little misleading—yes, there's an orangish spot on the crown, but it's usually concealed. Look instead for a small songbird that's not bright yellow like some other warblers but rather a comparatively blasé olive-green color with a bright-yellow undertail.

ID tips: A small songbird with a pointed bill and short, square tail. Plumage varies from gray to olive to yellow, with a broken eyering and yellow undertail. They're not as brightly colored as yellow warblers. Their bill is green and monochrome compared to that of common yellowthroats.

Locations: During spring and fall migration, look for them in mixed flocks with yellow-rumped warblers at places including Smith and Bybee Wetlands.

Wich-i-ty, wich-i-ty, wich-i-ty!
Photo: Kris Kristovich

Note the yellow on this female's throat.
Photo: Mark Lundgren

Common Yellowthroat *(Geothlypis trichas)*

Seen: April through Oct.

If you're just getting to know birds and specifically the world of warblers, this is a good starter species. Common yellowthroats are usually found close to eye level or below, and males are easy to recognize with their yellow throats and contrasting black face mask. Even when hidden in the vegetation, you can hear their distinctive and repetitive *wich-i-ty, wich-i-ty, wich-i-ty* song.

Common yellowthroat populations are declining, but for now they're still widespread, from Central America to every province in Canada. Like many other bird species, they feed largely on insects, so they don't arrive in Portland until spring and then spend much of their time foraging in dense vegetation at wetland areas.

ID tips: A small, chunky songbird with a rounded tail. Males are bright yellow below with a prominent black face mask and olive upperparts. Females are olive-brown, usually with yellow highlights on the throat and under the tail.

Locations: Any wetland area with thick vegetation will do, including Fernhill Wetlands, Vanport Wetlands, Sandy River Delta Park, and Sauvie Island.

Yellow Warbler *(Setophaga petechia)*

Seen: May–early Oct.

Just to make matters confusing, in Portland we have, among others, yellow-rumped warblers, yellow-breasted chats, common yellowthroats, and these yellow warblers—all of which have "yellow" in their names and are, to varying degrees, very yellow.

Yellow warblers are just that: gorgeous, golden-yellow birds that have a too-cute *sweet-sweet-sweet, I'm so sweet* song that they repeat over and over. Their populations are declining across Oregon, and in Portland they're uncommon except during peak migration in spring and fall.

Arthur C. Bent called them "a rich yellow flame."
Photo: Kris Kristovich

When those shoulder seasons roll around, look and listen for these brightly colored beauties near willows and other streamside vegetation.

ID tips: A small songbird, largely yellow all over, with olive tones on the back and crown. Male breasts have striking red streaks.

Locations: In dense trees and shrubs, especially among willows at sites including Sauvie Island and Sandy River Delta Park.

Yellow-rumped Warbler *(Setophaga coronata)*

Seen: Spring and fall migrant (occasional in winter)

Yellow-rumped warblers are the warbler you're most likely to see across Oregon. In April, large flocks of brightly colored "butter butts" stream through Portland, especially near budding maple and oak trees. Watch for the distinctive flash of yellow as they dart out from a branch to nab a flying insect, then flutter back to their perch.

The Audubon subspecies has a yellow throat.
Photo: Chuck Gates

Some yellow-rumped warblers stick around through winter, a rarity for area warblers that might be due to these birds' expansive diet of everything from insects to fruit. Especially in winter, look for the myrtle subspecies, with a white throat and black mask. The rest of the year, you're more likely to see the yellow-throated Audubon's subspecies.

ID tips: In summer, look for a blue-gray bird with a yellow crown, rump, and side patches. In winter, they're paler brown but still have a yellow rump and some yellow on the sides.

The myrtle subspecies has a white throat.
Photo: Kris Kristovich

Locations: Seen just about anywhere in migration, such as Mt. Tabor and Forest Park. In winter, they're thinly dispersed; put out a suet feeder and you might see small flocks in your neighborhood.

Black-throated Gray Warbler
(Setophaga nigrescens)

Seen: Early April–mid-Oct.

Here's an exception to the yellow bias among area warblers: Black-throated gray warblers are black, gray, and white, with only a small yellow spot in front of their eyes. These handsome birds are among the first species to arrive in spring, announcing themselves with a distinctive buzzy song *(zeedle zeedle zeedle zeet-chee)*.

In 1837, John Kirk Townsend became the first

Note the yellow mark in front of the eye.
Photo: Mark Lundgren

to describe black-throated gray warblers in English, after collecting one near Fort William, a fur trading post on Sauvie Island. Like many other pioneers, Townsend took advantage of Indigenous people on Sauvie Island and elsewhere, robbing their graves and earning credit for "discovering" species like this one that they had long known and had in some cases collected for Townsend.

ID tips: A small songbird with a gray back, white face and underparts, black mask, and two white wingbars. Look for the yellow square in front of each eye.

Locations: Mixed woods, especially those dominated by maples and oaks. Hotspots include Mt. Tabor and Powell Butte Nature Park, but they'll nest in any decent-sized park with maples.

A Townsend's warbler in winter.
Photo: Mark Lundgren

Townsend's Warbler *(Setophaga townsendi)*

Seen: Aug. through May

With their bright-yellow front and dark Batman mask, Townsend's warblers are one of the more attractive of our area warblers. They're most often seen during spring and fall migration, but they and yellow-rumped warblers are the most likely of local warbler species to tough it out through the long Portland winter.

Townsend's warblers are named after the same John Kirk Townsend who described black-throated gray warblers. On a three-year trip in the 1830s with botanist Thomas Nuttall, they collected thousands of species with the help of Indigenous people. Dozens of plants and animals are now named after Nuttall (including Pacific dogwood, *Cornus nuttalli*), and Townsend's name is attached to multiple birds, as well as to many small mammals.

ID tips: A small songbird with yellow on the face and chest, and stripes down the sides of the chest. Belly and undertail are white. Note the black cheek patch with yellow crescent under each eye.

Locations: In coniferous forests across the Portland area. Mt. Tabor is an ideal spot for watching them in spring alongside other warblers.

The yellow face and dark cap set them apart.
Photo: Mark Lundgren

Wilson's Warbler *(Cardellina pusilla)*

Seen: Late April through Sept.

Forgive me for saying so, but you might hear the descending whistles of a Wilson's warbler while walking waterside among willows in the Willamette Valley. These lemon-yellow beauties with dashing dark berets flit about shrubs and trees along many Portland-area waterways, especially in spring and fall.

Wilson's warblers are named after Alexander Wilson, the father of North American ornithology and the greatest American ornithologist before a guy named Audubon came along. They're the kind of bird you'd like to have associated with your name—bright, colorful, and hardy enough to fly to and from Mexico and Central America every year.

ID tips: A small, mostly yellow warbler with olive-green on the back. They're Portland's only warbler with a yellow face and dark cap. Males have a black cap and eyes; females have a smaller, usually olive-colored cap. Their song sounds like repeated attempts to get a car engine to turn over.

Locations: In riparian areas and near deciduous trees and shrubs. Common near streams in Forest Park. They breed in places including the Portland Audubon's Wildlife Sanctuary.

Western Tanager *(Piranga ludoviciana)*

Seen: Late April–mid-Oct.

It doesn't happen every May, but in fortunate springs Portland is flooded with a torrent of western tanagers, one of the most beautiful birds of this or any state. Males especially—with their flame-red heads, golden bodies, and colorful wings—look like they've lost their way from the tropics.

No wonder they grace the covers of so many bird guides. Photo: Mark Lundgren

Western tanagers spend winter as far south as Panama, and they range farther north than any other tanager. In between, they make a welcome appearance in the Portland area in spring and early fall, nesting in conifers at higher elevations outside the city.

ID tips: Bigger than most warblers, with lots of red. Males are yellow with a flaming orange-red head. Wings are black with two bright bars. Females sport yellow-green feathers on most of their bodies, set off by gray on the back.

Females are yellow-green with gray backs. Photo: Mark Lundgren

Locations: During migration, any park with a mix of trees will do. Look in Mt. Tabor, Forest Park, and Oaks Bottom Wildlife Refuge.

Black-headed Grosbeak
(Pheucticus melanocephalus)

Seen: Late April–mid-Sept.

It can be a little confusing, but in Portland we have two spring migrants that are both called grosbeaks (meaning "large beak") but are very different birds. Evening grosbeaks are classified with finches and are conifer-loving birds that typically fly over Portland at great heights.

That no-nonsense beak can crack open seeds and hard-bodied insects. Photo: Mark Lundgren

Black-headed grosbeaks are in the same family as cardinals and are far more common than evening grosbeaks. They're also more musical and can be heard singing like a robin, only better—or some say like a drunk robin doing a bit of improvisation. When you hear their pretty song, spring is in full swing and it's time to get outside.

A lighter-colored female with striped head. Photo: John Williams

ID tips: Big, stocky songbird with a stout bill. Males have a black head and bright-orange breast, neck, and rump. Females are buff with pale orange on the belly, a brown back, and a striped head.

Locations: In suburban areas and parks, especially where there are maple trees. Hotspots include Sauvie Island, Mt. Tabor, and Sandy River Delta Park.

A beautiful male perching on Himalayan blackberry.
Photo: Tracy Aue

Lazuli Bunting *(Passerina amoena)*

Seen: May–Sept.

Portland has only a few birds like this one that display striking blue feathers. Pronounce their name *"lah-ZOO-lee"* or *"LAZZ-you-lie,"* just don't miss out on seeing these blue-and-orange stunners in spring and summer.

Lazuli bunting males are also worth listening to. Each male mixes his own original song using a handful of notes sampled from nearby males. This practice leads to the creation of "song neighborhoods" where all the songs tend to contain similar parts. That makes it easy to recognize and exclude outsiders for singing songs that don't belong to the neighborhood.

ID tips: Small, stocky songbird with a cone-shaped bill and notched or slightly forked tail. Males have brilliant-blue heads, an orangish breast, and a white belly and shoulder patch. Females are grayish-brown above, with a blue tinge to their wings and tail.

Locations: They prefer undeveloped areas, so they're not found in the urban core. Sandy River Delta Park and Tualatin River National Wildlife Refuge are good places to look, along with Cooper Mountain Nature Park in summer.

Photo: Rick Derevan

Photo: Tracy Aue

Photo: Kris Kristovich

Photo: Kim Elton

Photo: Kris Kristovich

10 WAYS TO HELP BIRDS

Here are easy ways you can help make sure future generations get to enjoy Portland's birds:

1. Join the Audubon Society of Portland and donate to bird conservation.

2. Take part in a bird walk to learn to recognize birds (we care more about what we know).

3. Support politicians who value wildlife and Portland-area greenspaces.

4. Eliminate or minimize use of pesticides.

5. Introduce young people to birds and other wildlife, and model a respect for nature.

6. Keep cats indoors—they're a leading cause of bird mortality.

7. Plant insect- and bird-friendly native plants— and get your yard certified (audubonportland. org/issues/backyardhabitat).

8. Place a shallow bowl of clean water outside so birds can drink and bathe.

9. Put up nest boxes (the Audubon Society of Portland has details).

10. Discourage window collisions (again, the Audubon Society can help).

Photo: John Williams

Photo: Tracy Aue

Photo: Dave Reid

Photo: Rick Derevan

Photo: Alan St. John

Photo: Tracy Aue

Photo: John Williams

WILDLIFE

I realize that when you hear "Portland wildlife," you're more likely to picture the Naked Bike Ride than a mountain lion. Yet one of the great things about Portland is that it's still a little wild in the nature-related sense of the word, as coyotes patrol neighborhoods, deer browse on the outskirts, and even bears and bobcats occasionally stroll through.

To be fair, you're far more likely to encounter pint-sized wildlife than headline-grabbing large animals. From mice and moles to butterflies and bees, the city's small creatures thrive because they've learned to hide in plain sight: They're camouflaged,

Photo: Tracy Aue

Photo: M.A. Willson

Photo: Rick Derevan

Photo: M.A. Willson

Photo: Alan St. John

they come out at night, they live underground, or in the case of squirrels, they're so commonplace we forget about them until they knock out our electricity.

To the extent we notice urban wildlife in our everyday lives, it's often as a nuisance. But we live in a rapidly changing world in which wild land animals have lost an average of 60 percent of their members since 1970. Given that, it might be time to view the remaining animals as survivors we're fortunate to still have in the city. Maybe, too, we can continue working toward a Portland that's not a wildlife-free zone but rather an oasis for the relatively few remaining species.

Once you get to know the city's wildlife species, big and small, uncommon and ubiquitous, I think you'll agree they're at least as interesting and eye-catching as the people who pedal through town in their birthday suits.

AMPHIBIANS
FROGS

Look for the large skin fold right behind the eye. Photo: Tracy Aue

A great blue heron doing us a favor.
Photo: Jim Anderson

American Bullfrog (*Lithobates catesbeianus*)

In Portland and across the Pacific Northwest, the appropriate response to hearing the cow-like bellow of an American bullfrog is "uh-oh." That loud, low-pitched call means a highly invasive bullfrog has infested another wetland area—and where there's one, there are bound to be many, many more since bullfrogs lay 20,000 or so eggs at a time.

In the 1920s, folks from the southeastern U.S. brought bullfrogs to Oregon as a tasty treat. But here in our alligator-free waters, it's the bullfrogs doing the eating of native frogs, fish, snakes, birds, and baby turtles—all species that are having enough trouble surviving habitat loss, climate change, and other threats. Little wonder, then, that the Oregon Department of Fish & Wildlife lists bullfrogs as among the state's 12 most invasive animals.

To be clear, the half-foot-long bullfrog isn't a "bad animal." There's no such thing. It's just an animal that we introduced into an environment where it doesn't belong. Contact ODFW for guidance if these outsized frogs make an appearance in your neighborhood.

ID tips: They're huge! At about 6 in. long, bullfrogs are 2–3 times bigger than native frogs. Look for the large tympanum (eardrum) just behind their eyes that creates a distinctive circle.

Locations: They're in the Columbia Slough watershed, including at Sauvie Island, Whitaker Ponds Nature Park, and Bethany Lake Park.

Look for the black stripe through the eye. Photo: Alan St. John

Pacific Treefrog *(Pseudacris regilla)*

Summer, fall, and early winter, we hardly notice Pacific treefrogs (aka Pacific chorus frogs)—the smallest and most common frog in Portland and the state—as they quietly snap up spiders and bugs in our backyards and woodlands. But then February rolls around, and males hop en masse to wetlands where they inflate their throat sacs up to three times the size of their heads and repeatedly belt out one of the quintessential sounds of spring: *RIB-BET* (or *kreek-eek*, if you prefer).

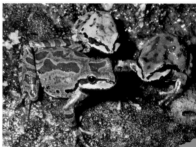

They come in many colors. Photo: Alan St. John

All that noise serves a distinct purpose: They're calling females to join them, and they're competing with each other to produce the more frequent calls the ladies prefer. When a female arrives, a male will climb on her back piggyback style, wrap his arms around her in an embrace called amplexus, and hang on (sometimes for hours) as he waits for her to lay a gelatinous mass of eggs in the water. When she does, the male sprays the eggs with his sperm, releases his hold, and goes back to calling for the next female who comes along.

Late in spring, head back to natural areas where you heard the chorus of males and look for tadpoles swimming in the water. The International Union for Conservation of Nature estimates that more than one in three amphibians is at risk of extinction, so the sight of the next generation of treefrogs is worth celebrating.

ID tips: Treefrogs are about 2 in. long. They're usually green or brownish but can be all sorts of colors (even blue); some can also change from one color to another. Look for their bulbous toe pads and a thick black stripe through each eye.

Locations: Common near wetlands and woodlands across the Portland area, including at Tryon Creek State Natural Area, Oaks Bottom Wildlife Refuge, Sauvie Island, and Tualatin Hills Nature Park.

> **"Some [frogs] sang so beautifully that you felt newborn,
> and banished all disagreeable thoughts; others so mournfully
> that one almost dies of melancholy."**
>
> — Carl Linnaeus in *Linnaeus: The Compleat Naturalist*

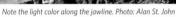
Note the light color along the jawline. Photo: Alan St. John

Their hind legs are especially reddish.
Photo: Alan St. John

Northern Red-legged Frog *(Rana aurora)*

The world-record distance for a migrating land animal is the 3,000 miles traveled annually by a particular herd of caribou in Alaska. By contrast, the northern red-legged frog's quarter-mile journey from Forest Park to a vernal pond in the little town of Linnton may seem quaint—until you realize that between the forest and their breeding grounds lies a four-lane highway.

To help hundreds of red-legged frogs (and some Pacific treefrogs) cross the road, a hardy band of volunteers known as the Harborton Frog Shuttle stands at the ready on rainy nights from about December through March. Their annual bucket brigade along Highway 30 is an example of how a few people can make a big difference, in this case for a dwindling population of colorful native frogs that have long been a part of Northwest forests.

ID tips: 2–4 in. long, grayish to reddish-brown with dark blotches (camouflaged to blend in with fallen leaves). Their rear legs and lower belly are usually reddish. Look for the dark facial mask and light stripe along their jawline.

Locations: Found in damp forests and forested wetlands and streams at areas including Tualatin Hills Nature Park, Sauvie Island, the pond near the Audubon Society of Portland, and Forest Park.

HOW TO HELP

To attract more amphibians to your property, ODFW recommends that you:

- Protect wetlands, meadows, shorelines, and other natural areas.
- Plant native vegetation along your watery areas.
- Protect paths between their breeding sites and upland areas.
- Leave some grass unmowed near their sites, and scout for them before you mow.
- Keep stumps, logs, leaf litter, and other debris that provide cover.
- Build a pond that offers both sun and shade and is deeper than a foot.
- Fence large ponds to keep livestock away and protect water quality.

SALAMANDERS

They're known for their bug-eyed look. Photo: Alan St. John

Ensatina *(Ensatina eschscholtzii)*

The Portland region is a hotbed, or really a moist bed, of salamanders, with more species (11) than in all the western plains and Rocky Mountain states put together. Especially with so many salamander species worldwide struggling to survive, it's worth getting to know our local species a little better.

The ensatina is one of many terrestrial salamanders that go through life entirely on land. The most common amphibian across most forests west of the Cascades, ensatinas live anywhere from under the debris of old-growth trees to inside the nooks and crannies of log piles. Instead of laying their eggs in the water like aquatic salamanders, ensatinas lay them in burrows made by small rodents and nightcrawlers.

Ensatina means "sword-like," which refers to how they brandish their tails like a sword at predators. The tall tail isn't so much a threat as an offering: If a predator rips off their tail (as opposed to their head), ensatinas can regrow it, as can most other salamanders. Sacrificing their tail is preferable to being killed, but it takes up to two years for them to regrow their lost appendage.

ID tips: Terrestrial salamander, about 3–5 in. long. There are lots of types and subspecies, but in the Portland area they're usually reddish-brown, like the rotting western redcedar logs where you might find them. They usually have yellow at the base of each leg (especially pronounced in juveniles).

Locations: Found in a variety of habitats, often under decaying logs. Look for them at Oaks Bottom Wildlife Refuge, the pond near the Audubon Society of Portland, and Tryon Creek State Natural Area.

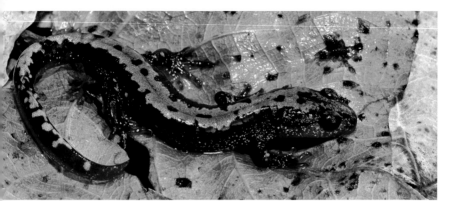

Check out those long toes on the back feet. Photo: Alan St. John

Long-toed Salamander *(Ambystoma macrodactylum)*

Salamanders are lizard-like in appearance but more closely related to frogs and toads. They start life as eggs, become larvae with gills and fins, and then metamorphize into moist-skinned, four-legged adults—or at least that's the usual story. There are more than 600 salamander species worldwide that we know of so far, each with their own unique adaptations.

The long-toed salamander—whose eponymous fourth toe is useful for grabbing onto vegetation—is one of the most widely distributed salamanders in North America, which tells you that this species has adapted to live in all sorts of demanding environments, even breeding in frigid waters in the Cascades. Adults can live up to 10 years if they manage to avoid garter snakes, birds, fish, and other predators.

ID tips: Aquatic-breeding salamander, about 1.5–3.5 in. long. They're dark overall with a greenish-yellow stripe on their back that can be irregular or mottled. There are sometimes light flecks on the sides and belly. Look for the long fourth toe on each hind foot.

Locations: In spring, adults can be found under logs and rocks or in the shoreline shallows of area rivers, streams, lakes, and ponds, including at Tryon Creek State Natural Area, Sauvie Island, and the Sandy River Delta.

FUN FACT

An early myth propagated by Pliny and Aristotle (and played on by J.K. Rowling in her Harry Potter books) was that salamanders are born and live in fires that they can extinguish at will with their cold bodies. If only! During fires, salamanders do what you'd expect, taking cover in their moist habitats; those that survive may appear to rise from the ashes. (This myth is also why top-fired broilers are called salamanders.)

Northwestern Salamander (*Ambystoma gracile*)

I know this is a little scandalous, but amphibians are naked! Birds rather demurely cover their skin with feathers, reptiles with scales, and most mammals with fur or hair like our own. But amphibians bare it all, which is why they usually live in cool, moist places where they can avoid drying out their exposed skin.

The reason these salamanders, as well as most other amphibians, aren't naked and afraid is that they protect themselves with poison glands in their skin. If attacked, a northwestern salamander—which can be nearly a foot long—will arch its back and tip down its snout in a sort of bucking-horse posture while oozing scary white drops of poison out the sides of its body.

I hope it goes without saying that nobody should annoy a salamander into oozing, or fail to wash their hands after touching one, but by all means lift a log or two to catch a glimpse of these big, naked salamanders.

Note the bulging gland behind the eye. Photo: Alan St. John

ID tips: Large aquatic-breeding salamander, up to about 9 in. long. They're brown, gray, or black, sometimes with flecks of lighter colors. Look for large glands right behind their eyes.

Locations: They live in moist forests and partly wooded areas and breed in permanent ponds, including at Sauvie Island, the pond near the Audubon Society of Portland, and Tryon Creek State Natural Area.

DID YOU KNOW?

If a predator rips off a salamander's tail or leg, the salamander doesn't develop a scab and scar tissue like we would. Instead, it regrows the entire body part. But that's not all: Salamanders also have the astounding ability to rebuild and regenerate damaged internal organs including their heart, eyes, and even brain.

The reason is that salamanders have specialized muscle cells that switch back and forth as needed between immature progenitor cells that can regrow tissue and mature cells that perform specialized tasks like contracting the heart. From early in our lives, we humans are stuck with mature cells only, although it goes without saying that scientists are trying to figure out how we too could someday regrow our organs and limbs.

These lungless salamanders breathe only through their skin. Photo: Mark Leppin

Western Red-backed Salamander *(Plethodon vehiculum)*

The forest-loving western red-backed salamander is one of the smaller and more abundant terrestrial salamanders. In a perfect world, a salamander called red-backed would have a red back, but in fact you'll find only a red stripe—or a tan or yellow stripe, or even no stripe at all.

The *vehiculum* species name is also a little odd—and it does refer to the word "vehicle." The name stems from their courtship ritual, in which a male will carry a female around while she holds onto his tail. Eventually he'll deposit a spermatophore (a gelatinous mass of sperm) on the ground, then walk forward so the female can absorb it into her system through her cloaca, although sometimes she will instead walk right on past.

They're much thinner than most other salamanders.
Photo: Mark Leppin

ID tips: Terrestrial salamander, about 3–4.5 in. long. Typically there's a colored stripe on the back, from the head to the end of the tail, that makes them look like a ribbon (they're much thinner than Northwestern and long-toed salamanders).

Locations: They prefer forests, rocky slopes, and riparian areas. Look for them under rocks and woody debris at sites including Tryon Creek State Natural Area, Oaks Bottom Wildlife Refuge, and Forest Park.

Their undersides are a pretty orange. Photo: Alan St. John

Rough-skinned Newt (*Taricha granulosa*)

Newts are technically a subgroup of salamanders, but people often use the two words interchangeably in a manner that may offend newts—something you really don't want to do. Compared to other salamanders, newts tend to move more slowly and have bumpier skin, although adults that spend a lot of time in the water have rather puffy and smooth skin.

The reason you don't want to offend newts is that they're one of the world's most poisonous animals. A single rough-skinned newt has enough toxin to kill you, as a man in his 20s found out in 1979, when he ate one on a bet at a bar in Coos Bay (he had a heart attack and died within hours). Birds and other animals will promptly spit out newts—all except some common garter snakes that have evolved an immunity to the toxin.

Rough-skinned newts are so toxic they don't bother with hiding or living the life nocturnal, which is why they're probably the most commonly seen salamander in Portland. Touching one won't kill you because their toxin is in their skin (not oozed out), but they can pick up salmonella and other diseases from polluted water. If you happen to touch a newt—or any amphibian or reptile—avoid touching your mouth and wash your hands as soon as you can.

A dangerous crossing. Photo: Alan St. John

ID tips: About 4–7 in. long. Look for the brown back with grainy skin (males look slicker when in ponds) and their vibrant-orange abdomen.

Locations: They live in forested, partially wooded, and developed areas, and breed in ponds, lakes, and backwaters. Newts are active during damp days in lots of places including Forest Park, the pond near the Audubon Society of Portland, and Tualatin Hills Nature Park.

222

INVERTEBRATES
BEES

A yellow-faced bumblebee (left) and honeybee.
Photo: Tracy Aue

FOUR EASY STEPS TO HELP NATIVE BEES

1. Find alternatives to herbicides like Roundup and systemic insecticides. Vinegar, boiling-hot water, and soapy water are among the cheap, nontoxic methods that work.

2. Ask nurseries and big-box stories if they treat their plants with systemic insecticides—labels may not tell you. If the plants have been treated, they'll be toxic to all insects, so don't buy them and ask the retailer to change their policy.

3. Be messy in parts of your yard. About two-thirds of native bees nest in bare soil, so leave some for them. Also helpful are overgrown grass, rodent holes, brush piles, dead wood, and leaves that can insulate bees over long winters.

4. Native bees need nectar and pollen from early spring to late fall, so plant a variety of native species (see table at right).

My sense is that Portlanders got aboard the native bee boat long before residents of most other cities. But I also sense some continued confusion about wasps, honeybees, and native bees, and why it's so important to support these and other insects that are, as naturalist E.O. Wilson says, "the little things that run the world."

To get oriented, it helps to know that bees are not wasps, and wasps are not bees—their lines diverged more than 100 million years ago, when bees went vegetarian and wasps continued to prey on insects and other animals. Wasps such as yellowjackets, mud daubers, and hornets look more armored than bees and have skinny, non-pollen-carrying legs. Some wasps have a nasty sting, but they're also helpful at eating garden pests and pollinating plants.

Among bee species, the most famous is the European honeybee (*Apis mellifera*), the subject of most bee-themed movies, books, and articles. Honeybees are not native to the U.S., but they're used extensively in agriculture. Beekeepers truck their honeybee hives around the country to pollinate everything from vegetables to almond orchards, a practice that's increasingly viewed as unsustainable and even dangerous, as much of our food supply depends on this one struggling species.

Mining bees like this one build nests in the ground.
Photo: Rich Hatfield

A western bumblebee on late-season goldenrod.
Photo: Rich Hatfield

Non-honeybee bees include about 3,600 native bee species across the U.S., and more than 150 species in the Portland area alone. We're talking about bumblebees, mason bees, sweat bees, cuckoo bees, leafcutter bees, tickle bees, carpenter bees, long-horned bees—everything but spelling bees. These native bees serve many functions, but they're most famous for pollinating plants.

Without native bees, we'd lose so much. There'd be far less produce available to eat (including tomatoes, pumpkins, cherries, blueberries, and cranberries), as well as fewer individual wildflowers and fewer species.

Especially as honeybee populations decline due to parasites, pesticides, and other factors, maintaining a diversity of native bee species is critical. Compared to honeybees, they pollinate different plants, fly at different times and in different places, and are often more efficient pollinators. Plus, they don't have to be transported all over the country—simply grow native plants, and a variety of native bees and other pollinators will find them.

YEAR-ROUND BLOOMS FOR NATIVE BEES		
WINTER & EARLY SPRING	**SPRING AND SUMMER**	**LATE SUMMER AND FALL**
Oregon grape	Cascara	Chicory
Osoberry	Common camas	Common yarrow
Red-flowering currant	Douglas spiraea	Douglas's aster
Western crabapple	Lupines	Goldenrods
Willows	Mock-orange	Oceanspray
	Pacific ninebark	Self-heal
	Native roses	Thistles (native)

ID tips: Honeybees have alternating black and brownish stripes on their abdomens (the bulbous back end of their body). Native bees vary greatly in appearance, with everything from honeybee lookalikes to brilliant green and blue species.

Locations: Any natural area—and your backyard, if you provide bee-friendly habitat.

BUTTERFLIES

These pages introduce you to some of the 50 or so butterfly species you might encounter in the Portland area—but it's really just the tip of the butterfly iceberg. Once you've got a handle on these common species, pick up a copy of *Butterflies of the Pacific Northwest* by Robert Michael Pyle and Caitlin C. LaBar to deepen your knowledge about the many other species found in the city.

SKIPPERS*

Skippers are butterflies that typically "skip" through the air in a stop-and-go pattern. They're notoriously difficult to tell apart, but look for brownish butterflies with short wings and stout bodies skipping along from flower to flower.

In spring, white-spotted **Juba Skippers** are fairly common in natural areas across the Portland area; their name is probably a misspelling that refers to California's Yuba River. **Woodland Skippers** don't come out till summer—August is your best bet—but they're the most common skippers in Portland. In late summer and fall, they may be our most common butterfly, period.

The **Propertius Duskywing** is the biggest and most strongly marked duskywing, and one of many butterflies you'll find in Portland's few remaining native oak woodlands.

Juba Skipper
(*Hesperia juba*)
Small (.75-1.25 in.)
April-Oct.
Photo: Sue Anderson

Woodland Skipper
(*Ochlodes sylvanoides*)
Small (.75-1.25 in.)
June-Oct.
Photo: Sue Anderson

Woodland Skipper (2)
Photo: Sue Anderson

Silver-spotted Skipper
(*Epargyreus clarus*)
Medium (1.25-2.5 in.)
April-Aug.
Photo: Sue Anderson

Propertius Duskywing
(*Erynnis propertius*)
Small-medium (.75-2.5 in.)
May-July
Photo: Linda Kappen

Two-banded Checkered Skipper (*Pyrgus ruralis*)
Small (.75-1.25 in.)
March-Sept.
Photo: Sue Anderson

* For clarity, I've capitalized species names for skippers and all other butterflies.

SWALLOWTAILS

Swallowtails are the butterflies of summer. They're big, eye-catching, and common both in backyards and parks such as Howell Territorial Park, Blue Lake Regional Park, and Cooper Mountain Nature Park.

The tiger-striped **Western Tiger Swallowtail** is the most conspicuous butterfly in Portland from April to September, but also keep a lookout for two similar butterflies: **Pale Tiger Swallowtails** are white with black stripes, and **Anise Swallowtails** have a thick black stripe paralleling their head in lieu of tiger stripes.

Clodius Parnassians are not as commonly known as the other swallowtails, but you might get a look at them if you plant bleeding hearts—the only plant the caterpillars eat. Most often, the butterflies are seen around clearcuts and along roads and streams in shaded forests. Watch for a white butterfly with a strong, gliding flight that's nearly twice as big as ubiquitous Cabbage Whites.

Western Tiger Swallowtail (Papilio rutulus)
Large (2.5–5 in.), April–Sept.
Photo: Kim Elton

Pale Tiger Swallowtail (Papilio eurymedon)
Large (2.5–5 in.), April–Oct.
Photo: Sue Anderson

Anise Swallowtail (Papilio zelicaon)
Large (2.5–5 in.), March–Sept.
Photo: Dave Rein

Clodius Parnassian (Parnassius clodius)
Medium (1.25–2.5 in.), May–Sept.
Photo: Lori Humphreys

Photo: Lori Humphreys

WHAT'S A WOOLLY BEAR?

Woolly bears (Pyrrharctia Isabella) are the most famous caterpillar of them all, found all across the U.S. and Portland. Contrary to myth, a wide orangish band on woolly bears doesn't suggest a milder winter ahead. Most are born with a narrow middle band that widens as they age through several life stages, or instars. The amount of black and orange thus varies largely based on how old they are.

In fall, watch for woolly bears crossing trails and roads to find safe places to spend winter, such as inside downed logs. In spring, they emerge from their cocoons as far less famous and rather drab tiger moths.

SULPHURS, MARBLES, & WHITES

These mostly white, orange, or yellow butterflies are among the most frequently seen butterflies in the world and can readily be seen patrolling open country, roadsides, and agricultural fields.

Cabbage Whites are the most common butterfly species in North America and one of the hardiest—they've even been spotted in downtown Manhattan. They're also one of only a couple non-native butterfly species in the Pacific Northwest, where their habit of nibbling on cabbage, kale, broccoli, and other garden veggies hasn't exactly endeared them to the masses.

Beginning in March, keep an eye out for the flash of orange on beautiful **Julia Orangetips** (formerly Sara's Orangetips) and the pale yellow to golden orange of **Orange Sulphurs.** As we converted much of the West to agriculture, Orange Sulphurs took advantage and became one of our most abundant butterflies. You can spot them all over agricultural fields, including on Sauvie Island.

Though sometimes considered agricultural pests, lepidopterist Robert Michael Pyle notes that sulphurs do little harm to plants and, unlike honeybees, they provide their pollination services for free.

Cabbage White (*Pieris rapae*)
Medium (1.25-2.5 in.), March–Nov.
Photo: Joan Amero

Julia Orangetip (*Anthocharis julia*)
Small (.75-1.25 in.), March–Sept.
Photo: Sue Anderson

Orange Sulphur (*Colias eurytheme*)
Medium (1.25-2.5 in.), March–Nov.
Photo: Sue Anderson

Margined White (*Pieris marginalis*)
Medium (1.25-2.5 in.), March–Oct.
Photo: Linda Kappen

> **"Do not call these organisms 'bugs' or 'critters.' They too are wildlife. Let us learn their correct names and care about their safety. Their existence makes possible our own. We are wholly dependent on them."**
>
> — E.O. Wilson in *The New York Times*

GOSSAMER-WINGED BUTTERFLIES

Purplish Copper
(*Lycaena helloides*)
Small (.75–1.25 in.)
April–Oct.
Photo: Sue Anderson

Brown Elfin
(*Callophrys augustinus*)
Small (.75–1.25 in.)
March–July
Photo: Sue Anderson

Gray Hairstreak
(*Strymon melinus*)
Small (.75–1.25 in.)
March–Oct.
Photo: Sue Anderson

Echo Azure (*Celastrina echo*)
Small (.75–1.25 in.), Feb.–Oct.
Photo: Sue Anderson

Silvery Blue (*Glaucopsyche lygdamus*)
Small (.75–1.25 in.), March–Sept.
Photo: Sue Anderson

Gossamer-wings are small, delicate-looking butterflies with wings that change color in different lights. They include the blues, which usually have iridescent blue wings; coppers, which are usually orange-red to brown; and hairstreaks (including elfins), which typically have thin, tail-like projections and narrow line markings on their wings.

Purplish Coppers are the most common and widespread copper species in the West. Their name comes from the fact that, although they often look orange and black, a purplish hue will pop out in the right light.

Of the several blues found in the Portland area, you're most likely to see **Echo Azures** (Oaks Bottom Wildlife Refuge is one place to look). Male Echo Azures have silvery to lilac-blue wings; females have less blue and more gray. Their caterpillars feed on native plants including red-osier dogwood, oceanspray, and madrone.

As early as February, look for **Silvery Blues** wherever vetches and native lupines grow, including at Cooper Mountain Nature Park. The bold blue hue of the "fresh" (newly emerged) male butterflies will catch your eye like few other species. Over time, the color of these and other butterflies fades and their wings get tattered and torn.

WHAT IS A LARVAL HOST?

Butterflies begin as eggs, become caterpillars (the larval stage), and metamorphose into butterflies. During their caterpillar stage, each species can only eat certain plants, which are known as their larval hosts. To support butterflies, plant their larval hosts and other nectar-producing plants in your backyard, and advocate for public lands where large swaths of these plants grow.

BRUSH-FOOTED BUTTERFLIES

The brush-footed family is named for these butterflies' shortened, brush-like front pair of legs—not exactly something you'll notice as you walk by them on the trail. Fortunately, a few common brush-footeds will catch your eye with their showy orange, brown, and black colors.

No brush-footed stands out quite so much as the **Monarch,** the most iconic and beloved butterfly in the world. The typical migratory path for western Monarchs does not take them through Portland, but they sometimes make an appearance, and any actions we take to support their struggling populations—like planting local, untreated varieties of pollinator-friendly plants—will also help other butterflies.

Summer's the time to look for **Lorquin's Admirals** and their stiff flap-flap-glide flight pattern. When you see these large butterflies, named after a French butterfly collector, stop for a while and watch what they're doing. They usually have a couple favorite perches they'll return to again and again, and you might get lucky and see one defending its territory—lepidopterist Robert Michael Pyle reports watching as they've chased off other butterflies and even birds.

In gardens and hilltops, you'll see various "ladies," including **Painted Ladies,** the world's most common and abundant butterfly. Painted Ladies live on five continents (all but Antarctica and South America). They and California Tortoiseshells are easy to confuse with Monarchs, so look closely at the differences in the photos.

Monarch
(*Danaus plexippus*)
Large (2.5–5 in.)
May–Oct.
Photo: Dave Rein

Lorquin's Admiral
(*Limenitis lorquini*)
Medium (1.25–2.5 in.)
May–Oct.
Photo: Dave Rein

Western Meadow Fritillary
(*Boloria epithore*)
Small (.75–1.25 in.)
March–Sept.
Photo: Sue Anderson

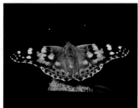

Painted Lady
(*Vanessa cardui*)
Medium (1.25–2.5 in.)
March–Nov.
Photo: Sue Anderson

Painted Lady (*2*)
Photo: Sue Anderson

Mylitta Crescent
(*Phyciodes mylitta*)
Small (.75–1.25 in.)
March–Oct.
Photo: Sue Anderson

BRUSH-FOOTED BUTTERFLIES (cont.)

California Tortoiseshell
(*Nymphalis californica*)
Medium (1.25–2.5 in)
Jan.–Nov.
Photo: Sue Anderson

Mourning Cloak
(*Nymphalis antiopa*)
Medium-large (1.25–5 in.)
Feb.–Nov.
Photo: Sue Anderson

Satyr Anglewing
(*Polygonia satyrus*)
Medium (1.25–2.5 in)
Feb.–Nov.
Photo: Linda Kappen

Red Admirable
(*Vanessa atalanta*)
Medium (1.25–2.5 in.)
March–Oct.
Photo: Sue Anderson

Ochre Ringlet
(*Coenonympha tullia*)
Small (.75–1.25 in.)
March–Oct.
Photo: Sue Anderson

Common Wood Nymph
(*Cercyonis pegala*)
Medium (1.25–2.5 in)
May–Sept.
Photo: Dave Rein

California Tortoiseshells are famous for their boom-bust population cycles in the Cascades. In some years, millions course along roads, waterways, and even the top of South Sister. There are several theories for what causes the fluctuations—winter weather? Larval parasites? Post-fire growth of snowbrush?—but researchers aren't sure. When another population spike happens, head to the mountains to see what the fuss is about—or stay at home, as their populations will also rise in Portland.

Mourning Cloaks are not actually made of velvet, though you'd be forgiven for thinking so. They're among the few butterflies that overwinter in cold, wet Portland as adults, not as eggs or in a chrysalis. That's why you'll occasionally see them staggering out of hibernation on warm days in winter. If you find them in your garage or garden shed, keep them safe and make sure they can escape in spring.

Satyr Anglewings and **Red Admirables** (aka Red Admirals) are found in many of the same habitats because they share the same larval host: stinging nettle. Like Mourning Cloaks, anglewings overwinter as adults, so you might see them on warm winter days and wonder what the heck they're feeding on with so few flowers in bloom. The answer is that the adults feed on tree sap, rotting fruit, and scat.

Small yellowish **Ochre Ringlets** and larger dark-brown **Common Wood Nymphs** have floppier flight patterns than most other butterflies in the Portland area, and they rarely fly more than a few feet off the ground. Caterpillars of both species feed on native grasses like Idaho fescue, so you'll see the adults in meadows at places including Cooper Mountain Nature Park and Powell Butte Nature Park.

DAMSELFLIES & DRAGONFLIES

A male tule bluet, with wings folded. Photo: Phil Nosler

Damselflies *(Varies)*

Damselflies and dragonflies are similar members of the insect order Odonata that have been darting around this blue planet of ours for at least 325 million years. They've evolved, adapted, and split off into more than 6,000 species (326 in North America), of which about 50 skim the waters of the Portland area.

Take a seat beside a wetland area in summer, and listen to the whir of these colorful carnivores as they hunt mosquitoes, flies, and other insects. Compared to dragonflies, damselflies are generally smaller and daintier, with thinner, whippet-like bodies and a noticeable gap between their eyes. When they land, damselflies usually close their wings over their bodies, while dragonflies manspread their wings, holding them out wide.

Because of damselflies' name and the fact that they tend to be smaller and thinner, people sometimes mistakenly assume they're female and dragonflies are male. That's not the case. They belong to different taxonomic groups, although as many a mosquito has discovered, they're both extremely fierce predators—Odonata is Greek for "toothed one."

Spreadwings like this one don't close their wings at rest. Photo: Phil Nosler

ID tips: Long, thin flying insects of varying colors (often iridescent blue) with space between their large compound eyes. Their eyes protrude on each side of the head. All their wings are similar in shape, narrowing toward the body (dragonflies have larger hindwings that broaden at the base). At rest, most fold their wings along or over their bodies.

Locations: May through October, look for adults flying along area waterways, including at Oaks Bottom Wildlife Refuge, Jackson Bottom Wetlands Preserve, and Fernhill Wetlands.

Dragonflies (*Varies*)

Dragonflies and damselflies are astounding animals that hatch from eggs in or on the water, live most of their lives as aquatic larvae, and then spend their brief adult lives hunting insects, defending territories, and reproducing.

Grab a pair of binoculars to watch these living helicopters in action. Not only do separate muscles control each pair of forewings and hindwings, but each of the four wings operates independently. That's how they can stop suddenly and hover, as well as fly straight up and down, briefly backward, abruptly sideways, and full-tilt forward, at speeds of 30-plus miles per hour.

Dragonflies have the best vision in the insect world. Each compound eye consists of 28,000 simple eyes that combine to give them nearly 360-degree vision. They can hunt much smaller insects not by chasing them down from behind but by predicting their trajectory, much like an outfielder anticipating where a pop fly will land.

ID tips: Heavy-bodied, strong-flying insects that show off brilliant iridescent and metallic colors in summer. Compared to damselflies, they have a thicker thorax (the body segment where wings attach). Their huge compound eyes take up almost their entire head, and they hold their wings out like airplane wings when at rest.

Locations: May through October, look for adults flying along area waterways, including at Oaks Bottom Wildlife Refuge, Jackson Bottom Wetlands Preserve, and Fernhill Wetlands.

A male eight-spotted skimmer, a common urban species. Photo: Dave Rein

A female widow skimmer, a species first recorded in Oregon in 1991. Photo: Evelyn Sherr

JUST SAY NO

Male dragonflies can be persistent—some might say harassing—in their attempts to mate with females. In a response noted by women the world over, some dragonfly females pursued by males take the rather dramatic step of dropping to the ground and feigning death. Researcher Rassim Khelifa observed 27 moorland hawker (*Aeshna juncea*) females plummeting and playing dead to avoid males; of those, 21 successfully avoided mating.

SLUGS

They breathe and defecate out of that hole on the right side of their head. Photo: National Park Service

Banana Slug *(Ariolimax columbianus)*

I can't tell you how happy it made me to walk the Reed College canyon trail with a four-year-old girl who loves slugs. "Look!" she said excitedly, sticking her hand out at me—not to offer a pretty flower but to show off the little slug that was sliming its way across her finger.

Maybe by the time Dot reads this she'll have adopted the typical, mistaken view that all slugs are yucky pests that gobble up our garden plants. The truth is that most native species do little or no damage to plants; it's the exotic imports, like European black slugs and red slugs, that stir up trouble. Of our natives, banana slugs are the biggest of all—the "king of slugs," second largest terrestrial slug in the world—and they'd much rather feed on forest debris than chew up your chard.

Let's hope that Dot and kids like her will hang onto their curiosity and openness to the wide world of nature, including its spineless, icky, sticky members. Banana slugs are most assuredly not cuddly, but they are among the many unheralded decomposers, or forest janitors, that break down dead plants, fungi, feces, and other organic material and turn it into the rich humus that forest life depends upon.

ID tips: Up to about 10 in. long. Colors vary but include yellow, green, tan, gray, and white, often (but not always) with spots.

Locations: Any forested area will have banana slugs, including Forest Park, Hoyt Arboretum, and Tryon Creek State Park.

A good-looking young bear. Photo: Dave Rein

American Black Bear *(Ursus americanus)*

Sightings of black bears in Portland were much more common decades ago. These days, the only bears you're likely to see are at the zoo, but every few years someone reports seeing a black bear wandering through a Portland neighborhood—just often enough to remind us that large animals still live near the city, if not in the midst of it.

Oregon used to be home to grizzly bears, but those much bigger animals were killed off by 1931, leaving the black bear as the only bear standing. It no doubt works in their favor that they can be as small as dogs and are solitary animals that prefer to stay as far away from humans as possible. The one exception is at parks and campgrounds where people leave out food and draw hungry black bears in for a snack. For their sake and yours, keep your food stowed when anywhere near bear country.

ID tips: They're the only bear you'll see in Oregon, and they can be brown, cinnamon, bluish-black, or other colors.

Locations: Buy a lottery ticket if you see a black bear in the Portland area, but rarely they pass through wild areas like Cooper Mountain Nature Park and Forest Park.

> **"If you find poop in the woods and it's tiny round balls, it's a rabbit. If the balls are larger, it is a deer or elk. If they are really large, you should come home."**
> — Brian Doyle in *Orion Magazine*

CATS

They're about twice the size of an average housecat. Photo: Buddy Mays

Note the black tips on the ears. Photo: Dave Rein

Bobcat *(Lynx rufus)*

Bobcats are the smallest and by far the most widespread wild cat in the Pacific Northwest, but you're not likely to see them in Portland or anywhere else in Oregon. That's because they're not big fans of the commotion people make and, like your housecat, they sleep through a large portion of the day.

Of course, there are always exceptions. Bobcats are seen in the suburbs, they've been photographed near Balch Creek, and they breed outside Forest Park along Cedar Mill Creek. In 2015, local TV anchor Jeff Gianola spotted a bobcat and her three kittens in his Northwest Portland front yard. If you're similarly fortunate, make sure to put your pets in protected areas since bobcats prey on small animals like rabbits, housecats, and chickens.

ID tips: Bobcats have tawny coats with dark spots. At about twice the size of the average housecat, they're still small compared to cougars. They have short tufts at the ends of their ears and roughly 6 in. tails (cougar tails are much longer).

Locations: Rarely seen in Portland, but they're in the suburbs across all sorts of habitats. Forest Park and Jackson Bottom Wetlands Preserve are likely spots.

They're by far the largest cats in Oregon. Photo: Buddy Mays

Mountain Lion (Cougar) *(Puma concolor)*

Most of us live distinctly urban lives, with buildings nearby, concrete underfoot, and phones in hand. Which makes it startling news when someone in or near Portland spots a five-foot-long cat swishing its long tail as it crosses a street—what is this brazen wildness penetrating our civilized urban oasis!

A young cougar showing off its tree-climbing prowess. Photo: Dave Rein

Here's the thing: Thousands of mountain lions live in Oregon, and like presidential candidates, they occasionally wander through the Portland area on their way to someplace else. The "Cougar Sighting!" headlines and rare tragedies grab our attention, but cougars don't view humans as a regular food source—bees, cows, jellyfish, mosquitoes, and many other animals injure and kill far more people every year. If you encounter a cougar, make yourself big and don't run or ride away from them, which could trigger their prey drive.

Knowing that attacks are extremely rare may not alter your primal response, but remember that mountain lions are part of the richness of Oregon. They and other apex predators are necessary for healthy ecosystems, and they're a helpful reminder that even relatively large cities like Portland are part of the natural environment, not separate from it.

ID tips: Don't go looking for cougars, but if you see a huge tan cat, look for the cougar's flowing, 3-foot-long tail, and note that overall it's way, way bigger than a bobcat.

Locations: Rarely seen in rocky, wooded places and the outskirts and suburbs of Portland.

COYOTES

Note the long legs, bushy tail, and slender face. Photo: Dave Rein

Trotting down Broughton Beach in the afternoon. Photo: Phil Nosler

Coyote (Canis latrans)

Chances are you either believe, as the Navajo did, that coyotes are "God's dog"—smart, adaptable, loyal, and playful—or you feel as the comedian Amy Schumer does: "If I made a list of the animals I care about more than coyotes, it would be a list of every animal."

Wherever you fall on the coyote continuum, it's worth understanding them, if only because you might be riding a MAX train with one sometime soon (that happened in 2002, when a coyote settled into a coveted window seat). Coyotes were rare west of the Cascades until the 1940s, and they weren't spotted in Portland until the 1980s. Now, they're a common sight across the Portland area, as detailed at portlandcoyote.com.

What's astounding about coyotes is that it's legal, and common, to shoot, trap, poison, and hunt them from planes—and yet since 1950 their range has expanded twice as fast as any other North American carnivore. In fact, there are more songdogs now than ever before. Where people kill coyotes, rodent populations skyrocket (up to six times, according to a study in Chicago), and coyotes inevitably get the last laugh.

When populations drop in a given area, existing packs split up and more males mate with more females. The females also have more pups in each litter—from as few as two per litter in areas with lots of coyotes to up to 19 pups when population density is low. Clearly, wily coyotes have adapted to us; the question is whether we're willing to adapt to them.

ID tips: Color and size can vary, but they tend to weigh less than 30 pounds. Look for erect ears, a pointy snout, and a bushy tail with no curve to it.

Locations: They're in Portland neighborhoods (even downtown) and wild areas including Forest Park, Sauvie Island, and Smith and Bybee Wetlands.

WILE E. COYOTE

Many folks of a certain age first encountered coyotes on Looney Tunes cartoons, where Wile E. Coyote kept trying to catch that elusive roadrunner. Wile E. first appeared in 1949, in a short called "The Fast and the Furry-ous," and last in 1994, in an episode called "Chariots of Fur." Over the years, animators variously referred to Wile E. as *Carnivorous vulgaris*, *Eatibus anythingus*, *Famishius famishius*, *Caninus nervous rex*, and *Overconfidentii vulgaris*.

Black-tailed Deer
(Odocoileus hemionus ssp. *columbianus)*

In a world that's becoming less and less wild, deer stand tall as the biggest, wildest creature many of us will ever encounter. They're the most common large mammal left in the wild, in part because we've reduced the numbers of predators like wolves that would naturally control their populations.

Hemionus translates as "half an ass"—referring to their donkey-like ears.
Photo: Dave Rein

In Portland neighborhoods and parks, you can see Columbian black-tailed deer, a subspecies of mule deer that lives between the coast and the Cascade Mountains. They're most often seen eating at dawn and dusk, and in fall you might get lucky and see males polishing their antlers on shrubs and small trees.

A couple tips: If you come across a fawn in spring, odds are the doe is somewhere nearby, so walk away unless you're sure the mother is dead. Also, don't feed deer. Human food isn't deer food, deer carry diseases, and those that hang around humans are more likely to get hit by cars.

A handsome buck.
Photo: Buddy Mays

ID tips: Smaller and darker than mule deer. Look for the dark forehead and large, wide, triangular tail that's dark brown or black on top with a white underside (only the tail tip is black on mule deer).

Locations: Found at forest edges and wild areas with shrubs for cover and forage, including Sauvie Island, Tryon Creek State Natural Area, Oaks Bottom Wildlife Refuge, Cooper Mountain Nature Park, and Tualatin Hills Nature Park.

DEER BY SEASON

- **Winter:** Deer mate and small groups travel together.
- **Spring:** Does give birth and hide fawns for a few weeks in brush.
- **Summer:** Does travel with fawns and yearlings; bucks are typically solitary or in bachelor groups.
- **Late fall:** Bucks go into rut, following does around and competing for the right to breed with them.

Elk graze on grass, shrubs, and tree shoots. Photo: Buddy Mays

Roosevelt Elk
(Cervus canadensis roosevelti)

At up to five feet tall and half a ton in weight, the regal Roosevelt elk is the single largest animal you might catch a glimpse of in the Portland area—although they'll do their best to keep that from happening. Unlike deer, most elk stay as far away from people as possible and are best viewed along the Oregon Coast.

Roosevelt elk are named after that famous conservationist and hunter, Teddy Roosevelt. At the start of the 1900s, he and others realized that elk were being hunted toward extinction and started working to protect them. As part of their efforts, they enacted hunting restrictions and formed elk preserves, including one that became (with the help of Teddy's fifth cousin, Franklin D. Roosevelt) Olympic National Park, where you can still see large herds of elk.

ID tips: They're a whole lot bigger than deer. Males have the largest antlers of all elk species (up to 4 ft.), with a 3-pt. tip or crown on the end. They have a tan body and dark-brown or black neck.

Locations: Occasionally seen in and near forested areas, including at Oxbow Regional Park, near PCC's Rock Creek campus, and at Tualatin River National Wildlife Refuge.

Jewell Meadows near the Oregon Coast is a prime viewing area. Photo: Buddy Mays

BRONZE ELK

The second-oldest sculpture in Portland is the 3,000-pound elk fountain on SW Main Street, which former mayor David P. Thompson gave to the city to provide a watering place for "bird, beast, and human." The downtown site used to be a feeding ground for elk, but hooved visitors are few these days.

RABBITS

Waking up is hard to do. Photo: Marlin Harms

Brush Rabbit (*Sylvilagus bachmani*)

Oh, the horror when my dog came wiggling up to me and deposited at my feet a tiny baby rabbit (technically called a kitten). My "helpful" pup had discovered a brush rabbit's litter hidden under a blackberry thicket in our side yard.

It's not surprising the litter was there—brush rabbits are famously homebound, rarely straying far from the brush piles and thickets where they live. Females reproduce like, well, you know, producing up to five litters a year of a few bunnies each.

Brush rabbits are a type of cottontail and are the only rabbit native to western Oregon. You might also see larger domestic rabbits (*Oryctolagus cuniculus*) of various colors that have escaped domestic life, and eastern cottontails (*S. floridanus*) with their eponymous fluffy white tails.

ID tips: Brush rabbits are small (10-14 in. long), brown to gray on the back, and white underneath. Their tail isn't prominent like a cottontail's, and the underside is gray, not white.

Locations: They prefer areas with lots of cover, especially blackberry and thimbleberry thickets, as found at Forest Park, Sauvie Island, and Tryon Creek State Natural Area.

Their ears are slightly pointed. Photo: Rick Derevan

240

RACCOONS & SKUNKS

Some have argued these clever, adaptable bandits are a better symbol of the U.S. than the bald eagle. Photo: Dave Rein

Northern Raccoon *(Procyon lotor)*

In a typical Portland encounter, a friend who lives near Grant Park walked out her door one morning and saw a raccoon strolling across a crosswalk on its hind legs. Upon hearing my friend, the raccoon looked over its shoulder and reluctantly dropped down to four legs, apparently deciding it should resume the charade of being a wild animal.

Keep trash cans secured, or they'll find a way in. Photo: Dave Rein

Raccoons are technically still wild, but they're also established urbanites and a prime example of a species that has learned to thrive among humans (the technical term is "synanthrope"). Oddly, raccoons, crows, pigeons, and other such urban-adapted animals—which use their intelligence to turn the lemon of losing their natural habitats into lemonade—are frequently vilified. In the case of raccoons, their reputation has fallen a long way since the 1920s, when President Calvin Coolidge carried a pet raccoon named Rebecca around his neck and gave her the run of the White House.

Raccoons are fierce when they have to be—"I've seen a male raccoon teach a German shepherd to climb trees," writes Oregon naturalist Jim Anderson—so be sure to secure your trash, keep your pet food and cats inside, and block entries to your basement, porch, and other areas. Otherwise, a clever bandit might arrive at night, possibly walking on two legs.

ID tips: About 10-25 pounds with that famous black mask over their eyes and dark rings around the tail.

Locations: Relatively common and well distributed all over, including at Sauvie Island, Forest Park, and Jackson Bottom Wetlands Preserve.

> **"As a people we Euro-Americans came here busting woods and taming rivers. Now that we've mostly done that, our sense of identity hinges on what we have left of woods and rivers. We could easily lose what is unique and beautiful about this place. Or we could learn to coexist with the creatures and features of the wild."** — Robin Cody in *Wild in the City*

Striped Skunk *(Mephitis mephitis)*

We've got it all wrong on skunks, focusing as we do on the unholy stink they occasionally release instead of on the everyday benefits they provide. Skunks are not at all aggressive, and they help us out by eating many garden troublemakers, from beetles and crickets to beetle grubs and cutworms, as well as larger prey including mice, moles, and rats.

While most wild animals try to blend in to their surroundings, Pepé Le Pews do their best to announce exactly where they are, in hopes that we and other animals will be smart enough to leave them alone. If we fail to pay heed, they'll spray an oily musk that will stink up its target for days. Their famously potent defense system doesn't work so well against the threat of onrushing vehicles, leading to the smelly roadkill we all know too well.

Fear not! Skunks prefer not to spray; they have limited "ammo" and it can take a week to reload. Photo: Sue Anderson

Trouble arises when skunks take refuge or form dens under houses, sheds, and porches. You can try to wait them out (they'll eventually move on) or contact the local Audubon Society for other options. As with other wild animals, prevention is best; avoid leaving food outside and block entries to your basement and other dark, quiet places that skunks might view as promising locations for a den.

ID tips: They have black bodies with two bold white stripes down their backs.

Such highly visible animals tend to have very good defense systems. Photo: Sue Anderson

Locations: Nocturnal and rarely seen, but they're found in a variety of habitats, including streambanks and forested areas at Sauvie Island, Forest Park, and Tryon Creek State Natural Area.

FUN FACT

Great horned owls are one of the few animals to prey on skunks. Not surprisingly, the owls do not have a well-developed sense of smell. Also not surprisingly, great horned owls and their nests sometimes smell really, really bad.

WEASELS

Weasels (*Mustela* spp.)

It's funny how we pick and choose certain animals to dislike. You wouldn't want to be skunked in a game or badgered on the witness stand—and you certainly wouldn't want to be called a weasel. It might be worth thinking about why, in the weasel's case, there's such acrimony directed toward a whip-smart, athletic animal that helps control rodent populations (you definitely don't want to be called a rat).

This long-tailed weasel walked right into the photographer's campsite. Photo: Alan St. John

One reason weasels aren't so beloved as, say, guinea pigs, is that they're ferocious hunters. Both long-tailed (*M. frenata*) and short-tailed (*M. erminea*) have thin fur and a high metabolism, so they have to work their brushy tails off to hunt and kill enough food—about 40 percent of their body weight each day. That's why they race through meadows, scale trees, and squirm through rock piles in a never-ending search for mice, squirrels, and other prey.

ID tips: Long-tailed are about 12–22 in. long (with tail of 3–6 in.); short-tailed are about 7–13 in. long (with 1–3 in. tail). Look for a long body and neck, short legs, black-tipped tails, and a flattened, triangular head.

Locations: Relatively common on city fringes, usually near water. Long-tailed prefer forests, while short-tailed prefer meadows, forest edges, and other places with voles and mice. Hotspots include Forest Park, Tryon Creek State Natural Area, and Smith and Bybee Wetlands.

Mink resemble river otters but are smaller, with a pointed snout. Photo: Phil Nosler

They're not the most agile of weasels, until they're in the water. Photo: Dave Rein

American Mink (*Neovison vison*)

While their fellow weasels are better runners and climbers, American mink have cornered the market on streams and rivers. They're svelte and semiaquatic, with webbed feet that help them dive to depths of 10 feet to snag a fish or muskrat.

The word "mink" comes from the Swedish *menk*, a charming term that means "the stinking animal from Finland." They win the award for foulest-smelling weasel thanks to anal glands that release a musk said to be as bad—or possibly worse—than that of a skunk (please report back). They're still trapped in Oregon and raised for their fur on mink farms.

ID tips: About 18–28 in. long (with tail). Glossy brown to blackish overall, with white spots on the chin and chest and a tapered tail. They're much smaller than river otters and have pointed snouts.

Locations: They prefer forested areas near water, including Smith and Bybee Wetlands, Sauvie Island, Oaks Bottom Wildlife Refuge, and Jackson Bottom Wetlands Preserve.

North American River Otter *(Lontra canadensis)*

There are three things to know when you see river otters in and along Portland waterways. One is that they're highly susceptible to environmental pollution, so when you see them close to the city, it suggests our efforts to restore and maintain water quality are succeeding.

Two is that we should be grateful for past and current efforts to protect populations of these and other wild animals. The river otter—a large member of the weasel family—is common enough now that we could easily forget how they were nearly wiped out by the early American fur trade. Their populations only rebounded with the help of habitat management, reintroductions, and limits on otter "harvest" (though they're still trapped).

Those long whiskers help them detect prey in murky water. Photo: Dave Rein

The third thing to know when you see river otters is that you should sit right down and watch them because they put on the best wild animal show in Portland. Scientists argue over whether river otters engage in something we can call play, but see what you think as they bodysurf in river rapids, turn somersaults, balance floating sticks on their noses, and drop pebbles in the water and dive down to retrieve them on their noses.

They can swim faster than the fastest humans. Photo: John Williams

You'll frequently see river otters in groups because they're much more social than their weasel kin. Adult males hang out in bachelor groups of a dozen or more, and family groups often have "helpers," including juveniles, yearlings, and unrelated adults. Let's hope we continue seeing large numbers cavorting in the Portland area.

ID tips: 3–4.5 ft. long (with tail). To distinguish them from other animals, look for the thick, tapered tail that's one-third their body length, and note that otters are much bigger than mink and stouter than beavers.

Locations: Fairly common in area watersheds, including Sauvie Island, Jackson Bottom Wetlands Preserve, and Smith and Bybee Wetlands.

BEAVERS & SIMILAR RODENTS

An eager beaver heading for the water. Photo: Dave Rein

American Beaver *(Castor Canadensis)*

No animal has lined more pockets and more hats than the American beaver. Oregon's original lumberjacks are the reason Euro-American settlers came here in the first place, and they continue to shape the wild world around us in broadly beneficial ways. So, yes, with all due respect to Ducks fans, the Beaver State got it right in naming the beaver our state animal and placing its visage on our state flag.

Pond Jovi's teeth never stop growing. Photo: Kim Elton

Dam it!

If you care about water issues in Oregon, you have to care about the American beaver, which author Ben Goldfarb describes as "the animal that doubles as an ecosystem." The bucktoothed builders cut down willow, cottonwood, alder, and other thin trees and drag them into waterways to slowly dam them up, spreading water out and slowing it down so plants and animals can squeeze out more use.

Beaver-created ponds and wetlands provide a nearly endless "stream" of benefits. They sponge up floodwaters, reduce erosion, filter out pollutants, stabilize streambanks, expand shelter for young fish (including threatened and endangered salmon and steelhead), and provide habitat for just about every wild animal you can think of.

The dam-building compulsion runs deep in busy beavers, which don't need a STEM-focused curriculum to learn how to engineer their environment. Research has shown that the mere sound of a babbling brook will send beavers into a flurry of stick stacking on top of the stereo making the noise.

Rodent gold

Europeans nearly trapped their own beaver to extinction because they couldn't get enough of the animal's fur and castoreum. The latter is an oily brown anal excretion that adds a musky depth to perfumes and used to be part of the "natural vanilla flavor" in ice creams and other foods that you may never want to eat again.

In the mid-1800s, Europeans were thrilled to "discover" about 60 million beavers in the New World. After decimating beaver populations in the eastern U.S., fur trappers headed west to get rich off the remaining hairy banknotes, pillaging Columbia River tributaries. The Hudson's Bay Company alone auctioned three million pelts from 1853 to 1877, and total populations dropped to an estimated 100,000. To avoid further losses, Oregon banned beaver trapping from 1899 to 1918, but it's been allowed ever since. From 2000 to 2015, 54,000 beavers were killed in the state.

Pelts to pests to partners

Beavers are a lot like us: They're intelligent, they like to live in fertile valleys, and they shape their environment to suit their interests—which makes it not at all surprising that conflicts arise. It's certainly much easier to be a beaver believer when they're not cutting down your trees, turning your backyard creek into a wetland area, or flooding your basement.

Not-so-subtle signs of beaver activity.
Photo: Tracy Aue

Fortunately, many homeowners and agencies are finding creative ways to live with our favorite rodents. We can landscape with plants that don't appeal to them, protect trees with fences, insert flow diverters to lower their ponds, or have the beavers moved someplace else where they can use their superpowers for good.

In other words, we can find ways to live alongside our state animal. And in doing so, we can allow beavers to make both urban and rural environments healthier places for wild animals as well as humans to thrive.

ID tips: Adults are 3-4 ft. long, 35 pounds and up (larger than nutria). They're chunky animals with reddish-brown to black fur, but the real giveaway, if you can see it, is their wide, paddle-like tail. They're rarely seen during the day.

Locations: Fairly common along area rivers, streams, and other year-round waterways. Look for dams, dens, felled trees, and runways where they've dragged trees to the water at sites including Jackson Bottom Wetlands Preserve, Smith and Bybee Wetlands, Sauvie Island, and Oaks Bottom Wildlife Refuge.

Muskrats can swim backward and forward—they even mate underwater. Photo: Buddy Mays

Common Muskrat *(Ondatra zibethicus)*

Can we get some muskrat love? To some, the muskrat is a poor man's beaver—a smaller version of our state animal that's not as attractive or compelling. But to many Indigenous people, the muskrat is a lucky and powerful animal sometimes credited with creating the world by bringing up a mouthful of mud from the depths of the sea.

Muskrats aren't undersized beavers but rather oversized voles (their cousin) that have adapted to the life aquatic by developing webbed feet and long, rudder-like tails. They can stay underwater for at least 15 minutes, swim backward and forward, and eat while submerged (their lips seal behind their incisors). They also mate underwater, or "do the jitterbug out in muskrat land," as the song would have it.

Although they don't construct dams, muskrats build lodges that are as complex as that of beavers, made entirely of vegetation (not sticks), with separate sleeping chambers for each family member. Turtles, frogs, snakes, and birds rest and nest in those lodges, and our native muskrats also create open water for wildlife by eating cattails, sedges, and other riparian plants.

ID tips: They're reddish-brown, with tawny-to-black guard hairs. Muskrats are about a foot long, much smaller than beavers and nutria. Their rat-like tail is nearly as long as their body, vertically flattened, and mostly naked. When they swim on the surface, they swing their tail back and forth like a rudder.

Locations: Uncommon, likely due to nutria, but look for them near slow-moving water, especially in marshy areas with cattails, such as at Smith and Bybee Wetlands and Fernhill Wetlands.

They're larger than muskrats and have more noticeable ears. Photo: Tracy Aue

Nutria (*Myocastor coypus*)

Let us hearken back to the 1930s to 1950s, when entrepreneurial Oregonians were tempted by advertisements for these "gold nuggets in fur." A century after decimating populations of our native beaver, here was a new opportunity to get rich quick off another animal, this time a "Rodent of Unusual Size" originally imported from South America. What could possibly go wrong?

Hundreds of Oregonians took the bait from sketchy organizations like the Purebred Nutria Association, paying up to $1,000 a pop for breeding pairs of these beaver lookalikes. Eventually, Oregon boasted more than 600 nutria farms. But then the fur industry declined, nutria meat never exactly caught on, and nutria farmers released their rat-like animals into local waterways—which is why Oregon's freshwater marshes are now said to have the highest density of nutria in the world.

They tear out plants with those dexterous forepaws. Photo: Tracy Aue

Nutria do not provide the same benefits as native beavers and muskrats. They cause a lot of damage by gorging on wetland plants and creating burrows that collapse banks and dikes. They also feast on crops, displace native animals like muskrats, and transport parasites and pathogens to other animals (including us). The encouraging thing is that we've learned our lesson about importing exotic animals for the sake of short-term economic gains ... right?

ID tips: Non-native. At up to 2.5 ft. long (with tail) and 20 pounds, they're smaller than beavers and bigger than muskrats. Their muzzle is covered with coarse white hair, and their tail is round, hairy, and pointed at the tip. Their hind legs are longer than their front legs, so they look hunched on land.

Locations: More common than we'd like at riverbanks, wetlands, and related areas, including at Sauvie Island, Tryon Creek State Natural Area, Fernhill Wetlands, and Jackson Bottom Wetlands Preserve.

BATS

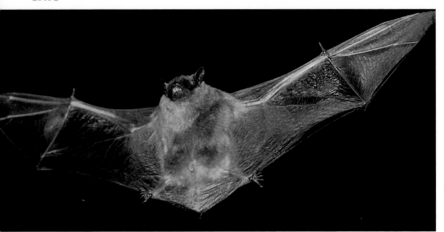

Myotis *means "mouse-eared." Photo: Jim Anderson*

Little Brown Myotis (*Myotis lucifugus*)

If a bat accidentally entered your home, would your response be to scream, throw a blanket over your head, and crawl madly toward an exit while whimpering and cursing? If so, you're not alone (I've seen it happen).

We've been told for centuries that bats are unclean (the Bible), devilish (Dante), witch-associated (Shakespeare), blood-sucking vampires (Bram Stoker). I don't know if it will get you out from under your blanket, but Oregon's 15 bat species eat insects, not blood or even fruit, and less than one-tenth of one percent of all bats carry rabies. Despite their terrible reputation, they're one of the most beneficial of all our wild neighbors.

The little brown myotis is one of the more abundant and widespread bats in Portland. During warm months, sit near a waterway at sunset to watch them flying about and sometimes swooping down for a sip of water. They also roost in barns and other human structures, so you might run across them; if so, see if you can't overcome the urge to duck and run.

ID tips: Body is about 2.5–4 in. long. Backs are brown and underparts are paler and grayish. Typical wingspan is about 9–11 in. Ears are small, black, and rounded.

Locations: Common in buildings and at just about any natural area with a pond, including Oaks Bottom Wildlife Refuge, Kelley Point Park, Commonwealth Lake Park, and Sauvie Island.

BAT FACTS

- Worldwide, there are about 1,000 bat species; 15 live in Oregon.
- Blind as a bat? Most bats can see at least as well as us.
- Bats are the only mammals that can fly.
- They can live up to 30 years.
- They can eat 600 insects an hour—and they routinely consume over half their body weight every night.

Townsend's Big-eared Bat (*Corynorhynus townsendii*)

The Townsend's big-eared bat isn't at all common these days, which makes it the perfect species to highlight the similar plight of many bat species.

You may have heard about white-nose syndrome, a deadly fungus that has decimated bat populations in the northeastern United States and has been documented in Washington. Oregon's bats are going to be in a world of hurt if the fungus gets here, so be sure to wear clean clothes and shoes when entering caves to ensure that you don't transmit the fungus.

Put up a bat house to attract insect eaters like this one.
Photo: Jim Anderson

White-nose syndrome is not the only problem facing bats. Townsend's big-eared bats are cave dwellers that need to hibernate without disruption. Winter disturbances are probably one reason these bats' populations are declining sharply across the western United States, including in Oregon, where they're classified as a sensitive species in the critical category.

ID tips: Body is about 4 in. long, and those large ears are tough to miss. Body is gray, brown, or black, and wingspan is about 12.5 in.

Locations: Rare, but they can still be found at a few locations such as Sauvie Island.

They don't drink blood, but they do eat insects.
Photo: Jim Anderson

FOUR WAYS TO HELP BATS

In addition to decontaminating your clothing after visiting places where bats roost, these are easy ways to help bats:

- **Avoid caves and mines where bats might be hibernating.**
- **Build a bat box, which will also help you control your insect populations.**
- **Go pesticide-free, replacing toxic quick fixes with natural alternatives like soapy water.**
- **Leave standing dead trees, or snags, that provide habitat for bats and other species.**

MICE, VOLES, & RATS

Look for perky ears and whitish bellies. Photo: Jim Anderson

Deer Mouse *(Peromyscus maniculatus)*

Portland writer Beverly Cleary has helped lots of kids (me included) turn their fear of mice into curiosity. But even if you like mice, you might wonder why there have to be so dang many of them scurrying around forests, parks, and backyards. The simple answer is that just about every predator larger than mice feeds on mice, which makes their prolific procreative powers essential to the circle of life.

Deer mice are the most widespread and abundant small mammal in North America, although their populations fluctuate annually. The 2012 Forest Park Wildlife Report found that deer mice made up two-thirds—two-thirds!—of the diets of the park's barred owls, great horned owls, and coyotes. The report also found that when there are lots of deer mice, northern pygmy-owls produce more young, illustrating just how valuable this one rodent is to the success of other species.

Important as they are in the wild, be very careful around deer mice because some carry a deadly and untreatable strain of hantavirus that can be transmitted to humans if we touch or inhale tiny particles of their urine, feces, or nesting material (as when cleaning out an attic or barn). The mouse in your house is likely a house mouse (*Mus musculus*) that's not known to carry hantavirus, but take precautions regardless.

ID tips: 4–6 in. long (with tail). Color, tail length, and markings vary. In general, their backs and sides are gray to dark brown, their bellies and feet are white, and their tails have hair (house mice have darker bellies and scaly, hairless tails). Their ears are essentially naked and usually held erect and directed forward.

Locations: Common across Oregon, nesting in burrows, rock crevices, logs, woodpiles, and more. They're nocturnal so they're not often seen, but they live in just about every park and in buildings near fields and forests.

> **"Ralph really felt sorry for the boy, hampered as he was by his youth and his mother."** — Beverly Cleary, *The Mouse and the Motorcycle*

Likely a creeping vole, the smallest vole around.
Photo: Phil Nosler

Voles *(Various* spp.*)*

Voles are little rodents easily mistaken for their mice relatives—the main difference to note at a glance is that voles have much shorter tails. Voles also tend to have smaller eyes and ears than mice, and they're active day and night whereas mice are usually nocturnal. Some voles are called meadow or field mice, but that's a dirty trick meant to confuse us.

Our native creeping vole *(M. oregoni)* is the smallest vole in the state. The other common native, the Townsend's vole *(M. townsendii)*, is the largest vole in North America, a two-story-tall monster that wreaks havoc across the continent (just kidding; they're up to about nine inches long). Townsend's are associated with moist habitats where they're noted for their ability to swim, dive, and build underwater entrances to their burrows.

ID tips: Creeping voles are 5–6 in. long, including their notably short tail. They have tiny eyes, gray to brown or nearly black fur mixed with yellowish hairs, and a gray or white belly. Townsend's voles are about 6.5–9 in. long (with tail) and have prominent ears. Vole species are tough to tell apart, even for experts.

Locations: Common at sites including Forest Park, Tryon Creek State Natural Area, and Sauvie Island.

Woodrats *(Neotoma* spp.*)*

Unlike non-native Norway rats, dusky-footed (*N. fuscipes*) and bushy-tailed (*N. cinerea*) woodrats are native rodents that have roamed this continent for at least 40,000 years, charming folks like John Muir, providing a boon to scientists, and supplying many other native animals with a convenient food source.

Check out those big ears! Photo: Buddy Mays

Woodrats are also called packrats because they're hoarders that stole flip-flops from my friend's porch and have a special fondness for shiny treasures, from gold watches to spoons to tinfoil. You can see their collected treasures in their nests, or middens, which can be 10 feet tall, added on to by generation after generation.

Some of the oldest and largest woodrat middens are highly valued by scientists who use the preserved contents to reconstruct thousands of years of changes in plants, animals, and the climate.

Packrats are among our more dapper rodents. Photo: Jim Anderson

ID tips: They're nocturnal so you're more likely to see (and smell) their middens, but they're handsome rodents with brownish coats and lighter bellies. They have big eyes, rounded ears, and tails about as long as their bodies. The dusky-footed's tail is sparsely covered with short fur; the bushy-tailed has, as you'd expect, a bushy tail covered in thick fur.

Locations: Rarely seen but they live in forest and other habitats, including at Sauvie Island and Oxbow Regional Park.

"Once, far back in the high Sierra, they stole my snow-goggles, the lid of my teapot, and my aneroid barometer. ... [When another started dragging off my ice hatchet], I threw bits of bark at him and made a noise to frighten him, but he stood scolding and chattering back at me, his fine eyes shining with an air of injured innocence." — John Muir, *Our National Parks*

They can slip into any space wider than their skulls. Photo: Andy and Helen Holt

Norway Rat *(Rattus norvegicus)*

Norway rats (aka brown rats) originated in Asia, not Norway, but they're now global citizens, living alongside people on every continent but Antarctica. They're the most common rats in the Portland area, in part because they reproduce like mad.

Females give birth to up to five litters a year, gestating for only three weeks, and all of the up to 14 rats in each litter reach sexual maturity within about 10 weeks. Many of those rats provide meals for hungry hawks and owls, but they also displace woodrats and other native wildlife species.

Brace yourself for this next part: Portlanders have been known to find Norway rats inside toilet bowls or hopping out of them to Netflix and chill. The rats are terrific swimmers that live in the city's main sewer system. After heavy rains, they're sometimes driven out of the main sewer line, into the lines that run to homes. There is no good news here, but you might be relieved to know that many of the rats drown once they reach the toilet bowl.

I think we all suspect that rats will rule the world once we're gone, or before, but you can take simple steps to slow their takeover. Keep your own nest clean by putting garbage in firmly closed bins and rodent-proofing home compost piles. It's also a good idea to keep your toilet seats down.

ID tips: About 13–20 in. long (including 6–10 in. tail), weighing up to a pound. Body is brown to gray, lighter underneath. Tail is bare and tapers to a point. Black rats have darker bodies and a tail that's longer than the body.

Locations: Common wherever people live, including in the urban core and natural areas. And sewer lines.

Shrew-mole photos are hard to find! The outward-facing front claws here suggest this is likely a mole, not a shrew-mole.
Photo: Ken R. Schneider

American Shrew-Mole (*Neurotrichus gibbsii*)

Look, I get it: You want your shrews to be shrews and your moles to be moles. But the American shrew-mole—the most commonly seen mole-like animal in Portland—steadfastly resists your binary constructions with its dense, shrew-like fur and mole-like head and teeth.

While moles' forepaws face outward as if they're ready to swim the breast stroke, shrew-moles place their feet flat on the ground. That's not ideal for digging—which is why you'll see shrew-moles in places with loose soil, where the digging is easy—but the tradeoff is that they're more agile than moles when they walk aboveground.

Like the several species of moles found in Portland, shrew-moles dig shallow tunnels just beneath the soil that are reused by all sorts of other animals. They also build permanent homes up to a couple feet underground—and, yes, shrew-moles and moles are the animals that churn up soil in your yard. Mole mounds are rarely appreciated, but their digging tills the soil in a helpful way, and shrew-moles and moles mostly eat earthworms and insects, not your plants.

ID tips: About 4.5 in. long (with tail). Blackish fur is dense and soft. Nose is flat and elongated. They don't have external ears, and their tail is about half as long as their body. Forefeet palms don't face out like that of moles.

Locations: Relatively common in forested, damp, or bushy areas, such as Forest Park, Jackson Bottom Wetlands Preserve, Tualatin Hills Nature Park, and Sauvie Island.

A vagrant shrew. By size, shrews have heavier brains than humans.
Photo: William Leonard

Shrews *(Sorex* spp.)

Portland writer Brian Doyle once joked that "a shrew is like a mouse with a bad temper." Shrews aren't known to be meaner than mice (although they look like they might be), but they are very different animals.

Unlike mice and voles, which are rodents that eat a largely vegetarian diet, shrews are classified as insectivores, but their varied diet also includes snails, small snakes, and even birds. Shrews tend to be smaller than mice, with pointier noses, smaller eyes, and shorter and furrier tails. Perhaps most strangely for a mammal, shrews have venom tucked into the grooves of their teeth.

The Forest Park Wildlife Report found that three-quarters of all shrews in the park were Trowbridge's shrews *(S. trowbridgii),* but there are also marsh shrews *(S. bendirii)* and vagrant shrews *(S. vagrans)* across Portland. The latter use high-frequency vocalizations—bat-like echolocation, in other words—to orient themselves and overcome their poor vision and sense of smell. Mice might look friendlier, but they can't do that.

ID tips: About 3–6 in. long. Look for a pointy snout and usually a brown body with varying underside colors. It's often necessary to look at the teeth to distinguish one shrew species from another, so let's leave that to the experts.

Locations: Common in forested areas across Portland, such as Forest Park, Tryon Creek State Natural Area, Marquam Nature Park, and Sauvie Island.

FUN FACT

Like hummingbirds, shrews live their lives in hyperdrive. They don't hibernate, their heart rates can reach 1,200 beats per minute, and they hardly sleep since they need to eat every few hours to keep their tiny bodies warm.

CHIPMUNKS

Almost all chipmunk species live in North America.
Photo: Tracy Aue

Townsend's Chipmunk
(Tamias townsendii)

Good luck getting a photo of a Townsend's chipmunk. Like most chipmunks—which are basically small ground squirrels—this one spends most of its time scurrying around like it's late for the bus. You would too, if you had to collect and store enough food to get you through Portland's long winters. Fortunately, our one native chipmunk has cheek pouches to help it carry a hundred or so seeds at a time.

ID tips: A large chipmunk (about 14 in. long, including tail), which is to say a very small squirrel. Their backs are striped, and telltale stripes run through their eyes. Their tails are grayish above and reddish below.

Locations: Not common in Portland but found in forested areas like Tryon Creek State Natural Area and Forest Park.

CHIPMUNK OR SQUIRREL?

Chipmunks are generally smaller than squirrels and have light-colored stripes on the head and particularly through the eyes. If there are stripes through the eyes, it's a chipmunk. If not, it's a squirrel.

GROUND SQUIRRELS

Note the dark saddle between the shoulders.
Photo: Claire Weiser

California Ground Squirrel
(Otospermophilus beecheyi)

California ground squirrels aren't widespread in Portland, but where you spot one of these natives, you can be sure lots more are nearby. They're homebodies that form large colonies and live in and near their communal burrows, each squirrel maintaining its own entrance.

Farmers don't appreciate the free tilling service provided by ground squirrels, but raptors, raccoons, coyotes, and other animals depend on them for food. In other regions, rattlesnakes try to make a meal of California ground squirrels, but the squirrels fight back in an ingenious way, sending blood to the end of their long tail and waving it about in an apparent attempt to redirect the snake's infrared sensors.

ID tips: Large ground squirrels with a distinctive dark patch on the upper back, white speckles on their mostly gray fur, and a tail about 6 in. long.

Locations: They live in a variety of habitats, including pastures, grain fields, rocky ridges, forested slopes, and oak savannas like those on Sauvie Island.

TREE SQUIRRELS

Populations are declining as we cut down mature forests. Photo: Mark Lundgren

Douglas Squirrel (*Tamiasciurus douglasii*)

Famed naturalist John Muir admired the Douglas Squirrel so much that he devoted a whole chapter of his book *The Mountains of California* to what he called "the squirrel of squirrels." After encounters with everything from polar bears to alligators, Muir described this small, common rodent as "without exception, the wildest animal I ever saw—a fiery, sputtering little bolt of life."

Also known as chickarees, Douglas squirrels are typically found in the canopies of conifers, looking down and giving us a piece of their mind. Muir further described this especially vocal tree squirrel as "the

"The wildest animal I ever saw."
Photo: Tracy Aue

mockingbird of squirrels, pouring forth mixed chatter and song like a perennial fountain; barking like a dog, screaming like a hawk, chirping like a blackbird or a sparrow."

Douglas squirrels have a lot to say because they're defending territories that contain the fruits, nuts, mushrooms, and other vegetation they need to survive. When we pass by on the trail, we're effectively invading their pantry. Along with listening for their scolds from a nearby branch, look for lots of ripe cones on the ground or heaps of seeds and cone scales that indicate you're trespassing in Douglas squirrel territory.

ID tips: Coat color varies, but in Portland they typically have an orangish belly and dark reddish-brown back. Also note the light-colored ring around each eye and the dark, bushy tail that often arches over their back.

Locations: Look and listen for them wherever there are conifers, including in Forest Park and Tryon Creek State Natural Area.

If you see a closed cone on the ground, chances are it's the work of a Douglas squirrel. In one minute, they can fell up to 12 Douglas-fir cones or 30 smaller cones.

Eastern Gray Squirrel (*Sciurus carolinensis*)

Populations are concentrated in the Willamette Valley. Photo: Phil Nosler

Eastern gray squirrels are healthy contributors to the local ecology of the eastern U.S., where each squirrel buries thousands of nuts taken from oaks, hickories, beeches, and other trees. Some caches get eaten and others become the next generation of trees. Red foxes, hawks, owls, rattlesnakes, and other predators also depend on the squirrels as a food source.

But Portland is not in the eastern U.S., and these squirrels cause a lot of problems here. Since they were brought west about a century ago, they've helped force out our native western gray squirrels (although, to be fair, we didn't help by cutting down the evergreens and oaks western grays prefer). Eastern grays are perhaps most despised in Britain, where they've decimated populations of their native red squirrels, which Beatrix Potter fans know as Squirrel Nutkin.

Eastern gray squirrels have exceptional senses of smell, better vision than our own, and enough ingenuity to outsmart most of us who try to keep them away from our bird feeders. Contact the Audubon Society of Portland for tips on how to reduce conflicts.

ID tips: At about 9–11 in. long, they have smaller bodies than western grays, as well as smaller ears and a shorter tail. They generally have a pale-gray coat with a noticeable reddish-brown wash on the face, back, and tail. Look for the white belly (not orangish-brown like on the fox squirrel).

Locations: All over the city, where they eat fruits, nuts, caterpillars, bird food, and anything else they can find.

Eastern Fox Squirrel (*Sciurus niger*)

They're redder overall than eastern gray squirrels. Photo: Calibas CC

Eastern gray squirrels were the first to populate most western cities, but the larger eastern fox squirrel is an up-and-comer. Together, the two non-natives are the most commonly seen squirrel species in Portland.

In the mid-1800s, squirrels weren't a common sight in cities—which might sound like a good thing, except the cities weren't terribly appealing to people, either. Frederick Law Olmsted popularized the idea of beautifying cities by creating idealized wilderness areas, such as Central Park in New York City. To that end, 68 squirrels were released in Central Park in 1877; six years later, there were 1,500.

I don't know of any strategies being considered to rid Portland of eastern fox squirrels (in Britain, they've introduced predators like pine martens). We may simply need to accept that it's our fault for bringing eastern squirrels in as pets and planting the deciduous trees they, and we, love. Now they're here to stay—in our backyards, trees, bird feeders, attics, and insulation.

ID tips: A large squirrel with reddish-brown coat, tan or rust-colored underside, and somewhat flattened tail. Look for the orange tip of the tail to firmly distinguish it from a gray squirrel.

Locations: In natural areas like Sauvie Island, as well as in urban areas.

They're slow and in constant danger on the ground. Photo: Carolyn Waissman

Western Gray Squirrel (*Sciurus griseus*)

If you need another reason to work to maintain, restore, and expand Portland's native oak habitats, consider the plight of the most beautiful and shyest of all our squirrels, the acorn-loving western gray.

Once the dominant squirrel in Portland, western gray populations are declining across Oregon, and they're on the state's sensitive-vulnerable list in the Willamette Valley. They've also been listed on Washington's threatened species list since 1993.

It's thought that western grays need about six acres of oak and conifer habitat to collect enough food and nesting material, which highlights the value of protecting the wild areas around Portland where this native squirrel still lives.

ID tips: At about 15 in. long (plus a 10 in. tail), they're the largest tree squirrels you'll see. Their silvery-gray coats, white bellies, and elegantly plumed tails lack any of the reddish color seen on eastern gray and fox squirrels.

Locations: They prefer oak savannas and mixed woodlands, so you'll find them at oak-rich sites including Sauvie Island, Cooper Mountain Nature Park, and Canemah Bluff Nature Park in Oregon City.

> "We cannot, of course, save the world because we do not have authority over its parts. We can serve the world though. That is everyone's calling, to lead a life that helps."
> — Barry Lopez in *Portland Magazine*

FLYING SQUIRRELS

Those big eyes help them see (and fly) at night. Photo: Alex Badyaev

Northern Flying Squirrel (*Glaucomys sabrinus*)

Look up in the sky on a moonlit summer night, and you might spot this squirrel soaring high above the city, wings spread wide, a mouthful of lichens dangling from its mouth as it dodges owls on its long flight home.

Nah, just kidding. The ambitiously named northern flying squirrel doesn't so much fly as float, or hang-glide, from tree to tree in a spectacular display. Long, fur-lined skin folds beneath their legs enable the "flights," which can cover hundreds of feet as the squirrels twist, turn, and spiral to avoid obstacles.

Most people have never seen a northern flying squirrel—and that is as it should be. They're nocturnal denizens of forests, where they perform the usual squirrel services of spreading fungal spores and plant seeds and serving as food for owls and other predators.

ID tips: Not seen during the day, but they have large, lustrous black eyes, a yellowish belly, and loose folds of skin that stretch from foreleg to hind leg on each side of their small body.

Locations: In areas such as Forest Park and Tryon Creek State Natural Area.

OTHER

Mountain Beaver (*Aplodontia rufa*)

Mountain beavers are also called boomers, which doesn't make a lick of sense since they're not closely related to American beavers and rarely utter a sound, much less a boom.

Relatively few people have seen these fern-eating furballs because they're nocturnal, live only in a narrow strip from California up to British Columbia, and spend most of their lives underground diligently digging their long tunnel systems.

Mountain beavers are descended from similar but smaller rodents that shared the planet with sabre-tooth cats, three-toed horses, and other ancient species. Today's species thrives despite being eaten by coyotes, bobcats, hawks, and owls. It helps that they're savage fighters with large front teeth, which might be why owls are occasionally missing toes.

Probably you and I will never see one of these loaf-sized rodents—although you might spot their burrows in Forest Park, at Mt. Hood, or in the Coast Range or Cascade Mountains—but it'd sure be cool if we did.

Consider yourself fortunate if you see a boomer.
Photo: Jim Anderson

ID tips: Chubby rodent (about 3 pounds), with a mole-like mug only a mother could love. They're about 1 ft. long, with almost no tail. Their face is heavily whiskered, and they have long claws and gray, brown, reddish, or blackish fur.

Locations: Rarely seen, but they've been known to live and breed in moist parts of Forest Park and at Canemah Bluff Nature Park in Oregon City.

They have small ears and eyes, and big claws for digging. Photo: Jerry Kirkhart

Pocket Gophers (*Thomomys* spp.*)*

Yes, gopher mounds are a nuisance in lawns, gardens, and agricultural fields, but before you go all Caddyshack on them, take a closer look at these little rodents and how they help the environment.

In Portland, you may well have walked on top of both Camas and western (aka Mazama) pocket gopher tunnels. Camas pocket gophers (*T. bulbivorous)* are common in urban orchards and farm fields, and much smaller western pocket gophers (*T. Mazama)* are found in open areas in the mountains and foothills of the Willamette Valley.

What good are these native pocket gophers? Well, their digging aerates soil, which encourages plant growth and slows water runoff. A single gopher is said to be able to bring over two tons of soil to the surface each year. All that churning mixes subsoil with topsoil, and reportedly played a key role in restoring green life to post-eruption Mt. St. Helens. It's also said to help alfalfa crops grow larger and healthier. Plus, gophers are a valued food source for many bigger animals.

ID tips: Squat, brownish rodents with thick tails that are almost hairless, long front claws, protruding incisors, and whiskers for navigating underground.

Locations: They till soil in backyards, golf courses, pastures, and natural areas including Sauvie Island and Forest Park.

Their panda-like ears are a redeeming feature. Photo: Mark R. Johnson

Virginia Opossum *(Didelphis virginiana)*

First, and least importantly, the correct word is "opossum," not "possum," when referring to this non-native, long-snouted animal. There are different animals on other continents that are the actual "possums."

Second, and most importantly, Virginia opossums are unusual and fascinating animals. They're the only marsupial in the United States—a 70-million-year-old relative of the kangaroo that lives in Portland! They're also the only animal besides humans and monkeys with a thumb-like opposable digit, which they use to climb trees. Don't even get me started on their forked penises, and yes, they sometimes do "play possum"—or "opossum"—by feigning death when threatened.

Opossum populations are believed to be declining in Portland. Although they're non-native, having originally been brought to Oregon in about 1915 as pets and a food source, they rarely transmit diseases to humans. Arguably, they do a lot of good in eating insects, mice, and especially ticks, but they can also be pests because they eat birds and other native animals.

ID tips: About the size of a housecat, with a triangular head, beady eyes, and a long, pointed nose. Grayish fur covers most of their body. Tail is hairless and rat-like.

Locations: Fairly common across the city, including in and around Forest Park, Tryon Creek State Natural Area, and Sauvie Island.

> **"... for everything in nature is lyrical in its ideal essence, tragic in its fate, and comic in its existence."** — George Santayana,
> *Soliloquies in England & Later Soliloquies*

REPTILES
LIZARDS

They're often seen atop boulders. Photo: Alan St. John

Western Fence Lizard *(Sceloporus occidentalis)*

Western fence lizards are the most common lizard in the Pacific Northwest, but they're also sun lovers that don't like urban areas or dense, wet forests. No surprise, then, that they're not very common in Portland.

If you get lucky and spot one, look for the fabulously blue patches on the bellies and throats of males. They're especially fun to watch when they flash those patches while performing pushups with their tiny T-rex arms. The display, intended to attract females and intimidate other males, closely resembles those you might see at some gyms in Portland.

A male with a blue belly and neck patches. Photo: Alan St. John

ID tips: About 7 in. long (with tail). Typically, their backs are dark with crossbars, often with white flecks. On males, look for blue on the throat and belly (the blue is dull or absent in females and juveniles).

Locations: Uncommon, but look for them basking on fence posts, rocks, or logs in sunny spots of oak woodlands, including at Sauvie Island and Cooper Mountain Nature Park.

Note the row of dark spots down the middle of the back. Photo: Alan St. John

Northern Alligator Lizard *(Elgaria coerulea)*

We may envision lizards as desert lovers, but they occupy a range of habitats—including cool, damp places like Portland. In the case of the northern alligator lizard, their preferred habitats range from the Oregon Coast (the only lizard you'll find there) to forested areas of the Willamette Valley.

Alligator lizards got their ambitious name from the fact that their scales are reinforced by bone, just as they are in alligators. Larger southern alligator lizards *(E. multicarinata)* display some alligator-like fierceness—as Oregon naturalist Jim Anderson notes, their diet is whatever will fit in their mouths, from bees and beetles to mice and baby gophers. Northern alligator lizards prefer to nosh on smaller fare such as insects, spiders, centipedes, and slugs.

ID tips: About 10 in. long (with tail). Their legs are short and their eyes are brown, not light in color like the southern alligator lizard's. Their back is usually brown, tan, olive, or grayish in color, with a row of dark spots down the middle. Look for pale-gray to white bellies, with no trace of the blue found on western fence lizards. Males have large triangular heads.

Locations: Look under logs and rocks in meadows, forest edges, and other sunny clearings. Populations are scattered around Portland, including at Sauvie Island and Powell Butte Nature Park.

> **"You will surely learn to like them, not only the bright ones, gorgeous as the rainbow, but the little ones, gray as lichened granite, and scarcely bigger than grasshoppers; and they will teach you that scales may cover as fine a nature as hair or feathers or anything tailored."**
> — John Muir, *Our National Parks*

SNAKES

Look for the yellowish stripe down the back. Photo: Alan St. John

Their stripes camouflage them in grassy areas. Photo: Alan St. John

Common Garter Snake *(Thamnophis sirtalis)*

There is nothing to fear from any of Portland's wild snakes—no rattles, no dangerous venom, no constricting of puppies. In the case of garter snakes, all they do is help us out by controlling populations of slugs, snails, rodents, and other small animals. The correct name is "garter," but you can think of them as "garden" snakes for the benefits they provide.

In Portland, most common garter snakes have a broad stripe, yellow to greenish-yellow, that runs down their back from stem to stern. Take a walk on a sunny day near any creek, lake, or other wet area to see and hear them slithering through the vegetation beside the trail.

ID tips: Up to about 4 ft. long with a darker head than body. Colors and patterns vary, but look for a wide yellow to greenish-yellow stripe down the back. Each side of the body usually has a row of orangish-red spots, and below that, a less vivid yellowish stripe.

Locations: Look for them near any area pond, lake, stream, or other waterway, including at Sauvie Island and Smith and Bybee Wetlands.

FUN FACT

It's thought that the word "garter" is either a corruption of the German word for garden *(garten)* or refers to the snakes' resemblance to the garters men used to wear to hold up their socks.

This one has an orangish stripe down the back. Photo: Alan St. John

Northwestern Garter Snake (*Thamnophis ordinoides*)

The Northwestern garter snake is another garter snake species you'll run across quite often in gardens and sunny clearings. Like common garter snakes, they come in a variety of colors, so don't be surprised if you see a red-striped snake—in Portland, that's a harmless garter snake, not a red racer or other species.

If you look closely at multiple garter snakes, you'll see that there are striped morphs as well as spotted morphs that lack a stripe down the back or have only a faint stripe. Studies have shown that striped morphs will flee when threatened—their stripes make it tough for predators to figure out the snake's speed and direction. Spotted morphs will instead hold still when threatened, likely in hopes that their spotted camouflage will enable them to avoid detection.

A reddish-orange morph. Photo: Alan St. John

ID tips: Adults are up to about 3 ft. long (shorter than common garter snakes, with a smaller head). Colors and patterns vary a lot, but the stripe down the middle of the back is usually wide, easy to see, and yellowish or red in color. For details, see Alan St. John's field guide *Reptiles of the Northwest*.

Locations: They're sometimes found near water, but they're mainly terrestrial, preferring brushy areas near forests. Look for them at Powell Butte Nature Park and Cooper Mountain Nature Park.

A yellow-striped morph. Photo: Alan St. John

It's easy to see how they got their name. Photo: Alan St. John

Rubber Boa (*Charina bottae*)

Yes, rubber boas are in the same family as boa constrictors and anacondas, but no, you have nothing to fear here. In fact, rubber boas are noted for being especially timid, gentle, and docile. They're pudgy-looking snakes that don't move fast and won't bite you.

When danger presents itself, rubber boas do what we've all done a time or two: They curl into a ball, conceal their heads from the world, and stick out their stubby tails as decoys (okay, maybe we don't do that last part).

Mild-mannered as they are, rubber boas have to eat to survive, so they use their constriction superpowers to subdue mice, shrews, and other small animals. They especially like to prey on infant rodents, sometimes using their hard-tipped tail to club the mother while they consume her infants. But, like I was saying, they're mostly very gentle animals.

ID tips: About 1.25–2.75 ft. long. Bodies are thick, with no stripes or other markings; they look like brown or grayish-brown rubber.

Locations: Rarely seen in the Portland area, in part because they spend so much time in rodent burrows and under rocks and logs, but they live in all sorts of habitats, especially forests.

This one's sticking its tail up as a decoy head. Photo: Alan St. John

TURTLES

Look for yellow stripes on their head and legs. Photo: Alan St. John

The colorful plastron. Photo: Alan St. John

Western Painted Turtle *(Chrysemys picta bellii)*

Painted turtles are America's turtle, a 15-million-year-old species found from sea to shining sea. As suggested by their name, painted turtles are especially colorful: Yellow stripes run along their neck and legs, and their gorgeous shell is greenish on top and a vibrant scarlet-red underneath.

The painted turtle's range in Oregon is limited to a narrow strip that runs north from the Salem area up to the Columbia River and then east. Portland is right in the heart of that range, and conservation efforts by the city, Metro, the Port of Portland, and others are ongoing, including measures to conserve and expand the wetland areas these turtles depend on. "Drain the swamp" may be a catchy political slogan, but it's the opposite of what the painted turtle and hundreds of other wetland-dependent species need right now.

ID tips: Shell is up to 10 in. long. Shell tops are olive-green to greenish-black and undersides (plastrons) are mostly red and beautifully patterned. Their legs and neck have yellow stripes, and their front feet have long claws.

Locations: Uncommon in sluggish water (marshy ponds, small lakes, slow-moving streams) with mucky bottoms, lots of vegetation, and logs for basking. To avoid having anyone collect them for pets, I'm avoiding giving specific locations.

SOME LIKE IT HOT

Turtle eggs—as well as those of alligators, crocodiles, and some lizards—develop into males or females depending on the temperature at which they're incubated. When temperatures are warmer (about 90 degrees Fahrenheit for red-eared sliders), eggs become females. With climate change heating things up, scientists are seeing some turtle populations skewing heavily female, which could lead to significant problems with reproduction.

Their beauty is humble, not flashy. Photo: Alan St. John

Western Pond Turtle *(Actinemys marmorata)*

Western pond turtles and western painted turtles are Portland's two native freshwater turtles. Of the two, it's safe to say the painted turtle got the better end of the stick when it comes to eye-catching good looks, but the pond turtle gets to live decades longer (up to 70 years).

At least half of all turtle species worldwide are in danger of extinction, and unfortunately the western pond turtle is among them. It's listed as a sensitive species in Oregon and endangered in Washington, where efforts are underway to restore habitat, remove invasive predators like bullfrogs, and rear quarter-sized hatchlings in captivity for later release.

ID tips: Shell is up to 9 in. long. The top of the shell is drab brown to nearly black, and the bottom is cream-colored to yellow with brown markings (not red as on the painted turtle). Their head and legs usually have some yellowish-white colors, but there are no stripes like on painted turtles and red-eared sliders.

Locations: Rare in streams, ponds, lakes, and wetlands. To avoid having anyone collect them for pets, I'm avoiding giving specific locations.

Photo: Mark Lundgren

DID YOU KNOW?

Western pond turtles like to bask on logs and rocks, but they're shy animals that will dive into the water if they see you coming (they can spot us at 100 yards). If you're quiet and patient, you might see one—or more than one, since they and other aquatic turtles stack one on top of the other when basking space is limited.

It's illegal to bring these non-native turtles into Oregon. Photo: Alan St. John

Red-eared Slider (*Trachemys scripta elegans*)

Sometimes I joke that my next pet will be a long-lived turtle because I can't bear the thought of burying another beloved cat or dog. Of course, this works both ways: Turtles may well outlive us, but that means we have to care for them for decades, even as they grow big as dinner plates and require large aquariums and constant maintenance.

Which leads us to the red-eared slider, which is native to the eastern U.S., not Oregon. Its other common name, "dime-store turtle," tells you how common it is as a pet (the Teenage Mutant Ninja Turtle craze made things worse).

When people tire of red-eared sliders, they sometimes release them into the wild, which is a problem because they introduce diseases and compete with our native turtles for food and habitat. They also lay their eggs a month earlier than native turtles, attracting predators that then prey on the nests of native species.

There's no red on the plastron, unlike on painted turtles. Photo: Alan St. John

ID tips: Shell is up to 14 in. long. Most have a distinctive red or orange patch behind each eye. The top of their shell is dark with a black-and-yellow line pattern. They have yellow or white stripes along their neck and legs. Unlike painted turtles, they have no red on the underside, or plastron, of their shell.

Locations: They sun themselves on logs in ponds, lakes, and other slow-moving waterways, including at Sauvie Island, Smith and Bybee Wetlands, Commonwealth Lake Park, and the Columbia Slough.

TREASURE HUNTS

I hope you enjoy reading about nature as much as I do, but the deeper pleasure is in experiencing what you've been reading about—the sound of sandhill cranes, the fuzzy feel of hazelnut leaves, the blue sea of common camas, the cucumber smell of an osoberry leaf. One of the wonderful things about living in Portland is that you can delight in all of those experiences, and so many more, just minutes from downtown.

This section highlights 10 parks and natural areas located both in the heart of Portland and to the east, west, north, and south of the city. You'll see photos of a couple dozen plants and animals that can be found at each location, as well as page numbers where you can learn more about each species.

These treasure hunts are meant to serve as a starting point for noticing, identifying, and appreciating the wild life located on either side of every trail in the city.

Map: Deb Quinlan, Deschutes GeoGraphics

1. **Cooper Mountain Nature Park**
2. **Fernhill Wetlands**
3. **Forest Park**
4. **Hoyt Arboretum**
5. **Mt. Tabor**
6. **Oaks Bottom Wildlife Refuge**
7. **Powell Butte Nature Park**
8. **Sauvie Island**
9. **Smith & Bybee Wetlands Natural Area**
10. **Tryon Creek State Natural Area**

Photo: John Williams

Photo: Tracy Aue

Photo: M.A. Willson

Photo: Tracy Aue

Photo: Steve Hersey

Photo: Tracy Aue

1. COOPER MOUNTAIN NATURE PARK

When you think about where to go to experience nature, southwest Beaverton probably isn't the first destination that springs to mind. But Cooper Mountain Nature Park will surprise you. It's one of the only places left in the Willamette Valley with upland prairie habitat and oak woodlands and savannas. Because of those rare habitats, it has rare species too, including checker lilies and western gray squirrels. Explore this park in spring or summer, and you'll wonder why you ever doubted Beaverton's natural wonders.

- Trails: 3.5 miles
- Dogs: No
- Accessibility: Limited
- Restrooms: Yes
- Steepness: Moderate

Pacific madrone
pg. 6

Ponderosa pine
pg. 8

Western crabapple
pg. 25

Mock-orange
pg. 33

Orange honeysuckle
pg. 34

Poison oak
pg. 39

Red-flowering currant
pg. 40

Western serviceberry
pg. 48

Western buttercup
pg. 79

Red columbine
pg. 91

Rosy plectritis
pg. 92

Oregon iris
pg. 95

Common camas
pg. 96

Lupines
pg. 97

Douglas's aster
pg. 102

Checker lily
pg. 103

Hutton's vireo
pg. 175

White-breasted nuthatch
pg. 186

Ruby-crowned kinglet
pg. 189

Swainson's thrush
pg. 190

Purple finch
pg. 195

Orange-crowned warbler
pg. 206

Yellow-rumped warbler
pg. 208

Lazuli bunting
pg. 211

Western Tiger Swallowtail
pg. 226

Julia Orangetip
pg. 227

Western gray squirrel
pg. 260

2. FERNHILL WETLANDS

Fernhill Wetlands lies a half-hour west of Portland, near Forest Grove, but it's worth the drive. November through March, you can see and hear thousands of waterfowl, and there are native plants galore. Not bad for a site that a couple decades ago featured 90 acres of sewage lagoons. Water is still treated here, but in a more natural way, with the wetlands filtering and cooling water before it's returned to the Tualatin River.

- Trails: Main loop is 1.1 miles
- Dogs: No
- Accessibility: Good
- Restrooms: Yes
- Steepness: Flat

Black cottonwood
pg. 15

Oregon ash
pg. 19

Willows
pg. 26

Red columbine
pg. 91

Chicory
pg. 101

Tundra swan
pg. 130

Northern shoveler
pg. 132

American wigeon
pg. 133

Green-winged teal
pg. 135

Ring-necked duck
pg. 136

Lesser scaup
pg. 136

Bufflehead
pg. 137

Pied-billed grebe
pg. 139

Spotted sandpiper
pg. 149

Greater yellowlegs
pg. 149

American white pelican
pg. 152

Great blue heron
pgs. 153–154

Great egret
pg. 155

Green heron
pg. 156

Bald eagle
pg. 161

Belted kingfisher
pg. 167

Purple martin
pg. 181

Tree swallow
pg. 181

Marsh wren
pg. 188

Red-winged blackbird
pg. 205

Coyote
pg. 237

Nutria
pg. 248

3. FOREST PARK

Probably you know how fortunate we are to have the nearly 5,200 acres of Forest Park in the city, but just to emphasize the point: It's one of the largest urban forests in the country, home to hundreds of animals and plant species, as well as thousands of human visitors who hike and bike the many trails, fire lanes, and forest roads. Part of the impetus for this book was to help you (and me) appreciate individual species in the park, instead of being overwhelmed by an undifferentiated mass of green.

- Trails: 80-plus miles
- Dogs: On leash
- Accessibility: Limited
- Restrooms: Varies
- Steepness: Varies

Douglas-fir
pgs. 3–4

Pacific yew
pg. 7

Western hemlock
pgs. 9–10

Western redcedar
pgs. 11–12

Bigleaf maple
pgs. 13–14

Cascara
pg. 16

Red alder
pg. 24

California hazelnut
pg. 28

Elderberry
pg. 30

False lily of the valley
pg. 55

False Solomon's seal
pg. 56

Vanilla leaf
pg. 58

Western trillium
pgs. 59–60

Baneberry
pg. 64

Pacific waterleaf
pg. 68

Wild ginger
pg. 104

Stinging nettle
pg. 106

Bracken fern
pg. 109

Lady fern
pg. 110

Licorice fern
pg. 110

Band-tailed pigeon
pg. 141

Black-capped chickadee
pg. 184

Chestnut-backed chickadee
pg. 184

Pacific wren
pg. 187

Pacific-slope flycatcher
pg. 174

Banana slug
pg. 233

Black-tailed deer
pg. 238

4. HOYT ARBORETUM

Hoyt Arboretum is located just a few miles from downtown but feels like a world away from the noise and commotion of the city. It's a living classroom for anyone who wants to learn more about plants, including the endangered species the arboretum's been conserving since 1928. You can see more than 2,300 tree and shrub species from around the world (and close to home) while walking the well-kept trails, or simply revel in the serenity of a beautiful place.

- Trails: 12 miles
- Dogs: On leash
- Accessibility: Good
- Restrooms: Yes
- Steepness: Gentle to moderate

Douglas-fir
pgs. 3–4

Western hemlock
pgs. 9–10

Western redcedar
pgs. 11–12

Blue elderberry
pg. 30

Oceanspray
pg. 33

Red-flowering currant
pg. 40

Salal
pg. 43

Salmonberry
pg. 44

Vine maple
pg. 47

False lily of the valley
pg. 55

Starry false Solomon's seal
pg. 56

Inside-out flower
pg. 57

Vanilla leaf
pg. 58

Enchanter's nightshade
pg. 63

Foamflower
pg. 66

Fringecup
pg. 67

Pacific waterleaf
pg. 68

Miner's lettuce
pg. 70

Strawberries
pg. 73

Pathfinder
pg. 76

Stream violet
pg. 80

Yellow monkeyflower
pg. 81

Wild ginger
pg. 104

Bracken fern
pg. 109

Lady fern
pg. 110

Maidenhair fern
pg. 111

Sword fern
pg. 111

5. MT. TABOR

Come for the views, stay for the birds. Mt. Tabor, a dormant cinder cone in southeast Portland topped by Mt. Tabor Park, provides outstanding views of the city. The butte also features huge old-growth Douglas-firs and bigleaf maples, but the main draw is the spring and fall migration of songbirds, when you can hear a couple dozen species tweeting messages to one another. If your eyes and ears need some help, the Audubon Society of Portland leads morning trips in spring to get you up to speed.

- Trails: 9 miles
- Dogs: On leash
- Accessibility: Good
- Restrooms: Yes
- Steepness: Gentle to steep

Douglas-fir
pgs. 3–4

Grand fir
pg. 5

Pacific dogwood
pg. 20

Snowberry
pg. 45

Inside-out flower
pg. 57

Trailing blackberry
pg. 72

Cooper's hawk
pg. 160

Great horned owl
pg. 166

Red-breasted sapsucker
pg. 168

Olive-sided flycatcher
pg. 172

Western wood-pewee
pg. 173

Pacific-slope flycatcher
pg. 174

Warbling vireo
pg. 175

Violet-green swallow
pg. 182

Chestnut-backed chickadee
pg. 184

Bushtit
pg. 185

Brown creeper
pg. 186

Bewick's wren
pg. 188

Golden-crowned kinglet
pg. 189

Hermit thrush
pg. 191

Varied thrush
pg. 192

Evening grosbeak
pg. 193

Golden-crowned sparrow
pg. 202

Black-throated gray warbler
pg. 208

Townsend's warbler
pg. 209

Western tanager
pg. 210

Black-headed grosbeak
pg. 210

6. OAKS BOTTOM WILDLIFE REFUGE

Over the years, portions of this wetland area on the east bank of the Willamette River have served as a landfill and been considered for everything from a parking lot to a motocross course. Fortunately, a coalition of nonprofits and farsighted individuals fought to protect what in 1988 became Portland's first official urban wildlife refuge. More than 120 bird species fly through Oaks Bottom, the city's first migratory bird park.

- Trails: 3.8-mile loop (with Springwater Corridor)
- Dogs: On leash
- Accessibility: On Springwater Corridor
- Restrooms: No
- Steepness: Mostly flat to gentle

Bigleaf maple
pgs. 13–14

Black cottonwood
pg. 15

Oregon ash
pg. 19

Oregon grape
pg. 35

Osoberry
pg. 36

Red-osier dogwood
pg. 41

Thimbleberry
pg. 46

Wapato
pg. 61

Fringecup
pg. 67

Canada goldenrod
pg. 82

Stinging nettle
pg. 106

Wood duck
pg. 131

Northern shoveler
pg. 132

Hooded merganser
pg. 137

American coot
pg. 146

Great blue heron
pgs. 153–154

Osprey
pg. 158

Belted kingfisher
pg. 167

Downy woodpecker
pg. 169

Cliff swallow
pg. 182

White-breasted nuthatch
pg. 186

Song sparrow
pg. 199

Pacific treefrog
pg. 216

Northern red-legged frog
pg. 217

Long-toed salamander
pg. 219

River otter
pg. 244

Nutria
pg. 248

7. POWELL BUTTE NATURE PARK

The remarkable thing about the eastside's largest natural area is that a single walk can take you through a mature forest, grassy meadow, oak savanna, and wetland area—which means you can experience a terrific variety of plants and animals. Powell Butte is an extinct cinder cone that sits atop a couple reservoirs that store the city's water. Along with the stunning mountain views, it's an especially good place for spotting raptors and the very occasional bluebird.

- Trails: 8-plus miles
- Dogs: On leash
- Accessibility: Some
- Restrooms: Yes
- Steepness: Gentle to moderate

Cascara
pg. 16

Oregon white oak
pgs. 21-22

Snowberry
pg. 45

Thimbleberry
pg. 46

Western serviceberry
pg. 48

Vanilla leaf
pg. 58

Pathfinder
pg. 76

Largeleaf avens
pg. 77

Canada goldenrod
pg. 82

Oregon sunshine
pg. 83

Wall lettuce
pg. 83

Tiger lily
pg. 85

Oaks toothwort
pg. 87

Lupines
pg. 97

Fuller's teasel
pg. 100

Northern harrier
pg. 159

Red-tailed hawk
pg. 162

American kestrel
pg. 163

Northern flicker
pg. 170

Hammond's flycatcher
pg. 174

Black-throated gray warbler
pg. 208

Pacific treefrog
pg. 216

Painted Lady
pg. 229

Red Admirable
pg. 230

Brush rabbit
pg. 240

Townsend's chipmunk
pg. 257

Garter snakes
pgs. 267–268

8. SAUVIE ISLAND

Don't miss this nature haven a dozen miles north of downtown. A Manhattan-sized island bordered by the Columbia River to the east and Multnomah Channel to the west, Sauvie Island is home to about 1,100 year-round residents (compared to 1.6 million on Manhattan). The nude beach and pumpkin patches get more attention, but the island's natural wonders are awe-inspiring, including 300-year-old native oaks and a bevy of raptors and large waterfowl.

- Trails: 8-plus miles
- Dogs: On leash
- Accessibility: None
- Steepness: Mostly flat
- Restrooms: Varies by trailhead

Bigleaf maple
pgs. 13–14

Black cottonwood
pg. 15

Cascara
pg. 16

Oregon white oak
pgs. 21–22

Red alder
pg. 24

Wapato
pg. 61

Snow goose
pg. 129

Cinnamon teal
pg. 132

Ring-necked duck
pg. 136

Sandhill crane
pg. 147

Western sandpiper
pg. 148

Double-crested cormorant
pg. 151

Great blue heron
pgs. 153–154

Great egret
pg. 155

Osprey
pg. 158

Northern harrier
pg. 159

Bald eagle
pg. 161

American kestrel
pg. 163

Barn owl
pg. 165

House wren
pg. 187

Savannah sparrow
pg. 198

Golden-crowned sparrow
pg. 202

Common yellowthroat
pg. 207

Yellow warbler
pg. 207

Northern raccoon
pg. 241

River otter
pg. 244

Garter snakes
pgs. 267–268

9. SMITH AND BYBEE WETLANDS NATURAL AREA

Smith and Bybee is the place to go for planes, trains, and pelicans. At the largest protected freshwater wetland in an American city, you can see nearly all of Portland's waterfowl and shorebirds. Not bad for a natural area wedged alongside Marine Drive in north Portland. Metro had the foresight to protect these 2,000-plus acres, about 240 of which used to be the St. Johns Landfill. Walk the brief but beautiful Interlakes Trail or kayak the lakes to appreciate this inspiring environmental success story.

- Trails: About 1 mile (connects to more)
- Dogs: No
- Accessibility: Good
- Restrooms: Yes
- Steepness: Gentle

Oregon ash
pg. 19

Douglas spiraea
pg. 29

Red-osier dogwood
pg. 41

Snowberry
pg. 45

Wood duck
pg. 131

Cinnamon teal
pg. 132

Northern shoveler
pg. 132

Gadwall
pg. 133

Northern pintail
pg. 135

Green-winged teal
pg. 135

Ruddy duck
pg. 138

Pied-billed grebe
pg. 139

American coot
pg. 146

Killdeer
pg. 148

Western sandpiper
pg. 148

Spotted sandpiper
pg. 149

Greater yellowlegs
pg. 149

American white pelican
pg. 152

Great egret
pg. 155

Red-breasted sapsucker
pg. 168

Pileated woodpecker
pg. 171

Cliff swallow
pg. 182

Pacific treefrog
pg. 216

Woolly bear
pg. 226

River otter
pg. 244

American beaver
pgs. 245–246

Common muskrat
pg. 247

10. TRYON CREEK STATE NATURAL AREA

This natural area in southwest Portland is not a pristine old-growth forest—large western redcedar stumps hint at the logging done by the former owner, Oregon Iron Works. But it is the only state park in Oregon located within a major metropolitan area, and you can spend hours trying to identify the many native (and, yes, invasive) species. The forest best known for its trilliums is an urban oasis for all sorts of plants and animals, including humans.

- Trails: 8 miles
- Dogs: On leash
- Accessibility: Limited
- Restrooms: Yes
- Steepness: Mostly gentle

Douglas-fir
pgs. 3–4

Grand fir
pg. 5

Pacific yew
pg. 7

Cascara
pg. 16

Pacific dogwood
pg. 20

California hazelnut
pg. 28

Red huckleberry
pg. 31

Orange honeysuckle
pg. 34

Oregon grape
pg. 35

Pacific ninebark
pg. 37

Poison oak
pg. 39

Hooker's fairybell
pg. 54

False Solomon's seal
pg. 58

Western trillium
pgs. 59–60

Bedstraws
pg. 63

Baneberry
pg. 64

Largeleaf avens
pg. 77

Skunk cabbage
pg. 84

Self-heal
pg. 98

Piggyback plant
pg. 105

Stinging nettle
pg. 106

Barred owl
pg. 166

Pileated woodpecker
pg. 171

Ensatina
pg. 218

Long-toed salamander
pg. 219

Banana slug
pg. 233

Douglas squirrel
pg. 258

PHOTO CREDITS

Nagi Aboulenein is a computer engineer in the Portland area. He is passionate about birds and bird photography. Other interests include diving and underwater photography.

Joan Amero is a volunteer photographer for the Deschutes Land Trust, Friends & Neighbors of the Deschutes Canyon, and Friends of the Metolius. Joan lives in Sisters.

Sue Anderson is a published nature and portrait photographer and butterfly enthusiast living in Sisters with her naturalist husband, Jim. celastrinasue@gmail.com.

Jim Anderson is an Oregon writer, naturalist, and photographer. When not chasing bugs and birds or writing nature columns, he and his wife, Sue, are in Oregon's outback surveying Golden Eagle populations.

Tracy Aue has gained a love for the outdoors through a lifetime of camping and hiking adventures. Photography has become an extension of his appreciation for the beauty of the natural world as well as an excuse for taking more breaks while hiking. See more of his photos on Instagram @tracy.m.aue.

Susan Berger is a photographer, writer, graphic designer, and active member of the High Desert Chapter of the Native Plant Society of Oregon.

Travis Chaney is a photographer, writer, birdwatcher, and jazz aficionado. He lives in Portland. More of his work can be found at www.travischaney.com.

Char Corkran is a naturalist, writer, and photographer specializing in amphibians and birds. She is the co-author, with Chris Thoms, of *Amphibians of Oregon, Washington and British Columbia.*

Gerald D. Carr is Professor of Botany Emeritus of the University of Hawaii. He is now affiliated with OSU as a contributor to the Oregon Flora Project. Many thousands of his Hawaiian and Oregon plant images can be seen by following links at www.botany.hawaii.edu/faculty/carr/ofp/ofp_index.htm.

For Creative Commons photo licenses: creativecommons.org/licenses.

Rick Derevan is an amateur (but avid) bird and wildlife photographer living on the Central Coast of California.

Alice Doggett is a landscape photographer inspired by nature and wildlife. Her images capture the intense natural beauty of the Pacific Northwest, where she divides her time between a home in Central Oregon and a boat in Anacortes, Wash. You can reach Alice and see her work at her website: www.alicedoggettphotography.com.

Sue Dougherty is a passionate wildlife photographer and veterinarian living, working, and thriving in Bend. Sue shows her many images in the Red Chair Gallery in Bend and at shows throughout the year. www.offleashphotography.net.

Kim Elton—former journalist, commercial fisherman, and politician—now uses a camera to celebrate the flora and fauna of public lands.

Chuck Gates is a retired biology teacher, longtime Central Oregon birder, and the author of "The Oregon Birding Site Guide" website. www.ecaudubon.org.

Marlin Harms is a nature photographer whose work can be seen at flickr.com/photos/marlinharms.

Rich Hatfield is a senior conservation biologist with the Xerces Society (www.xerces.org) and a founder of www.BumbleBeeWatch.org.

Steve Hersey is a lifelong conservationist and amateur photographer whose work can be seen at www.flickr.com/photos/sherseydc.

Lori Humphreys, retired, has worked as a wildlife biologist and professional gardener, and now does volunteer work with native bees and butterflies.

Ed Jensen is an award-winning educator and photographer based in Corvallis. His popular books include *Trees to Know in Oregon* and *Shrubs to Know in Pacific Northwest Forests.*

Linda Kappen is a naturalist who lives in southern Oregon and specializes in the lepidoptera of Oregon and Monarch butterflies.

Kris Kristovich is a nature/landscape photographer living in the Sisters area since 1970.

Tom Lawler lives in La Pine, Ore. www.avianpics.com.

Mark Leppin is a naturalist in Corvallis. He is currently a master's student at Oregon State University where he is examining the natural history of the northern rubber boa *(Charina bottae).*

Mark Lundgren is a wildlife photographer from Portland.

Buddy Mays is a travel and natural history photographer, zoologist, and the author of 24 books including *The Butterflies of Bend & Central Oregon* and the award-winning novel *Hard to Have Heroes.* https://buddy-mays.pixels.com or https://fineartamerica.com/profiles/buddy-mays.

Dr. Randall Moore is an ecologist in the Dept. of Fisheries and Wildlife at Oregon State University and has been studying streaked horned larks since 2003.

Phil Nosler is an entomology student and local wildlife photographer.

Mark R. Johnson is a photographer whose work can be seen at www.flickr.com/photos/27381338@N03.

Dave Rein has resided in Bend since 1975 and has journeyed the globe seeking to photograph wildlife naturally in wilderness situations for the benefit of conservation. His photographs have illustrated the pages of *Audubon, National Wildlife, Wild Planet, Outdoor Photographer, Cascades East,* and *Bugle.* He authored *Great Fishermen*, comparing the similar lives of brown bears and river otters.

Al Schneider is the author of the app Colorado Rocky Mountain Wildflowers and the website www.swcoloradowildflowers.com. Al retired in 1998 after careers as an English professor, Ozark trail planner for Missouri State Parks, backcountry guide, and computer-based teacher with the Ute Mountain Ute Indian Tribe. Al, his wife, Betty, and pup, Pepper, are often out hiking the wildflower trails of the Four Corners region.

Ken Schneider is an entomologist, birder, and volunteer at the California Academy of Sciences. www.flickr.com/photos/zonotrichia.

Evelyn Sherr is a Professor Emeritus of Oregon State University with an abiding interest in Pacific Northwest flora and fauna.

Rick Shory has worked as a field botanist from the North Slope tundra to the Florida Keys. He has many plant and landscape images from identification and documentation. https://rickshory.wordpress.com.

Paul Slichter is a nature enthusiast, hiker, and photographer.

Alan St. John is a Bend-area nature writer/photographer and author of *Reptiles of the Northwest* and *Oregon's Dry Side: Exploring East of the Cascade Crest.*

Carolyn Waissman is a wildlife photographer featured at Artists Gallery Sunriver. You can also find her work at www.imagesbycbw.com.

SELECTED BIBLIOGRAPHY

Ackerman, Jennifer. 2016. *The Genius of Birds.* Penguin Books.

Anderson, Jim. 1992. *Tales from a Northwest Naturalist.* Caxton Press.

Corkran, Charlotte C. and Thoms, Chris. 1996. *Amphibians of Oregon, Washington and British Columbia.* Lone Pine Publishing.

Cornell, Joseph. 1979. *Sharing Nature with Children.* Dawn Publications.

The Cornell Lab of Ornithology. allaboutbirds.org.

Czerski, Helen. 2016. *Storm in a Teacup: The Physics of Everyday Life.* W.W. Norton & Company.

Deshler, John. Forest Park Wildlife Report, Dec. 2012. portlandoregon.gov/parks/ article/427357.

Deur, Douglas. 2014. *Pacific Northwest Foraging.* Timber Press.

Dietrich, William. 2003. *Natural Grace: The Charm, Wonder, & Lessons of Pacific Northwest Animals & Plants.* Univ. of Washington Press.

Dungy, Camille T. 2009. *Black Nature: Four Centuries of African American Nature Poetry.* Univ. of Georgia Press.

Eder, Tamara. 2002. *Mammals of Washington and Oregon.* Lone Pine Publishing.

Fagan, Damian. 2006. *Pacific Northwest Wildflowers.* Falcon Guides.

Goldfarb, Ben. 2019. *Eager: The Surprising, Secret Life of Beavers and Why They Matter.* Chelsea Green Publishing.

Haskell, David George. 2012. *The Forest Unseen: A Year's Watch in Nature.* Penguin Books.

Houck, M.C. (author) and Cody, M.J., editor. 2011. *Wild in the City: Exploring the Intertwine: The Portland-Vancouver Region's Network of Parks, Trails, and Natural Areas.* OSU Press.

Houle, Marcy Cottrell. 1996. *One City's Wilderness: Portland's Forest Park.* Oregon Historical Society Press.

Houle, Marcy Cottrell. 2019. *A Generous Nature: Lives Transformed by Oregon.* OSU Press.

Jensen, Ed. 1999. *Trees to Know in Oregon.* OSU Press.

Jensen, Ed. 2013. *Shrubs to Know in Pacific Northwest Forests.* OSU Press.

Johnson, Nathanael. 2016. *Unseen City: The Majesty of Pigeons, the Discreet Charm of Snails & Other Wonders of the Urban Wilderness.* Rodale Books.

Johnson, Thomas H., ed. 1983. *The Poems of Emily Dickinson.* The Belknap Press of Harvard University Press.

Kemper, John. 2002. *Southern Oregon's Bird Life.* Outdoor Press.

Kimmerer, Robin Wall. 2003. *Gathering Moss: A Natural and Cultural History of Mosses.* OSU Press.

Lichen, Patricia K. 2001. *Passionate Slugs and Hollywood Frogs: An Uncommon Field Guide to Northwest Backyards.* Sasquatch Books.

Lloyd, T. Abe, and Chambers, Fiona Hamersley. 2014. *Wild Berries of Washington and Oregon.* Lone Pine Publishing International.

Maser, Chris. 1998. *Mammals of the Pacific Northwest: From the Coast to the High Cascades.* OSU Press.

Mathews, Daniel. 2017. *Natural History of the Pacific Northwest Mountains.* Timber Press.

Mighetto, Lisa (editor). *Muir Among the Animals: The Wildlife Writings of John Muir.* 1986.

Moran, Robbin C. 2004. *A Natural History of Ferns.* Timber Press.

Muir, John. *The Mountains of California.* 1894.

Native Plants for Willamette Valley Yards, from Metro and local partners. oregonmetro.gov/sites/default/files/native_plants_for_willamette_valley_yards_booklet.pdf.

Native Plant Society of Oregon. npsoregon.org.

Nisbet, Jack. 2010. *The Collector: David Douglas and the Natural History of the Northwest.* Sasquatch Books.

Oregon Flora Project. oregonflora.org.

Pojar, Jim, and MacKinnon, Andy (Eds.). 2014 (2nd ed.). *Plants of the Pacific Northwest Coast.* Lone Pine Publishing.

Portland Plant List 2016. portlandoregon.gov/citycode/article/322280.

Pyle, Robert Michael, and LaBar, Caitlin C. 2018. *Butterflies of the Pacific Northwest.* Timber Press.

Russell, Sharman Apt. 2003. *An Obsession with Butterflies.* Basic Books.

Safina, Carl. *Beyond Words: What Animals Think and Feel.* 2015.

Shewey, John. 2017. *Birds of the Pacific Northwest.* Timber Press.

Sibley, David Allen. 2009. *The Sibley Guide to Bird Life and Behavior.* Knopf.

Steelquist, Robert. 2016. *The Northwest Coastal Explorer.* Timber Press.

St. John, Alan D. 2002. *Reptiles of the Northwest.* Lone Pine Publishing.

Swanson, Sarah, and Smith, Max. 2013. *Must-See Birds of the Pacific Northwest.* Timber Press.

Tekiela, Stan. 2001. *Birds of Oregon Field Guide.* Adventure Publications.

Thayer, Samuel. *The Forager's Harvest: A Guide to Identifying, Harvesting, and Preparing Edible Wild Plants.* 2009.

Tualatin Riverkeepers (Susan Peter, Shirley Ewart, Barbara Schaffner, Eds.). 2002. *Exploring the Tualatin River Basin: A Nature and Recreation Guide.* OSU Press.

Turner, Mark. 2006. *Wildflowers of the Pacific Northwest.* Timber Press.

Wildlife of Portland. City of Portland Environmental Services. portlandoregon.gov/bes/article/371508.

INDEX

ABOUT THE AUTHOR

LeeAnn Kriegh grew up picking strawberries, catching crawdads, and helping woolly bears cross the road in St. Helens. After earning bachelor's and master's degrees in English, she wrote for *The Oregonian* and various magazines while living on Sauvie Island for nearly 15 years. She's the author of multiple nature guides (okay, two) and now pays for her nature-writing habit by writing and editing for businesses and nonprofits nationwide. LeeAnn's passion is helping readers deepen their connections to the natural world through a unique blend of facts, stories, and humor. To order her books, learn about upcoming events, and share your favorite nature puns, go to www.natureofbooks.com.

ABOUT THE DESIGNER

Sarah Craig has loved the outdoors from the moment her mom pushed her outside and told her, "Don't come home until dinner." For Sarah, it was the beginning of a life full of nature explorations and the continual pursuit of the next amazing vista. When LeeAnn asked for help creating a nature guide, Sarah jumped at the chance to design what she initially thought would be a pamphlet. It was only after about 100 pages that she realized what she had gotten herself into. And how grateful she is to have gotten the chance to connect more with her surroundings and help others do the same, learning and laughing the whole way. To see more of Sarah's work, go to www.sarahcookdesign.com.